SELF-INTELLIGENCE

JANE RANSOM

SELF-INTELLIGENCE

THE NEW SCIENCE-BASED APPROACH FOR REACHING YOUR TRUE POTENTIAL

FOREWORD BY
JACK CANFIELD, COAUTHOR OF THE INTERNATIONAL
BEST-SELLING CHICKEN SOUP FOR THE SOUL® SERIES

FAIR WINDS

Brimming with creative inspiration, how-to projects, and useful information to enrich your everyday life, Quarto Knows is a favorite destination for those pursuing their interests and passions. Visit our site and dig deeper with our books into your area of interest: Quarto Creates, Quarto Cooks, Quarto Homes, Quarto Lives, Quarto Drives, Quarto Explores, Quarto Gifts, or Quarto Kids.

First Published in 2019 by Fair Winds Press, an imprint of The Quarto Group,
100 Cummings Center, Suite 265-D, Beverly, MA 01915, USA.
T (978) 282-9590 F (978) 283-2742 QuartoKnows.com

Fair Winds Press titles are also available at discount for retail, wholesale, promotional, and bulk purchase. For details, contact the Special Sales Manager by email at specialsales@quarto.com or by mail at The Quarto Group, Attn: Special Sales Manager, 401 Second Avenue North, Suite 310, Minneapolis, MN 55401, USA.

22 21 20 19 18   1 2 3 4 5

ISBN: 978-1-59233-857-3

Digital edition published in 2019
eISBN: 978-1-63159-624-7

Library of Congress Cataloging-in-Publication Data is available

Cover Design: Landers Miller Design
Cartoons: Written and designed by Jane Ransom, drawn by David Fletcher

Printed in China

The anecdotes and dialogue in this book are based on Jane Ransom's extensive experience working with clients. Names and identifying information have been changed. Some case histories use composite characters to illustrate concepts.

Knowing others is wisdom,
knowing the self is Enlightenment.

—LAO-TZU

We never know how high we are
Till we are called to rise;
And then, if we are true to plan,
Our statures touch the skies.

—EMILY DICKINSON

CONTENTS

FOREWORD

Jack Canfield

If you are reading this, count yourself lucky to have found this book. It contains some of the most fascinating information and material you will ever read. I have been teaching people a holistic model of personal growth and development for almost fifty years. I have read more than 3,000 books and have attended hundreds of seminars, workshops, and trainings. I have been a high school teacher, teacher trainer, self-esteem expert, psychotherapist, success coach, corporate trainer, professional speaker, and best-selling author. And yet, I found new information and helpful insights on almost every page of this book.

Jane Ransom is a self-described "science nerd," a competent hypnotherapist, and in my opinion a great writer. She has the uncanny ability to look at tons of research and extract the most important useful concepts and processes that can be used to enhance your life. In chapter after chapter she sheds light on both the truths and the myths of human transformation.

Jane has synthesized all of her academic research and clinical experience into an original, holistic model of Self-Intelligence, a model that is based on up-to-date science, and, I was happy to discover, also validates my life's work. Jane has spent seven years research-ing and testing her model, distilling and synthesizing scientific findings from many diverse fields, including research and insights from positive psychology, neuroscience, hypnotherapy, high-tech neurobiology, behavioral economics, and even game theory. Jane has mastered this knowledge, and she has used it to create dozens of transforma-tional tools that you can put to immediate use in your life.

One thing that makes this book so accessible is that Jane uses all of the insights she has learned in the actual presentation of the material in the book. She uses powerful stories, pictures, and engaging humor (including cartoons) to actively engage all of your senses. She follows that up with practical action steps that you can take immediately to apply the principles that you are learning. All of this keeps you turning the pages . . . and remembering and applying what you are learning.

What I also love about this book is that Jane addresses many of the myths and misunderstandings that abound in the world of personal development, human happiness, and achievement. She approaches everything with an open mind, and yet with the integrity of someone looking for the real truth. I find that refreshing in a world where there is so much hype and hyperbole.

My staff and I sometimes joke that a person could spend all day working only on their inner self—reading, meditating, writing and repeating affirmations, visualizing, etc.— and ultimately end up getting nothing done. That's why Jane and I both teach people the importance of setting realistic and measurable goals and then *taking action* to achieve those goals. We also stress that genuine success must be holistic—encompassing among other things our relationships, our health and fitness, our fun and recreation, and our happiness, as well as our careers and our finances, none of which can be improved by only focusing inward. Therefore, I'm pleased that Jane's five-part model of Self-Intelligence addresses the whole person, from the hidden reaches of the *subconscious self* to the outer world *striving self*, which takes action to achieve those quantifiable goals.

I love that Jane is an ardent academic researcher, but she also happens to be a fine storyteller. To powerfully lock in what she is teaching you, she shares stories of transformation from her own personal life, as well as from the lives of public figures you will recognize, including how Michael Phelps used the power of visualization to win more Olympic gold medals than anyone in history, and how I used that same power to create a bestselling book series that has sold more than half a billion books. But mostly Jane writes about her clients, usually regular folks with regular problems, yet their case histories will fascinate you. And, although only one chapter in the book focuses on hypnosis, throughout the book you will get an insider view on Jane's intriguing work as a professional hypnotist.

I first met Jane in 2010 at my annual Breakthrough to Success training, just two years after she'd opened her hypnosis office. During the training she half-jokingly confessed to being a "recovering intellectual" still relatively new to the world of self-transformation. Over the subsequent years while Jane was developing her multifold model of Self-Intelligence, I watched her learn to embrace her own multifaceted uniqueness. As a result, she's now still a serious scholar, but she is also a playful presenter and a passionate agent of positive change.

I am excited knowing that this book will now enable her to help far more people than she's previously been able to serve, because I know that's her heartfelt aim and her true passion. Writing this book was the BHAG (Big Hairy Audacious Goal) that she set back in 2010 at the Breakthrough to Success training. Now, because she practices what she teaches, the book is a reality. It is the culmination of a committed seven-year journey. But her journey's not over—and neither is yours—for as long as we live, the path to becoming all we can be continually opens before us.

I wish you well on *your* journey and congratulate you on your decision to read *Self-Intelligence*. By implementing the strategies here, you truly can change your life. Therefore, don't just read this book. Use the tools that are offered. Take action and commit to the never-ending process of your own personal growth.

Best wishes for a meaningful and fulfilling journey.

Jack Canfield, cocreator of the *New York Times* #1 bestselling Chicken Soup for the Soul® series and *The Success Principles™: How to Get from Where You Are to Where You Want to Be*; founder of the Transformational Leadership Council

INTRODUCTION

Welcome to the Party!

Propped against the basement wall of my childhood home was a makeshift bookcase, where as an adolescent, I happened to discover, nearly hidden behind a pile of magazines, two tantalizing paperbacks. One touted so-called extrasensory perception or ESP—the author claimed to bend spoons with his mind—and the other extolled hypnosis as a surefire way to impress people. I devoured both books.

Well, I never managed to bend spoons using only my psyche. But I did learn how to hypnotize willing schoolmates, and became a hit at slumber parties. For us kids in rural Indiana, this passed as great entertainment. One friend in particular, named Susan, went into a trance very easily. Looking back, I recognize that she was what we professional hypnotists call a *high-hypnotizable*.

One night I told Susan under hypnosis that she was walking along the beach. After coming out of her trance, she reported having *felt* the soft sand beneath her bare feet. She had *seen* the glittering waves collapse into foam against the shore. She had *heard* the plaintive cries of gulls. She insisted that she had not merely daydreamed her walk on the beach. Somehow, hypnotized, she had *lived* it.

Feeling slightly jealous, having never experienced a trance myself, I asked her to hypnotize me by employing the same technique I'd used with her. She tried it, gently massaging my temples while counting backward. To my dismay, nothing happened. I began to suspect her of exaggerating her trance experience. After all, by then the proclaimed spoon-bender had been exposed on television as a fraud. Maybe hypnosis wasn't completely real either? Maybe it was just hocus-pocus. I decided that at best it was child's play, and moved on.

Fast-forward to the twenty-first century. Web-browsing one lazy Sunday morning at home in San Francisco, I saw a mention of the first accredited college of hypnosis in the United States. This shocked me enough to google "hypnosis scientific research." The results amazed me. Among many other things, I found studies that showed hypnosis could help people to quit smoking. That hit home, because just months earlier my father, a heavy smoker, had died of cancer. Years before that, both my mother and stepfather also had succumbed to lung cancer related to smoking. Shortly before he left this world, Dad told me that although he'd been able to finally quit drinking after a life of alcoholism, he hadn't managed to kick cigarettes. It was too hard. Now I wondered: Could hypnosis have helped?

I love the internet. It feeds my learning addiction. Soon I became convinced—due to hundreds upon hundreds of scientific studies—that hypnosis was quite real indeed. Rigorous research showed that by influencing the subconscious self, hypnosis not only could help people quit smoking, it could be used to treat everything from chronic pain to poor study habits . . . from eating disorders to phobias . . . from high blood pressure to sexual dysfunction. The news seemed almost too good to be true. But I was receptive to it because I'd recently read a book that opened my mind about, well, my mind.

It was *The Brain That Changes Itself* by Norman Doidge, one of the first books for nonscientists on *brain plasticity*. You see, in recent decades computerized brain-imaging technology has wrought a neuroscientific revolution by revealing that our brain "maps" are constantly shifting. We each have about 100 billion neurons, or thinking cells, that communicate with one another through synaptic connections. Contrary to earlier belief, those connections never get irreversibly set in place but instead remain *plastic*, that is, able to remap throughout our lives—which is why, it turns out, people at any age really can change. Brain plasticity grants us the astonishing ability to literally re-form our own brains by strategically choosing our thoughts, actions and experiences.

What that book hadn't told me—but what I learned while web-diving hypnosis re-search—was that the same neuro-imaging technology that revealed brain plasticity also had helped validate hypnosis as a powerful tool for remapping the brain. Scientists can look at the brain under hypnosis and see that it's a measurable phenomenon far beyond mere imagining. (We'll explore how you can use hypnosis in chapter 4.)

Helping My Self to a Science Smorgasbord

So it was that a decade ago, the skeptic in me surrendered to new science. Not only could people transform themselves, but hypnosis could help them. I knew I had a knack for it. I enrolled in the United States' first accredited hypnosis college to train as a master hypnotist and hypnotherapist, while earning additional certifications from the American Hypnosis Association in specialties such as smoking cessation and weight loss. In 2008 I opened an office in downtown San Francisco on Market Street near Union Square.

Soon I was helping people reach all sorts of goals, from kicking addictions to acing difficult exams to boosting their sports performance. It was exhilarating . . . and humbling. I began to feel in over my head. While hypnosis provided a magic bullet for some clients for some issues, it didn't always solve everything, and clients began bringing in problems I hadn't trained for. A client would come in to do one thing—say, quit chewing their nails—and then ask my help to do something else totally unrelated, such as improve their marriage or get a promotion.

Did I tell you that I love the internet? Each day I'd come home from my office to look up scientific studies, order books, take massive notes on whatever I read, and write out synopses of what I'd learned, thereby managing to stay a step or two ahead of my clients.

I began to accumulate what the philosopher John Dewey might have called a very big toolbox—all sorts of positive-change tools drawn from all sorts of disparate disciplines, from game theory to neurobiology to behavioral economics to various fields of psychology. Not only did this stuff work, but it was way-cool science. It felt to me like a fabulous party too good to miss, and in my nerdy, obsessive way I began sharing this brain candy with everyone. Or maybe oversharing.

"Do you know *everything*?" my client Larry said accusingly. "You're cluttering my mind. Can't you just connect the dots to make one pretty picture to hang on my refrigerator?" (All clients' names in this book have been changed to protect confidentiality.)

A sixty-five-year-old charmer, Larry was both a deep thinker and a playful tease. (You'll meet him again in chapter 15.) He liked to get my goat. Now he made a show of stretching out on his back in my office recliner, which was just big enough to hold his six-foot-two frame. He put his hands behind his head and closed his eyes as though taking in the sun. "Instead of 1001 brainiac facts to keep me up at night, how about just a quickie system to help me understand myself? As much as I enjoy this comfy chair, no relationship lasts forever. Give me something I can wrap my head around and take with me when we break up."

He'd come in many months earlier to quit smoking, after which we'd tackled various other issues. He was a wonderful client, open-minded and proactive, and he was right: As we had moved from one challenge to the next, in my zeal to be helpful, I'd been throwing science at him willy-nilly. My big toolbox contained lots of valuable instruments, but it was a disorganized mess.

"You're a heartbreaker, Larry," I teased him back. "Okay, I'll work on it."

That evening in my home office, surrounded by an ever-expanding collection of articles and books, I pondered how to meet Larry's request for a single system to, as he'd said, "help me understand myself." I realized that despite the diversity of their challenges, all of my clients wanted to understand themselves. People came to me because they felt confounded by how hard it was for them to reach certain goals—goals they knew they could achieve.

They never asked for help to walk through walls or grow a foot taller or turn invisible. They wanted to kick a habit, conquer a phobia, improve a relationship, win a golf tournament, or up-level their lives in some doable way. Whatever the goal was, they knew they had it in themselves to succeed. And they knew it was something about them*selves* that had so far stopped them.

Honing a Holistic Five-Part Model

My clients wanted to understand and master the *self*. Could I help them to do that in more than a piecemeal fashion? Thousands of years ago, the Greeks had inscribed a maxim in the Temple of Apollo at Delphi: *Know thyself.* Given that the mystery of the self might be as old as humanity, I wasn't arrogant enough to imagine I could solve it. But I was lucky enough to recognize that a multitude of modern-day scientists, equipped with ever-advancing neuro-imaging technology, were discovering secrets of the self that the ancients never dreamt of. These scientists were providing pieces of the puzzle that had never previously come to light.

Already there were too many pieces for any one person to fully master. And more discoveries are being made every day at an ever-faster pace. I had no illusions about creating a grand theory of everything. I just wanted to design an accessible, holistic model to serve my clients.

I'd already found that it served them to think of the whole self as containing multiple sub-selves, including the *conscious self* versus the *subconscious self*. For example, Larry's *conscious self* had, for many years, wanted to stop smoking . . . but Larry only succeeded after we used hypnosis to bring his *subconscious self* also on board. That very explanation enabled him to let go of guilt about his past inability to quit. (We'll learn how guilt inhibits willpower in chapter 20.) Later, when we'd begun to address Larry's relationship issues, he'd wanted to know which self was at play; I told him that we'd be targeting his *social self*.

"My social self," he'd mused. "That may need upgrading. People so often baffle me."

I'd found early on that this approach empowered clients. It helped them to understand there was nothing wrong with *them*, per se—for we are all infinitely complex, multifaceted individuals. It was simply that some specific part of their whole self happened to need adjusting.

With clipboard, paper, and pencil in hand, I settled onto my sofa to make a list of the most effective science-based tools I'd been using in my practice, noting beside each one how I might describe which "self" that tool addressed. The list grew too fast. For there were seemingly endless possibilities—the spiritual self, the professional self, the romantic self, the artistic self, the public self, the private self, the creative self, the logical self, and so on and so on.

I decided to channel my client Lynn.

Lynn's a professional home-organizer. (You'll meet her again in chapter 17.) She had once shared with me her *organize-by-five* rule. "You've got to control chaos through categories, but unless you want more chaos filling your house and head, never try to impose more than five main categories. Doesn't matter whether it's a closet, a company, or a system of government. If you want to crush that chaos, you've got to be able to tick off the top categories on the fingers of one hand. Even my grandkids can do that. *Organize-by-five* works for everybody."

There's a long-standing theory in psychology, called Miller's Law, which says that most people can hold in their minds (specifically, in working memory) only between five and nine items at a time. Lynn's rule struck me as sound in that regard. Plus, the childlike image of counting fingers appealed to my penchant for keeping things basic (we'll visit the science on that in chapter 19).

The evening grew long as I labored to formulate a model of the whole self, comprising no more than five main categories whose proverbial umbrella would cover the rest. Holding in mind that, historically, conceptualizing the *self* was as much a philosophical ambition as a scientific one, I kept my goal modest. While the transformational tools I share with clients are science-based and backed by research, I am neither scientist nor philosopher. I just wanted a practical model to help ordinary folks master their selves. "Pracademics" over academics, as they say.

Down the rabbit hole I went, working past midnight and falling asleep on the sofa. As I caught myself drifting off, I invited my subconscious to brainstorm while I slept (more about dream-programming in chapter 1). Over the next few days a five-part model of Self-Intelligence emerged. It isn't a rigid model made of discrete pieces. In keeping with brain plasticity, the parts are flexible, overlapping, and interconnected. None of them stands alone, but all fit together to comprise an inviolable whole. Since then I've found the model helps with virtually any client issue because every aspect of personal change fits under the umbrella of the five sub-selves.

Along with the *subconscious self,* the *conscious self* and the *social self* are two others which seemed at first less obvious: the *embodied self* and the *striving self.*

The *embodied self* refers to your physical being, but not in the classic mind-versus-body manner. In fact, just the opposite. It denotes the continuous body-brain "loop" of mind and physicality that shapes you inside and out. This mind-body oneness has attracted recent scientific attention, including in neurobiology and in the field known as "embodied cognition."

The *striving self* gets things done. I believe that irrespective of age, profession, or background, all healthy humans are strivers. By reading this book, you prove you're a striver. Regardless of your personal aim—whether it's to learn more about Self-Intelligence, or to make a specific change, or to completely turn your life around—you are taking action this very moment in pursuit of a goal. Any model of Self-Intelligence worth its salt must support you in becoming an ever more successful striver, ever more able to realize your dreams.

"What if all I want to do is lie on the beach?" objected Larry when I gave him an early-draft printout of the categories, including the *striving self.*

"Wear sunscreen," I smiled. Larry sometimes professed to be a beach bum, but he ran a lucrative construction business. His *striving self* was highly functional.

"You give me this." He theatrically waved the printout. "I wanted a pretty picture to hang on my fridge. Can you at least add phone numbers? I do like the idea of being able to call on any of these selves to get me out of trouble."

> **Self-Intelligence is the ability to master one's whole self by influencing the five main sub-selves that govern well-being.**

Larry had immediately recognized that the model draws strength from its flexibility; each and any of the five sub-selves presents a portal to positive change.

The Self-Intelligence Model

Self-Intelligence is the ability to master one's *whole self* by influencing the five main sub-selves that govern well-being. Any of these five interconnected selves can be targeted to achieve positive change through the use of science-based tools. Each affects the others in a holistic process of personal transformation, which can be accomplished through:

1. programming the *subconscious* self;
2. conditioning the *conscious* self;
3. thinking through the *embodied* self;
4. integrating the *social* self; and
5. vitalizing the *striving* self.

If the model isn't crystal clear to you yet, please don't worry. It will come together as you read through the book's five parts (each addressing one of your sub-selves) and as you begin to use the powerful science-based Self-Intelligence tools offered throughout.

Meanwhile, it's enough to note that, as Larry observed, whenever you're "in trouble"—that is, feeling blocked, stuck in a rut, or otherwise off track—you have various selves to call on. Your multidimensional nature grants you tremendous flexibility (what neuroscientists might call *self-plasticity*), along with multiple ways to solve any problem.

Larry dropped the printout into his briefcase and got up to go. But the sparkle in his eyes suggested that he wasn't quite finished with me. "You say the positive changes I've been making all fit under one umbrella. You know I refuse to carry an umbrella. Too cumbersome!"

I rose to walk him out. Beside my waiting room exit was a bronze bucket holding several spare umbrellas for my clients' convenience. Although it was true Larry didn't carry an umbrella, he sometimes borrowed mine.

"Larry," I said, "Think Mary Poppins."

He bounced on his toes, turned, and gave me a hug. "A flying umbrella! Why didn't you say so? Everybody needs a flying umbrella."

An Invitation to Fete Your Potential

Over the years I've become convinced that everyone indeed needs Self-Intelligence. I've grown determined to spread the word. Mastering the self is better than magic. It's real. And yes, it's truly uplifting. It was in a seminar with my mentor Jack Canfield, author of *The Success Principles*, that I decided to write this book. Jack may not be best known for cutting-edge science, yet for forty-some years he's been helping people all over the world to achieve personal breakthroughs. In many ways, new science is now validating what transformational leaders such as Jack have been doing all along.

Whether you identify as a seasoned self-helper, a personal-growth newbie, or a previously skeptical intellectual, may this book empower you. May it expand your sense of who you can be and what you can do. The model of Self-Intelligence is yours for everyday application and long-term transformation. It's a big-picture, nonlinear model designed to be flexible.

Some of the topics here may appeal to you more urgently than others, and you should feel free to read the chapters out of order. See what sparks your interest, then follow that spark. Every chapter provides proven strategies that you can use immediately, along with solid science that may surprise you. For example, one way to lose weight is to get more sleep (chapter 12). Want to build your self-discipline? Banish self-shame. (See chapter 20.) Prefer to catch fewer colds? Make more friends (chapter 13).

Is this book the final word on Self-Intelligence? Nope, and there won't ever be one. Your brain encompasses a network of more than 100 trillion neural connections. That's a thousand times the number of stars in the Milky Way. Your *self* turns out to be a mighty vast subject, which scientists will be studying for a very long time. Why, you could say this shindig never ends.

So let's start celebrating. While you're here, you'll meet some of my clients, plus I'll share a little of my personal story, so that you can shorten your learning curve by benefitting from my mistakes. In retrospect, I believe my biggest mistake lay in adopting a cynical attitude as a young adult toward self-help. Now we know that, due to brain plasticity, anyone can build their Self-Intelligence to attain lasting change. That's why you'll find your name on the A-list of invitees no matter where you were before on the transformational spectrum. There's exciting science here for all our guests, plus plenty of party favors in the form of quirky quizzes, scintillating sidebars, actionable takeaways, bite-size chapter summaries, and goofy cartoons.

Are you ready to have some brain fun, learn some new life moves, and open up some surprise ideas that you can actually use? Let's get this party started!

PART ONE

PROGRAMMING YOUR SUBCONSCIOUS SELF

Neuro-imaging technology not only has confirmed the fact of brain plasticity, it also has created new scientific respect for the subconscious self. Because we can now spy on the secret life of the brain, we can discuss the subconscious as a real, even observable, entity. Of course, I'm particularly fond of the subconscious because I'm a hypnotist. But, as you'll discover in this part, hypnosis is just one of many tools you can use to directly program your subconscious self.

We'll investigate the extraordinary problem-solving power of your dreaming mind and how you can harness that power while you sleep. We'll talk about how to take your performance in a certain area from good to great by practicing visualization the scientific way. We'll discuss your brain's visual cortex, explain why what you *see* so deeply affects your subconscious, and explore what you need to do about it for greater success. Naturally, we'll pull back the curtain on hypnosis, my specialty and a scientific topic of great mystery.

Research indicates that you will more easily learn the scientific content here if you prime your subconscious self by asking questions beforehand. Thus, we begin every chapter with a quiz.

Remember, you can read the chapters in whatever order suits you best. While each one focuses on a particular topic, you'll find that ultimately those topics all interconnect, just as do the five sub-selves. Therefore, as you enjoy the specific stories and strategies shared in each chapter, you simultaneously will be building, within your mind, the big-picture model of Self-Intelligence.

What you prevent yourself from doing and
force yourself not to do,
the dream will do
with all the lucidity of desire . . . .

—SALVADOR DALI

CHAPTER 1

DREAMS

Wake Up to Their Power

Prime-your-mind Quiz

Research says you'll remember this chapter better if you test yourself now. How will the answer affect *you*?

Dreams can be particularly useful because they . . .

a. enable the brain to stop thinking and to conduct cellular repair while engaging in random neural activity.

b. allow us to release repressed psychological urges, especially in the areas of sexuality and aggression.

c. process problems in a highly visual and disinhibited manner, fostering greater creativity than might occur when awake.

You've probably heard that some Silicon Valley high-tech companies offer ideal places to work. They provide free food, free gyms, perhaps even free time just to think up brilliant inventions. Such policies attract super-smart achievers—the geeks of the geeks. So it's not surprising that new employees feel intense pressure to prove their worth. If they succeed quickly, they enjoy prestigious assignments and social esteem. If they fail to impress, they may be sidelined, looked down on, or even resented as the weakest link.

When Mary first called me, she sounded mortified to be seeking help. "My team can't know about this. Some of them were on my hiring committee. For me to be seeing a hypnotist would create the wrong impression." Once in my office, Mary explained that her team included software engineers creating an upgrade of a popular product. It was Mary's job to program a particular new feature.

"My code looks really awful right now," she said. "It does some things okay, but I'm almost surprised it works as well as it does. It's really inelegant. I keep trying to force it because I can't afford to wait. Usually my code is much better than this. They hired me because I'm good. But to try adding onto what's there, to get it to do the rest of what it needs to do, will be like asking a donkey to be a racehorse. It's as if my mind's paralyzed by what my team will think of me. There's really got to be some nice, economical way to write this code. If I had a lot more time, it would come. Ideally, I should just start over, but five months have gone by already, with only one month to nail it. I'm desperate."

Frankly, her one-month deadline scared me too. New hires in any profession tend to suffer performance anxiety, and if Mary had come in sooner, I could have helped her to get comfortable with her job in time to prevent a crisis. Instead, she had backed herself into a corner. Now she slumped in her chair, sighing, "There's probably nothing you can do."

No, I couldn't promise anything. But just maybe, I told her, she could solve this problem for herself in her sleep. "Think of it this way," I said. "We're going to program your subconscious to deliver your answer in a dream."

Historically, dreams at night have often saved the proverbial day. Dmitri Mendeleev spent years trying to systemize the atomic weights of the elements, until the periodic table came to him in a dream. India's late great math genius Srinivasa Ramanujan dreamt up many of his solutions. He said that a Hindu goddess regularly visited his sleep to give him answers. The chemist Friedrich August Kekulé discovered the tetravalent nature of carbon while dreaming, as well as the circular structure of benzene, which appeared to him as a snake biting its own tail. Two Nobel laureates, neuroscientist Otto Loewi and physicist Niels Bohr, both attributed their prizewinning discoveries to dreams.

Numerous great artists have credited dreams for directly inspiring some of their best work. These dreamers include painters Salvador Dali and Jasper Johns; poet William Blake; author of *Frankenstein*, Mary Shelley; and musical composers from Beethoven to Billy Joel.

Thinking Through Dreaming

Despite dreaming's long track record as an idea-generator and problem-solver, for centuries the science of dreams remained in the dark. Dreams were difficult to test, allowing theories to proliferate without much evidence. Many people asked, "What are dreams for?" Freud suggested that dreams express forbidden desires, especially sexual and aggressive impulses. More recently, scientists hypothesized that dreams randomly generate images while our brains rest.

But now, new brain-imaging technology has illuminated the function of dreams. We've discovered that a dreaming brain is not on vacation but hard at work. Simply put, dreaming is just another form of thinking. As Harvard dream expert (and fellow hypnotist) Dierdre Barrett points out, it's silly to ask what dreaming is for, because, like thinking in general: "It is for *everything*." (Check out her book on dreaming, *The Committee of Sleep*.) Thanks to positron-emission tomography (PET) scans, we finally know why in some cases we think better in dreams than when awake. But let's return for a moment to Mary, who experienced this benefit firsthand.

Prior to hypnotizing her, I asked Mary to write a description of the ideal code she wished to create—what it would do, how it might look, even how she would feel after completing it. (She wrote, "Elated!") Later, under hypnosis, she listened to me read her own words out loud. I also suggested that the insight she needed would come to her soon in a dream. Afterward, she took her written description home, with instructions to review it every night at bedtime. Then while lying in bed, she was to think about this ideal code, so that it would be her last thought before falling asleep.

One week went by with no results. Nevertheless, on her second visit she told me she'd been experiencing a strange sensation of hopefulness, which she couldn't quite explain. "I think we should keep trying," she said. So during her second session we repeated everything we'd done the first time. Four days later, on a Sunday evening, she emailed me the following:

> Dear Jane,
>
> Good news. Yesterday morning I woke early feeling anxious and certain I could not go back to sleep. But then I found myself sort of floating around the room where I grew up. On the floor was a toy I remember my cousin owning that I used to play with. It was a toy race car track that could be bent into curves and loops. Here I saw it splitting and looping and coming back together in many places. It was very elaborate, really gigantic and intimidating, but there was also something right about it. I felt that if I could understand the structure I would be okay. I kept floating around the form looking at it from all sides. Sometimes it seemed really complex but then it would seem obvious. Suddenly I understood the structure was the program I needed to write. In a way it was really simple, but it was also taking a whole different turn from what I'd been working on. It was really 'out there.' Anyway, I woke up and as you had told me to do in case of a dream, I lay in bed while I remembered it and went over it in my mind. Before getting out of bed, I drew a picture of the track in my

notebook. Then I told myself sternly to get up in a calm manner and to get to work before I forgot anything. That is what I did. As soon as I sat down at the computer, the code began coming to me really fast. It is elegant. It is not finished but it will not take long now and already I know it will run smoothly. Thank you for your help.

So what was happening neurologically in Mary's brain that allowed her to do her best thinking in a dream? PET scans show that while dreaming, we undergo intense brain activity that differs from our waking thought in key ways. Certain cortical areas that generate visual imagery become even more active. This allows dreams to be visually richer than waking thoughts. In Mary's case, her solution came to her as the image of an elaborate racecar track.

Meanwhile, as the brain dreams, part of the dorsolateral prefrontal cortex takes a break. Think of this part as the brass-knuckled bouncer who, when awake, shoos away inappropriate thoughts—those it perceives as immoral or antisocial or illogical. At dream time, the bouncer goes off-duty, so all those crazy ideas and taboo fantasies get free entry. That's why we can do forbidden stuff in our dreams. It's also why dreaming allows us to come up with great ideas that, when we're awake, might get barred from conscious thought as being, in Mary's words, too "out there." Dreaming enabled her to solve her puzzle by taking "a whole different turn."

Priming for Supine Problem-Solving

It may not surprise you that, historically, artists of all stripes have drawn on dreaming, from composers to painters to writers to filmmakers. Barrett in her research has found we can even use dreaming to solve personal dilemmas such as where to attend graduate school. In my practice, I give dream suggestions to many of my clients, including the athletes. I remind them that in 1964 the legendary golfer Jack Nicklaus came back from a slump after having a dream.

"Wednesday night I had a dream and it was about my golf swing," he told the *San Francisco Chronicle*. "I was hitting them pretty well in the dream and all at once I realized I wasn't holding the club the way I've actually been holding it lately . . . . So when I came to the course yesterday morning I tried it the way I did in my dream and it worked. I shot a 68 yesterday and a 65 today."

Next time you encounter some seemingly intractable problem, one that puzzles you and that you haven't been able to think your way through, consider tackling it while asleep.

Priming your mind with hypnosis might speed things up, but you also can learn to direct dreams on your own by following these steps:

1. Write down what it is you want to discover through dreaming. Rather than describe the problem, describe in one sentence the solution you seek. "I want to come up with an exciting, profitable new product line for my business," or "I want to make a funny video to show at our next family reunion that will help heal old wounds" or "I want to throw a great dinner party for 18 people on a budget of $100."

2. Set up some easy way to record your solution in the middle of the night, in case that's when inspiration strikes. I sometimes give clients a "light pen" with a small LED light that enables writing in the dark. But you might prefer speaking into your smartphone. Whatever method you choose, make it easily accessible so that you don't have to get out of bed to capture your dream-born insight.

3. Just before going to sleep (preferably when you're already in bed), read your solution description out loud. Repeat this process nightly.

4. Whether it's during the night or the next morning, record any interesting dreams before getting out of bed, even if they don't make immediate sense; later, their symbolic meaning may become clear. Remember, Kekulé discovered the circular structure of benzene by dreaming of a snake biting its own tail.

Trust your subconscious. Be patient, knowing that eventually you will get results. With disciplined practice, anyone can wake up to the power of dreams. What shall you do with yours?

Use Your Self-Intelligence

Once you get the hang of directing your dreams, the possible uses are limitless. Here are but a few suggestions to inspire you.

With problems at the workplace, our prefrontal cortex tends to go on overdrive, smothering inspiration. Invite yourself to literally dream your way to successful solutions, just as Mary did.

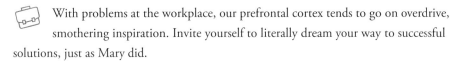

Recall golfer Jack Nicklaus's dream breakthrough. Is there a sport or physical exercise you're well trained in, yet know you could improve with a better strategy? Dream on it! The next chapter, on visualization, will also help you reach the top of your game. And for best results, please get enough sleep. (See chapter 12.)

Wondering what you and your partner or loved ones should do on your next big holiday? Dream up your dream vacation. On another note: aim to avoid arguing at bedtime. Follow the old adage to "sleep on it," for we often resolve conflicts in our dreams, even if the next day we don't remember the dreams, but simply wake up feeling better about everything.

Next time you wish someone would invent a gizmo to do this or that, take the initiative and give it a shot yourself. Ask your subconscious to design your invention while dreaming. Many entrepreneurs make money licensing their ideas to companies that develop them.

Quiz answer: Dreams can be particularly useful because they . . .

 c. process problems in a highly visual and disinhibited manner, fostering greater creativity than might occur when awake.

In a Nutshell

When you dream, your brain continues to think, and in some ways it thinks better than when you're awake—particularly in terms of visual problem-solving. Your sleeping brain stops censoring your thoughts, which allows your creativity to expand. This is why so many inventors, scientists, and artists have discovered breakthrough solutions while dreaming. Anyone can learn to direct their dreams. Practice programming your mind to work for you while you sleep.

Humans excel at visual imagery. Our brains evolved this ability to create an internal mental picture or model of the world in which we can rehearse forthcoming actions, without the risks or penalties of doing them in the real world.

—NEUROSCIENTIST V. S. RAMACHANDRAN

CHAPTER 2

VISUALIZATION

Use Your Brain to Reach the Top of Your Game

Prime-your-mind Quiz

Research says you'll remember this chapter better if you test yourself now. How will the answer affect *you*?

To employ visualization most effectively, one should . . .

a. include only visual imagery, because engaging other senses may dilute the effect.

b. treat visualization as a form of mental practice by bringing to it discipline and focus.

c. fantasize that everything effortlessly turns out great, because this will attract success.

O
n August 13, 2016, when Michael Phelps approached the pool for the final swim of his Olympic career, he was feeling choked up. Only two years earlier, he had been considering suicide. Now, here he was in Rio de Janeiro, completing a comeback.

And when his final race arrived—the third leg of the men's medley relay—the Americans were trailing the Brits by .61 seconds. For Phelps, there would be no easy swan song. The pressure was intense. One hundred meters of his butterfly stroke later, the Americans led by .41 seconds, allowing teammate Nathan Adrian to bring in the gold. Once again, Phelps had come through.

Phelps acknowledged afterward to ESPN: "Walking down the warm-up pool deck, I started getting choked up thinking this is my last 'this,' this is my last 'that.'" Phelps closed his Olympic career as the most decorated champion of all time, with twenty-eight Olympic medals, twenty-three of them gold.

The journey had taken him from boy to man. He swam his first Olympic race at fifteen, and his last as a thirty-one-year-old father. Over time, the stress of celebrity, and a troubled relationship with his own dad, had driven Phelps to abuse drugs and alcohol. After facing charges of a second DUI in 2014, he retreated to his bedroom for several days without food or water and waited for death. But life won. Phelps sought help, he found his higher purpose, he reconnected with his father, and he began training one more time for the Olympics.

How is it possible that throughout his Olympic career, from the depressive youth whose dad had deserted him to the caring adult he became, Phelps consistently performed to near-perfection? Yes, he met all those requirements we'll explore in chapter 18: he began swimming at an early age; he worked hard; he had a great coach. But as a child he also learned another skill to which he himself credits much of his superhuman success: visualization.

His coach, Bob Bowman, made it a top priority. "When I was thirteen or fourteen, Bob started asking me to play a race in my head as though it were a video," recounts Phelps in his book *No Limits*. "Visualizing like this is like programming a race in my head, and that programming sometimes seems to make it happen just as I had imagined it."

Both he and his coach agree that "visualization . . . makes me different." Different, indeed! Visualization has played a part in making Phelps not just great, but *the greatest* Olympic athlete in history. However, I should mention that the term *visualization* can mean various things. Here, we'll explore only one kind—a scientifically validated form of mental practice. This is the kind that Phelps himself employs. It is the kind my clients also have used to become better golfers, speakers, musicians, sales representatives, and more.

Why Visualization Flies and Fantasy Flops

Let's look at some science related to visualization. Before researchers discovered *why* visualization works, a famous 1989 experiment dramatized how well it works. Seventy-some college students were tested on their dart-throwing ability at the beginning and end of an eight-week study. Those assigned to a control group didn't practice at all and, understandably, did not improve. A second group physically practiced dart-throwing daily for eight weeks. The remaining participants put in the same amount of time, but alternated between physical and mental practice, that is, visualization. One day they'd physically throw darts; the next day, they'd practice only in their minds. In other words, they physically practiced half as much. And guess what? They improved the most.

That's right: Those who skipped physical practice every other day, using that time to visualize instead, improved more than those who physically practiced every day. Since then, other studies have confirmed that visualization tends to be extremely effective, and that combining it with physical practice produces stellar results. (Perhaps more shocking, research shows that in some instances, merely visualizing the use of a muscle can, over time, improve muscle strength. This is because visualization activates neurons in both the brain and the body.)

In 2011, some headlines declared that visualization was a bust. But it turned out those studies were really about fantasizing, which is a whole different animal. Two New York University psychologists had asked subjects to fantasize about happy outcomes, from winning a contest to achieving weekly goals. This daydreaming may have felt good but it encouraged passivity—which, the researchers concluded, made the participants less likely to achieve anything at all.

When done correctly, visualization is quite distinct from fantasizing. It means using one's mind not to daydream about—but to *rehearse*—the achievement of a goal. It's a form of mental *practice*, and therefore like all effective practice requires focus and discipline. This activates thousands upon thousands of synaptic connections, creating and strengthening neural maps throughout the brain and body for peak performance. That is why a meta-analysis of 35 studies including more than 3,000 subjects found that, when done properly, visualization significantly boosts success for an astonishingly wide range of activities.

Think about your own tennis serve, or your public speaking, or guitar playing, or some other skill you've learned. Let's say you "know how" to perform perfectly, but at the moment of execution, you fall short. That's because your conscious knowledge—of what you should do—hasn't been fully mapped into your subconscious mind. What's worse, if you keep committing the same mistakes in real-life practice, those mistakes get reprogrammed into your body and brain. In contrast, visualization allows you to practice error-free every time, thereby programming the subconscious for automatic perfect performance. See how that works?

For example, to improve a particular golf shot, my client first visualizes it several times in slow motion, which enables her to mindfully attend to all the details of an impeccable swing. Only after she has mastered perfection does she mentally rehearse that same shot at a faster pace.

It's also key that in order to create strong cellular connections, she makes her experience feel as real as possible. So even before practicing the shot itself, she sets the scene. First, she creates a vivid image—for example, picturing not only the golf course landscape,

THE BASIC DRILL

1. Decide what you want to practice—nailing your tennis serve, playing Bach's *Prelude in C Major*, or giving a public talk . . . . Whatever it is, choose something you've already trained for in real time and now want to improve.

2. Choose a place and time that will allow you to comfortably relax. Close your eyes. Get calm. If you have a favorite relaxation technique— such as abdominal breathing—go ahead and use it. Aim for a steady calm that will allow you to mentally focus.

3. Begin by setting the scene. Where does this activity take place? First focus on the visuals, adding whatever details you know of, to make the picture more vivid: colors, lighting, architecture or landscape, furniture or equipment, an audience or others who will be present, and so on.

4. Bring into your mind, as best you can, whatever sounds you would hear in that situation: maybe the rustle of clothing, the hum of an air conditioner, or a murmuring crowd . . . .

5. Weave in physical sensations. Will you be sitting in a certain chair that feels a certain way? Holding something in your hands? Sensing the warmth of the sun? How will your feet feel in your shoes? This part of visualization doesn't need to be perfect. Just do the best you can.

6. If particular tastes or aromas will be part of your experience, then bring those into your mind as well. Will you experience the flavor of Gatorade? The scent of freshly mown grass?

7. Once you've constructed the setting, it's time to practice performing at your absolute best. This is the most important aspect of visualization. You may want to begin in slow motion to get it right. Remember to include kinesthesia, strongly imagining all the body sensations relevant to your success. Intensify your focus, always aim

for a flawless execution, and carefully rehearse your top performance. As you start to feel more sure of yourself, you can speed up your practice.

8. Congratulations, you've done the hard work. Now, invite into your mind and body the positive emotions you associate with getting it right. For example, you might feel confidence, pride, or joy. Retain this emotional state as you let go of your visualization, open your eyes, and return your awareness to the present moment.

9. Good job! For maximum results, visualize regularly, alternating between real-time and mental practice.

Bonus tip: Sometimes a beginner will find it hard to conjure up mental images. Here's an easy exercise that can help. Look at something, then close your eyes and immediately recall the image in your mind. For example, if you glance up from this book, what do you see? Take in your surroundings, then close your eyes and mentally re-create the scene as vividly you can. Next, open your eyes, note any details you missed in your first re-creation, then close your eyes and do it again . . . and so on. You also can practice using photographs. Over time your mental-imaging ability will noticeably improve. Get an extra benefit by practicing with beautiful, uplifting images, to give yourself an emotional boost. (In the next chapter, we'll explore the sometimes strange influence of images on your subconscious self.)

but also details such as the very texture of the golf ball. Plus, she brings to mind other sensations—the smell of the grass, or the coolness of fresh air against her skin.

As she executes her perfect shot, she taps into kinesthesia (a concept we'll explore in chapter 10), imagining every relevant bodily sensation. She imagines the position of the club in her hands, the movement of her hips, and the muscles in her arms as she swings. She feels the impact as her club strikes the ball with a *thwack* before she watches it land exactly where she aims.

During our sessions, my client does her mental practice while under hypnosis—visualization on steroids, as it were. But visualization also works fine on its own. One famous example is Glenn Gould, the world-class pianist who did most of his daily practice not at the piano keys but in his head. You can use mental practice to improve any number of skills, with one caveat: you must be already trained in that skill. If you've never picked up a guitar, then visualization won't turn you into Jimi Hendrix. It can't teach you how to swim. But if you do quality hands-on training, then visualization can help make you a master.

Using Good Sense to Prep for Bad Events

Sometimes clients ask me if it's dangerous, while mentally practicing, to visualize bad luck—a windy golf tournament, say, or raucous onlookers—because they're afraid it might "manifest" or "attract" that bad luck. Not to worry. Visualization offers an ideal opportunity to train for hard challenges. Phelps reports that, "It's a good thing to visualize the bad stuff. It prepares you. Maybe you dive in and your goggles fill with water. What do you do? How do you respond? What is important right now? You have to have a plan."

People also ask me, why is it called *visualization* if we're bringing in other input besides images? Well, as we'll discuss in the next chapter on *Images*, sight dominates the senses. The visual cortex is a powerhouse of the brain—even for blind people. For them, because there's no visual data coming in, the visual cortex instead ramps up the brain's processing of other input, such as sound or touch. In fact, visualization works just as well for the blind as for the sighted.

Many years ago, while living in San Juan, Puerto Rico, I knew a blind man who regularly practiced visualization (although he didn't call it that). Sightless since birth, Don Carlos was a happy husband and dad who owned a profitable laundromat. Don Carlos radiated goodwill. He enjoyed chatting, and easily recognized anyone he'd met before by the sound of their voice. He repaired all the laundry machines himself by using his senses of hearing and touch.

While interviewing him for a news article, I asked for his secret to well-being. "Before getting up from bed, I take a moment each morning to go over how I will behave that day," he told me. "Especially the manner in which I will treat my wife and children. I practice it in my mind—being a very good man. This way, when the time comes, I *am* a very good man. This is why my family loves me. My laundromat pays the bills. It is my family's love that makes me happy."

Knowing that visualization can work for all of us, what skills would you like to improve? In what endeavor do you want to go from good to very good, or perhaps to great, or even to greatest? Remember, it's not just for sports. It can help you hone any performance skill you're already trained in but need more practice at, from making cold calls to busting a dance move to doing stand-up comedy. My mentor Jack Canfield—a mega-millionaire and world-renowned author and trainer—attributes much of his own success to visualization. He still practices it every day in order to stay at the top of his game in all areas of his life, consistently conquering greater challenges and achieving bigger dreams. It will take you just minutes to learn this powerful technique. Follow the nine steps in the sidebar "The Basic Drill," then enjoy alternating between physical and mental practice. Before long, your performance will astonish you.

Use Your Self-Intelligence

Visualization can help you achieve top performance in a wide variety of activities. Once you learn the technique, you'll find it easy to use throughout every area of your life.

 Anxious about an upcoming business talk? Add visualization to your prep. Of course, do plenty of actual, out-loud rehearsal in real time. But also rehearse in your mind; deliver the entire talk in your imagination, including varying your vocals, making physical gestures, and seeing the audience in your mind's eye. Alternate between these two forms of practice—real and visualized—so that each reinforces the other. Rehearse both out loud and in your mind enough times that you begin looking forward with excitement to the real event.

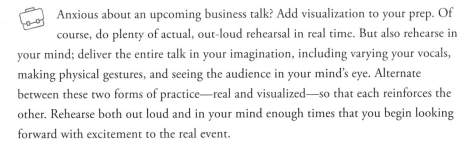 Do you ever struggle with overeating? Before a lavish meal—say, Christmas—visualize taking moderate portions, chewing slowly, savoring your food, saying

no to that second piece of pie, and feeling great about yourself afterward. In this way, you will strengthen your neural maps for automatic healthy habits. Self-discipline will be far easier.

 Follow Don Carlos's example. If you mentally rehearse treating your loved ones well—then it will become second nature. You *will* treat them well, and reap the rewards.

If you're in sales, visualization provides a risk-free way to perfect your pitch. When you practice, include feelings of genuine *liking* toward the person or group you're addressing. You will be more effective—and enjoy your job a whole lot more—when you access your heartfelt connection with clients.

Quiz answer: To employ visualization most effectively, one should . . .

b.   treat visualization as a form of mental practice by bringing to it discipline and focus.

In a Nutshell

The kind of visualization that's been proven to work is a form of highly focused mental practice that includes multiple senses—for example, sight, hearing, touch, and kinesthesia. This activates synaptic connections throughout the brain and body, forming strong neural maps for success. Visualization can be used to improve all sorts of skills, including athletic and musical performance, as a complement to quality training. To start with, choose one skill to improve by adding daily visualization to your practice. Soon you will be amazed by your results.

I will not be just a tourist in the world of images,
just watching images passing by which I cannot
live in, make love to, possess as
permanent sources of joy and ecstasy.

—ANAÏS NIN

CHAPTER 3

IMAGES

What You See Is
What You "Get" Deep in the Brain

Prime-your-mind Quiz

Research says you'll remember this chapter better if you test yourself now. How will the answer affect *you*?

If you watch a video of someone saying "Ga, ga," but the audio has been dubbed over with the sound "Ba, ba," you will actually hear . . .

a. the sound "Da, da," because the senses are integrated to work together, with sight wielding the strongest influence.

b. the sound "Ga, ga," because your eyes will completely fool you.

c. the sound "Ba, ba," because the brain is compartmentalized so that each of our senses functions independently.

Tom had moved from Idaho to the Bay Area hoping to land a high-end restaurant job. A culinary school graduate and certified sommelier, he had chosen San Francisco, a mecca of foodies, as the ideal place to further his hands-on education for a few years. Eventually, he wanted to open his own eatery back in Boise. To save money while job-scouting, he was renting a cheap studio in the notorious Tenderloin district.

"It's just me, my bed, my laptop, my dumbbells, my cell phone, and four walls that have kind of creepy stains on them," he told me when he called. "And one little window with bars. That's what I'm looking at, here. Not too pretty. A friggin' jail, basically."

Like many prospective clients, Tom was seeking a mental boost. "Normally I'm high energy, and usually I don't mind applying for work because I really like people and interview well. But now I'm feeling too blah staring at these walls to convince anyone to hire me. I'm still doing my push-ups and lifting my weights, but mentally . . . . Don't know what's hit me, really."

I asked what his home had been like in Boise. "Beautiful! Tall windows, great view of the river. But I've always wanted to live in San Francisco. Of course it's a bore looking at this friggin' room, but it's not a big deal."

I asked, "How about putting up some pictures?"

"Pictures?" He sounded incredulous. "I just want a mental recharge to get my energy back."

The Irresistible Influence of Images

Many people wish for a quick fix from hypnosis, not realizing that, in most cases, they must take steps to make change last. Yes, hypnosis could lift Tom's spirits. But if he continued staring at the dingy walls and barred window of his prisonlike studio, any good mood would likely fade. Why? Because the images that we see every day wield a big emotional impact. Vision is so dominant in primates—and in humans especially— that it sometimes overrides all the other senses. Because Tom had emphasized what his place looked like, I felt certain that it did in fact matter to him, even though he wasn't conscious of it.

When we met, there was an immediate sense of good rapport. "Fantastic office!" he exclaimed. He noted the Tiffany wall sconces and my framed arrangements of four-leaf clovers (see chapter 6 to find out why I might have so many lucky clovers), as well as the charming view below of Yerba Buena Lane. As much as he liked what he saw, he still didn't quite believe me when I began to explain the importance of images.

"I don't really care about what I'm looking at. It's my energy level I care about," he insisted. "Let's just get to the hypnosis." Tom turned out fairly easy to hypnotize, thoroughly enjoyed his session, and left feeling, as he put it, "friggin' fantastic!"

However, the following week, he called again. "It seems to be wearing off," he said. "I'm back to staring at the ugly walls. Let's do another session to make it stick." I asked Tom if he thought the ugly walls might be a factor. He laughed. "Nah. You ladies are sensitive to décor. Even strong, smart ladies like you."

Tom was on a budget and in a hurry. As we set our second appointment, an idea came to me of what to do. I decided to carry out my plan only if it seemed right when the moment arrived, because it involved two lies—what you might call "white lies," although technically one was green and the other red. Allow me to explain:

It used to be thought that the brain analyzed visual signals cognitively before processing them emotionally. But we now know it's the other way around. The optic nerve goes straight to the thalamus, which turns out to have a direct, synaptic connection to that emotional hot spot, the amygdala. That means that our emotion-driving limbic system reacts to images before we can think about it. For example, experiments show that simply seeing a genuine smile triggers an instant positive response in most people. The sight of someone cringing in terror will trigger fear. This is called *emotional contagion*, our built-in neurological tendency to automatically "catch" the emotions we perceive in others. It involves more than sight (see chapter 8 and chapter 14), but sight is its strongest trigger.

The fact that we're emotionally affected by images may seem obvious. After all, it's a regular practice of scientists to show people evocative pictures in order to induce in them whatever specific emotions the researchers wish to study. Want to know how people's neurons behave when they're upset? Show your test subjects an upsetting photo, then use brain-imaging technology to see how that emotion plays out in their heads. Yet, it's all too easy for us as individuals to make the same mistake Tom did, of imagining oneself as somehow exempt from this neurological reality.

What's more, we respond emotionally even to images we never consciously perceive. This has been dramatized in studies of people with healthy eyes who've suffered damage to their visual cortex, the brain area where most visual stimuli are processed after passing through the thalamus. People with this unusual condition, called *blindsight*, consciously see nothing at all. Legally, they are 100 percent blind. Yet research shows that visual stimuli continue to reach other, subconscious parts of their brains. A blindsighted man will deftly navigate an obstacle course—say, a hallway strewn with office equipment—but later will not know how he did it, having consciously seen neither the hallway nor the obstacles. Other experiments find that, just like the rest of us, blindsighted people experience image-induced *emotional contagion*, automatically emoting when presented with photos of people who are, for example, crouching in fear or jumping for joy.

For full-sighted folks, the effect is so strong that vision dominates all the senses, profoundly influencing even those experiences we don't normally associate with sight. The research on this is mind-boggling. Which is why, getting back to Tom's story, I wanted to boggle his mind just enough that he'd do something to improve the images he was taking in.

My plan was unoriginal. I re-created a common experiment by using one bottle of clear cherry-flavored sparkling water and one of lime. Using food dye, I colored the cherry soda green, and the lime soda red. And I just hoped that Tom would react the same way most people do who've undergone this test in science labs.

When he came in, I asked if he'd mind taking a "sensory-acuity test" before we did any hypnosis, because it would help me demonstrate something helpful. Tom good-naturedly agreed. I poured us each one cup of the red sparkling water, and one of the green. Here's where I lied—as it were, by omission. I said, "One is cherry-flavored sparkling water and one is lime. Please tell me what you notice." And then with genuine curiosity, I tasted mine too. The wrong-colored drinks tasted odd even knowing the experiment!

Tom tried both of his, shrugged, and shook his head as if to indicate there was nothing to say. I asked him to please try the cherry again and, understandably, he picked up the cup of *red* sparkling water.

"A little bland," he said.

I requested that he retry the lime. He picked up the *green* drink, and tried it again too. "Losing its fizz. Already going flat. Nothing to write home about."

I had never before (nor have I since) conducted any experiments on clients. So it was with real trepidation that I explained to him what was up. To my great relief, Tom broke out laughing. I then showed him the little bottles of food coloring, and the large bottles of sparkling water with their labels exposed so that he could see which flavor was which.

Tom retasted each drink with eyes open and then, at my suggestion, with eyes closed. "That's bizarre," he concluded. "They taste normal only when I don't look—and I'm a friggin' sommelier!"

I handed him a printout about a scientific study involving wine tasters at the University of Bordeaux in France. The researcher found that even these would-be connoisseurs, aiming to detect every intricacy of aroma, will mistake a white wine's "nose" for a red wine if it is dyed red. Because our visual sense trumps all the others, and because science proves that it so deeply affects our emotions, I beseeched Tom to consider putting something nice on his walls. By then, it was time for hypnosis. Afterward, he left my office feeling great.

> **The reason that sight can trick our senses of taste and smell is that the brain is far less compartmentalized than scientists once assumed.**

When he phoned a month later, he was still feeling good. He explained that he never took my suggestion to hang pictures because he'd come up with something better. He had decided to stop looking at his room, period. "I'm doing more video calls with friends to see their faces. I've been to two art museums. I've started working out in the park. I'm down at the Ferry Building right now, admiring the bay. I'll be moving soon and will make sure to find a place with a view because this city is beautiful." He was happy to report that once his energy had lifted, he'd intensified his job search and gotten hired as a hotel restaurant prep chef. "Everyone in my business knows that presentation is important. But now I really get it."

Auto-Filling in the Blanks

The reason that sight can trick our senses of taste and smell is that the brain is far less compartmentalized than scientists once assumed. All our senses interact, each relying on the others for cues—and in humans, sight reigns supreme, with the visual cortex being one of the most powerful parts of the brain. (Cup your hand around the middle of the back of your head; it's right there.) Vision measurably influences our sense of touch—which is why it's best to *not* watch that vaccination needle plunging through your skin—and even can distort the sounds we hear. Cognitive scientist Harry McGurk discovered this back in 1976 after an assistant accidentally dubbed a video with a mismatched phoneme during a study on how babies perceive language. When he and his assistant played the video back, the adults were astonished to hear a third phoneme that was neither the one mouthed, nor the one spoken. It turns out that if we see someone saying "Ga, ga," synced to an audio of "Ba, ba," what we hear will be a compromise: "Da, da." This is now known as the *McGurk effect*.

If you want to remember the McGurk effect, you'd be wise to watch a YouTube video demonstration. My favorite is by developmental molecular biologist John Medina, author of the *Brain Rules* book series. Why should you see the video? Because doing so will hugely boost your memory retention. Research finds that when you add visuals to your learning, you remember up to six times as much. This phenomenon, which scientists call the *picture superiority effect*, or PSE, is well documented and put to lucrative use by advertisers. Alas, in our schools most books and lectures still rely too exclusively on words. "Human PSE is truly Olympian," says Medina. "Tests performed years ago showed that people could remember more than 2,500 pictures with at least 90 percent accuracy several days post-exposure . . . . Accuracy rates a year later still hovered around 63 percent."

Medina is a big proponent of using more images in the classroom. Why aren't educators doing so? Possibly because they don't know the research on PSE. Another obstacle may be the widespread myth that each human being fits neatly into of one of three learning categories: visual, auditory, or kinesthetic. Given this notion, some teachers may believe it's unfair to privilege visual resources over other kinds. However, while some early studies seemed to support this catchy each-to-their-own theory, controlled research just does not bear it out. What studies do prove is that pictures increase memory retention for virtually everyone. That doesn't mean it would help to put *words* on a blackboard or in a PowerPoint slide. It means adding *images*—photos, artwork, videos, computer animations, or cartoons—to illustrate the lessons at hand.

If, like Tom, you've grown accustomed to thinking of images as external phenomena, irrelevant to the internal workings of your mind, it may help to understand what scientists now know: Vision is a brain activity. We don't see with our eyes, not really. We see with our *brains*. We don't see what's *out there*. We see what our neurons concoct in our noggins, and hopefully, most of the time, it matches what's out there.

Consider this: You have in each eye a blind spot, literally, which takes in no visual information. It's at the very back, where the optic nerve leaves the retina on its way into the brain. If it were your eyes that did your seeing, you'd notice this blind spot. If you closed one eye, you'd clearly perceive the other eye's black patch of nothingness interrupting your view. But we never do perceive our blind spots, because our brains compulsively fill them in with invented information. That's right, the visual cortex shamelessly makes up stuff to fill the holes, much the same way you might use Photoshop to fill in missing pixels on your granddad's tattered portrait.

But here's what's weirder. In a very real sense, your brain is making up everything you see, extrapolating images not only out of new data coming in, but also out of bits and pieces of memory data on hand. That's why, during a vivid dream, you are genuinely *seeing*, neurologically speaking. It's just that what you're seeing has no external counterpart outside your brain.

Or consider this: If you lost your eyes right now, you could learn to see again through a camera attached to your forehead that would deliver visual information, via tiny electrical impulses, to your tongue. (They say it feels like champagne bubbles.) Amazingly, your brain would figure out how to translate the tingles into images that you'd *see*. You wouldn't see very well, because the technology can't transmit as much data as can your million-plus optic nerve cells . . . but regardless, you would *see*. You don't need eyes to see. You do need your brain.

Once we fathom what a brainy process vision actually is, we may find it easier to respect the influence of images. Take a moment to contemplate: Is what you see every day depressing you or inspiring you? Have you, like Tom, been telling yourself that you don't care what you're looking at? Sciences proves that we *do* care, and that our happiness may, to some extent, depend on it. Choose to live in a world you love to behold.

Use Your Self-Intelligence

What would you like to literally *see* more of in your life? Decide now to make it happen.

Take a good look at your work area. How could it be more pleasing to you? Studies show that improving décor with wall art and potted plants tends to boost productivity. If you're the boss, take note in chapter 7 that allowing employees to customize their own workspaces doubles that effect.

The images that you see at bedtime will wend their way into your subconscious mind and affect your sleep. (Good sleep is key to your overall health, as we'll discuss in chapter 12.) Avoid gory movies late at night. At day's end, look at something soothing. Go glance at your garden in the moonlight, or take note of the serene expression on your sleeping cat. No garden or cat? Try a nature show or book of art.

Research has found that viewing photos of smiling loved ones sets off neural rewards far beyond the standard pretty picture. Keep such photos on hand (they make great screensavers) and enjoy them regularly. This will make you feel better in general, as well as more positive about your relationships in particular.

When you sell personal property, whether it's a house, a bicycle or a yacht . . . it's worth having it spruced up before you put it on the market. Studies show buyers *think* they judge logically, but subconsciously they estimate value based on appearances. A clean car sells for more than one with garbage on the floor. A coat of paint will boost a house price by many thousands of dollars.

Quiz answer: If you watch a video of someone saying "Ga, ga," but the audio has been dubbed over with the sound "Ba, ba," you will actually *hear* . . .

   a. the sound "Da, da," because the senses are integrated to work together, with sight wielding the strongest influence.

In a Nutshell

The limbic system—your brain's processor of emotions—responds powerfully to whatever you see, even when you don't consciously realize it. Images often go straight to the subconscious, influencing your mood and behavior without your conscious consent. Exploit this fact by taking in images that elevate your well-being.

In effect, hypnosis is the epitome of mind-body medicine. It can enable the mind to tell the body how to react, and modify the messages that the body sends to the mind.

—JANE E. BRODY, *NEW YORK TIMES*

CHAPTER 4

HYPNOSIS

It's Real and It Works, so Don't Be a Chicken

Prime-your-mind Quiz

Research says you'll remember this chapter better if you test yourself now. How will the answer affect *you*?

In many documented cases, people have undergone pain-free surgeries without chemical anesthesia, using only hypnosis to maintain comfort, and what scientists now say about this is . . .

a. hypnosis works by altering our bodies' magnetic fields.

b. hypnosis works by shutting down the nervous system.

c. hypnosis works, but we don't know how or why, nor even exactly what hypnosis is.

K athy is a high-energy high school principal, but the first time we met she looked haggard, with dark circles under her eyes and a distracted frown, as though she couldn't quite focus.

"I'm exhausted," she explained. "I go to bed on time, but either I can't fall asleep, or if I do, within a few hours I'm wide awake for the rest of the night. This has been going on for weeks. I'm getting more and more worried. I'm forgetting things. It took me half an hour this morning to find my car keys, which is totally unlike me. I can't keep my mind clear. I'm not even sure it's safe to drive, although . . . " she laughed ruefully, "there seems to be no danger of my falling asleep at the wheel! It's weird. When it began, it was just one night that I had some difficulty sleeping, but nothing terrible. The next day I worried about it happening again, and it did happen again, only worse. Since then, it keeps happening and I'm getting more and more scared. I tried some sleeping pills, but they don't help much, and they make me woozy the next day."

I asked if she'd ever been hypnotized.

"Oh yes!" she exclaimed. "Each year a hypnotist performs in the school auditorium. For some reason, I always end up on stage doing funny things. The kids love it."

This was joy to my ears. "You're going to sleep well tonight, and from now on," I announced. And indeed she did, and reportedly has ever since.

How could I know it would be so easy? Because Kathy is a *high-hypnotizable*, or so-called *somnambulist*. And how did I know that? Because it's the somnambulists whom any good show-hypnotist will invite up on stage. (It's fairly easy to spot them in an audience by observing their reactions to certain suggestions.) Their participation makes hypnosis seem almost supernatural, because somnambulists can drop into a deep trance within seconds, then blithely comply to seemingly outrageous commands on stage—whether it's performing Elvis's *Love Me Tender*, or behaving like some other species altogether.

It's because of those silly stage shows that when strangers meet me, a hypnotist, at a cocktail party, they're liable to jump back, shield their eyes, and implore, "Please don't make me cluck like a chicken!"

But even if I wanted to carry out such dastardly deeds, most people are not highly hypnotizable enough to be turned into farm animals. Somnambulists make up only an estimated 10 percent of the population. And not even they can be *forced* to do anything under hypnosis. Hypnosis helps them to shed inhibitions about performing in public, but given a command they really don't like, they'll refuse. Yet it's true that for them, therapeutic hypnosis can create instant, dramatic results. On the flip side, because these people are so *suggestible* all day long, negative thoughts can lodge in their subconscious minds and wreak havoc. Thus, Kathy's worry that she might not sleep had snowballed into a subconscious directive to *not*-sleep.

The Highs and the Lows of Hypnotizability

In my professional training, I learned that to free somnambulists from their subconscious programming, one must put them into a deep trance—deeper than the suggestible states they naturally experience on their own. Over a two-hour session I led Kathy into deep hypnosis, then offered her a new directive: "You will find it easy to sleep well every night and throughout the night, comfortably and soundly, enjoying your sleep, and you will awake each morning well rested with plenty of energy to start the day." From then on, Kathy had no problem sleeping.

Oh, those lucky somnambulists for whom hypnosis can be a fast *and* permanent fix. But what about the rest of us? Are we a lost cause? For example, me—I'm a low hypnotizable, perhaps in the lowest 10 percent, the opposite of Kathy. Well, in my experience, hypnosis can help just about everybody who truly wants to change. Indeed, hypnosis helped to cure me, too, of insomnia—in fact, of chronic insomnia, which had plagued me for decades.

For me, having sessions with another hypnotist was not enough to do the trick. It took several weeks of also practicing self-hypnosis every night for me to gain control of my sleep. (For my free mini-course on self-hypnosis, visit self-intelligence.com.) Many years later, my continued success depends on regularly using self-hypnosis to maintain my subconscious conditioning. One payoff is that the more those neural pathways become reinforced, the quicker the process works. Now, instead of up to half an hour, it typically takes me less than a minute to drop into dreamland.

Most of my clients fall near the middle of the range, between low- and high-hypnotiz-ability. Often, they ask me, what makes one person more hypnotizable than another? Preliminary studies indicate it may be related to brain structure, and to a propensity for mental absorption—that is, the capacity to become so fully engaged in a particular mode of thought that outside stimuli fade away. But all scientists know for sure is that hypnosis works.

Science, Suspicion, and the Secret We Don't Yet Know

Thousands of people have used hypnosis to quit smoking, shed phobias, pass difficult exams, boost creativity, stop panic attacks, increase self-confidence, play better ball, and so on. Many famous figures have credited hypnosis for their personal or professional breakthroughs. (See "Celebrity Hypno-Cases.") Top athletes tend to combine it with visualization, the technique we tackled in chapter 2. The use of hypnosis among athletes and other celebrity performers is far more widespread than most people imagine. Such clients tend to treat hypnosis as their "secret weapon," insisting on confidentiality. (That's fine with me, as I believe it's only fair to respect my clients' privacy.)

Most of the hundreds of scientific studies on hypnosis have focused on health care. Over the last decades, scores of controlled experiments have found hypnosis to be effective for a plethora of medical issues, from pain relief to improved surgery results to weight loss to dispelling allergies to curbing psoriasis. Because of these scientific results, hypnosis is now embraced by virtually all top medical institutions, including the National Institutes of Health, the Mayo Clinic, Kaiser Permanente, Harvard Medical School, Stanford University Medical Center, the American Cancer Society, the American Dental Association, and the American Psychology Association.

CELEBRITY HYPNO-CASES

Countless famous folks have used hypnosis to achieve their goals.

Here are a few:

Ellen DeGeneres, Matt Damon, and Ben Affleck all used hypnosis to successfully quit smoking. DeGeneres celebrated it on her own show; Affleck raved about it on *Oprah*; and Damon told Jay Leno, "I went to that hypnotist . . . It worked. I swear to god it worked. It was the greatest decision I ever made in my life!"

Actor Aaron Eckhart used self-hypnosis to kick both cigarettes and alcohol. He told the London *Telegraph*, "I couldn't be happier with that decision. I recommend it to anybody."

Irish heavyweight boxer Kevin McBride used hypnosis to prep for his fight with former world champion Mike Tyson in 2005. McBride told *USA Today* before the match, "What hypnosis does is send out signals to the subconscious mind that makes you leave nothing behind. I'm going to take it to Mike Tyson with a 100% effort." Tyson became so dispirited he quit in the seventh round; McBride won.

In the year 1900, Russian Romantic composer Sergey Vasilyevich Rachmaninoff was too depressed to write music, until he went to see hypnotist Nikolai Dahl. Rachmaninoff later said in his published *Recollections*: "Although it may sound incredible, this cure really helped me. Already at the beginning of the summer I began again to compose . . . . Dr. Dahl's treatment had strengthened my nervous system to a miraculous degree. Out of gratitude I dedicated my second Concerto to him."

Tiger Woods began mental training at age 13 with hypnotist Jay Brunza, who worked with him for several years. Woods told *Golf Digest* in 2002 that as an adult, he uses self-hypnosis to play his best by "willing myself into the zone," and that hypnosis is simply "inherent in what I do now." But keep in mind that everything we do affects the subconscious mind. When Woods's personal life swerved off track, so did his game.

Nevertheless, hypnosis still arouses suspicion even among many otherwise educated folks. A tech-savvy woman at a chic San Francisco gathering told me, "I don't believe in hypnosis." That's a bit like saying, "I don't believe in sound waves." Had she ever read any research studies on it, or even a single article about hypnosis in a respected science magazine? No, she said. But she remained sure of her opinion.

Hypnosis boasts a long, colorful history (See the sidebar "Hypno-History"), and often has met with scorn, usually for one of three reasons:

1. Early hypnotists made fantastical claims about what they could do and why.

2. The legitimate effects of hypnosis were sometimes so dramatic as to appear fraudulent.

3. Over the last century, the association of hypnosis with entertainment has made it seem literally laughable.

So far, the U.S. government does not regulate hypnosis. A few states do, but its potential uses are so vast and varied that they're hard to codify. Recent brain-imaging experiments indicate that hypnosis triggers more powerful activation of more parts of the brain than can be achieved by merely imagining something.

Okay, but you still may be wondering, "What *is* hypnosis?" We don't know!

You could define it as a highly suggestible state, but that's pretty vague. It often involves deep relaxation, but doesn't have to. A person could be hypnotized while reclining with eyes closed, or while swinging upside down from a jungle gym. There are countless ways to hypnotize people, using visual or auditory cues, verbal suggestions, touch, or some combination.

Hypnotists watch for physiological shifts that indicate a trance state, such as rapid eye movement, changes in breathing or skin pallor, or an unconscious parting of the lips. Or, you can simply do a test—say, by directing a client to experience numbness, after which you pinch them hard and they don't feel a thing. But those are only the *effects*. Why or how hypnosis does what it does remains a subject of study, and a mystery for now. Of course, the same is true of gravity; we still don't know exactly what gravity is, nor how it works, but hey, it seems to work.

HYPNO-HISTORY

Hypnosis goes back more than 4,000 years to the "sleep temples" of ancient Egypt, where priests used chanting to lead patients into deep trance states, then gave suggestions for healing and health. But its modern history begins in the 1770s with *mesmerism*. The Austrian physician Franz Anton Mesmer discovered he could heal people by making "passes" with his hands. He hypothesized that an invisible magnetic fluid was at play.

He gained considerable notoriety for his curative ability, counting among his fans Wolfgang Amadeus Mozart and the French queen Marie Antoinette. In Paris, Mesmer conducted salons with dim lighting, music, and incantations. He would move his hands about, reportedly healing many people of various ills. But both his social popularity and his theory of "animal magnetism" aroused suspicion among the intelligentsia, including the queen's husband, Louis XVI. The king appointed an investigating panel, on which served the American Ambassador Benjamin Franklin.

The panel demanded a demonstration. Perhaps wary of going himself, Mesmer sent an apprentice to Franklin's home outside Paris. The apprentice dutifully "magnetized" a tree, then "magnetized" a boy, blindfolded the boy and told him to find the tree by sensing its magnetic attraction. The youth reported feeling extremely strong sensations indeed, but walked in the wrong direction, away from the tree—and promptly fainted. Mesmer's reputation was ruined.

Yet, because of its powerful track record, mesmerism continued to inspire followers even while ridiculed by the scientific establishment. One practitioner was James Esdaile, the Scottish surgeon who in the mid-1800s performed hundreds of major surgeries using only mesmerism to keep his patients pain-free. Meanwhile, another Scottish surgeon, James Braid, began experimenting with mesmeric techniques while rejecting the theory of animal magnetism.

Braid found that he could produce the same trance state in patients by having them focus on a moving object (hence the cliché movie image we have today of a swinging watch). Braid observed that it was the patients' psychological responsiveness and expectations that led them into trance. He called this process "hypnosis," which means *sleep* in Greek. Later, when he realized hypnosis was not actually sleep, he tried to change the name, but to no avail; the term had become too popular.

Sigmund Freud studied hypnosis, but became disenchanted by his own inability to put his patients into a deep trance. He eventually settled on using psychoanalysis instead, which took up to 600 sessions to produce results rather than, say, six.

In the twentieth century, American psychiatrist Milton Erickson became famous for creating dramatic changes in his patients through hypnosis, as well as for his brilliant techniques. He could, for example, put someone into a hypnotic trance with only a handshake. His methods were foundational in the development of Neuro-Linguistic Programming (NLP) which, like hypnosis itself, is now practiced worldwide.

Tested Benefits from Drug-Free Surgery to Better Sex

Long-standing evidence indicates that virtually anyone desiring to be hypnotized *can* be, given world enough and time. The nineteenth-century British doctor James Esdaile performed hundreds of documented surgeries without chemical anesthesia, using only hypnosis to block pain, with each of his patients reporting a pain-free experience. This sounds bizarre until you consider that his hypnotic inductions were so laborious, it's no wonder that even the lowest hypnotizables would have succumbed. Esdaile hired assistants to carry out the process (back then called *mesmerism*), which involved numerous hypnotic techniques administered several hours daily, for ten or twelve consecutive days, leading up to surgery. Whew.

The use of hypnosis for pain-free surgery was phased out in the 1800s by the development of ether and chloroform. But recently, *hypno-anesthesia* has regained popularity as a way to supplement and reduce the use of drugs. Now many surgical teams employ hypnotic inductions that require only minutes to deliver instead of days. (For medical professionals, I highly recommend former Harvard radiologist Elvira Lang's book *Patient Sedation Without Medication*.)

Multiple studies at Harvard Medical School, involving more than 700 patients, prove that hypnosis significantly reduces pain, lowers anxiety, decreases blood loss, and helps prevent complications from surgery. Just as impressive, the research shows that hypnosis promotes quicker healing. Even broken bones mend faster following hypnosis.

If you're a big do-it-yourselfer, you can do your own hypno-prep for surgery. In 1994, a thirty-six-year-old British hair-loss specialist named Andy Bryant made headlines by choosing to undergo a vasectomy with no chemical anesthesia at all, using self-hypnosis instead. He reported a painless procedure and went back to work the next day.

Lest you get the impression that hypnosis always causes numbness, it does not. Hypnosis enables your brain to create what you want, whether it's less sensation—or more. For example, hypnosis has helped several of my female clients become more orgasmic by heightening their reaction to touch. And hypnosis can help men to dial down sexual arousal in order to combat premature ejaculation, or to dial up arousal if that's what they need. In a controlled experiment of 79 men with impotence of unknown origin, only hypnosis proved more effective than a placebo, improving sexual function by 80 percent.

So now you have it—hypnosis is not only legitimate, it's sexy.

Choose a personal issue over which you would like to gain more control. Whether you seek out a professional hypnotist or learn self-hypnosis—or get the best of both by combining the two—hypnosis will help put you firmly in charge of your own life. As *Scientific American* explains, "Under hypnosis, subjects do not behave as passive automatons but instead are active problem solvers who incorporate their moral and cultural ideas into their behavior while remaining exquisitely responsive" to suggestions for positive change.

Knowing that there's nothing to be afraid of, and everything to gain, what are you waiting for?

Use Your Self-Intelligence

You can begin by learning self-hypnosis (download my mini-course for no charge at self-intelligence.com), or by seeking out a hypnotist. Given that hypnosis can resolve a wide variety of problems, choose just one personal issue to start with. For example:

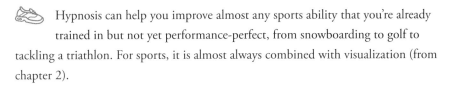 If there's someone at the office whose very presence annoys you, hypnosis can lower your reactivity so that interacting with them doesn't bother you. You can program yourself to find their physical appearance highly amusing. Sounds funny, and it is, but it works.

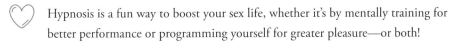 Hypnosis can help you improve almost any sports ability that you're already trained in but not yet performance-perfect, from snowboarding to golf to tackling a triathlon. For sports, it is almost always combined with visualization (from chapter 2).

Hypnosis is a fun way to boost your sex life, whether it's by mentally training for better performance or programming yourself for greater pleasure—or both!

If you're like most people, you may suspect your subconscious of harboring some limiting belief that's sabotaging your efforts to build wealth. Use hypnosis to get comfortable with the idea of making a lot more money.

Quiz answer: In many documented cases, people have undergone pain-free surgeries without chemical anesthesia, using only hypnosis to maintain comfort, and what scientists now say about this is . . .

    c.   hypnosis works, but we don't know how or why, nor even exactly what hypnosis *is*.

In a Nutshell

 Science has rescued hypnosis from the fringe, finding it to be a reliable tool for fixing a wide variety of problems and for generating improvement across numerous areas. Much of the research has been in health care, where studies show that hypnosis can help people to kick bad habits, reduce bodily pain, speed up physical healing, enjoy better sex, and more. Scientists still don't fully understand hypnosis but because the science proves its power, the most highly respected medical institutions advocate its use. It's also the secret to success for many top athletes and other performers. Feeling frustrated with some aspect of your life? Try hypnosis.

PART TWO

CONDITIONING YOUR YOUR CONSCIOUS SELF

My mentor Jack Canfield has been teaching people for almost half a century to improve their self-talk. By now, there's a whole lot of science to back him up. From owning your choices to rewriting your inner autobiography to "reframing" difficult situations, this part offers a variety of scientifically proven ways to change your life by changing what *you* tell *you* throughout the day, thereby conditioning your *conscious self*.

Don't worry, we're not leaving the subconscious self behind. We couldn't even if we wanted to, because all your sub-selves are inextricably intertwined. By conditioning your *conscious self*, you will positively influence your *subconscious self*. Another side effect is that you will improve the health of your physically *embodied self*. Oh, you'll be strengthening your relationship skills too, thus supporting your *social self*. And yes, all this leads to greater success for your *striving self*. Talk about interconnected!

Some people believe the phenomenon of interconnection to be so vast that it creates a direct link between your mind and the workings of the universe. This could someday prove to be true, but for now this particular belief exceeds the purview of science. Given that there's passionate disagreement about this issue, in chapter 6 I'll address some common misunderstandings about quantum physics, while being careful to encourage an open mind.

Alright already! Let's go ahead and talk about what we talk about when we're talking to ourselves.

There is no psychology;
there is only biography and autobiography.

–PSYCHIATRIST THOMAS SZASZ

CHAPTER 5

YARN

Oh, That's a Good One

Prime-your-mind Quiz

Research says you'll remember this chapter better if you test yourself now. How will the answer affect *you*?

Recent studies of how our minds process stories show that . . .

a. if we know a story is fictional, it loses the power to strongly influence our opinions or actions.

b. our opinions and actions are deeply influenced even by stories we know to be untrue.

c. we are somewhat influenced by stories, but much more so if hard data backs them up.

O nce upon a time, a beautiful woman appeared in my office without an appointment. Miriam was tall, with long, light-brown hair, coffee-colored eyes, strong cheekbones, and flawless skin. Although she could have been a model, she moved self-consciously, hunching her shoulders and dropping her head when she spoke. When she introduced herself, she almost seemed to be apologizing.

As I was taking a break between sessions anyway, I invited her to sit down and tell me about herself. It turned out she worked for an internet company a few doors down the hall. She had a fetching French accent. In response to my questions, she shared that she'd grown up near Paris, was an only child, and had lost her father when she was twelve. She said she felt close to her mother.

"I wish I could be more like her. She is so much fun. She is always laughing and singing and full of energy. But ever since I was little, I have been shy and reserved, what you call a stick in the mud. My father was like that too, but my mother says this is attractive in a man. As a woman, I should smile and be outgoing. I know my mother is correct. She is the life of the party." Miriam gave me a worried smile. "I thought maybe you could help me."

Intrigued, I asked her to explain.

"My mother is coming to visit next month. I don't know why, but I am anxious. My boyfriend Sharif and I began living together last year, so she will stay with us. Maybe I am afraid that when he meets her, she is so lively that he will see what he is missing with me. I am twenty-five, and he is my first serious boyfriend. Of course my mother says that is part of my problem, always being afraid. Maybe you can help me be less afraid?"

Over the next month, we worked to reduce Miriam's anxiety and to strengthen her confidence. She appeared to be making progress, yet still clung to much of her habitual timidity. Then we took a week off during her mother's visit.

When Miriam returned after that visit, something had changed. She grinned hello, then without waiting for an invitation, tossed her jacket onto the wall hook, signaled me to pour her a cup of water, claimed her chair, and instead of needing me to ask her questions, started right in.

"My mother was fooling me all this time." Miriam clasped her hands together as though to contain her own energy. "There is nothing wrong with me. Maybe you were trying to tell me that before, but I have found out for myself."

Her chin was up. Her eyes shone. Even her voice sounded different, more clear and resonant. "You've transformed yourself," I said. "How did you do it?"

"I was believing the wrong story," said Miriam. "I thought I was too quiet and my mother was so full of life. But Sharif pointed out to me how she always needs to be the center of attention. He said he loves me because I am much more considerate of other people." Miriam's eyes widened with excitement. "That made it easy for me to be happy and cheerful around her, the way she has always wanted, but something very strange happened. My mother did not like me being happy and cheerful! I think she could not criticize me for being too reserved, so she began to criticize everything else—my job, my clothes, my cooking, even my relationship with Sharif. It made me see that she has always needed to criticize me for something. Sharif told me she is jealous of my youth and my beauty, and that is why she must put me in my place. Whether or not this is true, I don't know. But what I used to think, about my mother being positive and me being negative—" Miriam threw her hands apart, "it fell into pieces."

Then she reached out and playfully tapped my knee for emphasis, something I could not have imagined her doing before.

Until then, I had helped many clients to shift their perspectives or let go of old beliefs. But before Miriam's discovery, I had not understood the full power of autobiography, the almost magical way in which self-stories create who we are. More importantly, I hadn't realized the ability we have to *rewrite* our autobiographies. The same brain plasticity that allows us to restructure our brains enables us to revise our lives, backward and forward through time, in order to choose and move in a better direction. Miriam's metamorphosis inspired me to learn the latest science on how our brains are wired for narrative.

Why We Won't Stop Telling Tales

Across every culture throughout history, we humans have told stories. Such a universal behavior, scientists now conclude, must be rooted in biology. Researchers today investigate how exactly telling tales has helped us to survive. Is it by teaching us morals, wisdom, and social skills? Or is it by preparing us to handle challenges, the way a flight-simulator prepares a pilot to fly? Or is it by creating community bonds so that we understand one another and stick together? Or is it *all* those things? At this point, we only know for sure that our brains have evolved a yearning for yarns.

I like the word *yarn* because it suggests that there's something creative in every tale, something "spun." It's not just data we're after but *meaning*, the satisfying *sense* that a story weaves from mere facts. Think about your own life. Maybe you haven't written down your autobiography but, I bet that if asked, you could tell a condensed version on the spot. You would naturally connect key life events to explain your evolution through time, how you became the person you are. Yet it's likely that even your best friend would relate "your" story quite differently, mentioning other events altogether or interpreting the same ones from another angle. Both tales would be true; which one would you choose?

Please think about this: What life story are you telling yourself now? Is your current version sabotaging you or serving you? Does your inner autobiography make you feel like a loser or a winner? Unlucky or lucky? Helpless or able? Could you revise your story so that it better supports you?

In Miriam's first account, she was a stick in the mud compared with her vibrant mother, who rightly criticized her. In the revision, Miriam emerges as a considerate, positive person compared with her too-critical, self-aggrandizing mother. This new yarn has freed Miriam from chronic low self-esteem, boosting her energy and joy.

But is the second version the Truth? It clearly holds some validity, but shouldn't Miriam try harder to check for absolute accuracy? Let's look at the science.

Delusions of Being Non-Delusional

Psychologists once assumed that to be well-adjusted, one must see oneself as realistically as possible. That may seem obvious . . . only, it's not so. A slew of studies proves that nearly all of us (at least in the United States) are delusional. Some 90 percent of drivers believe they're better than average on the road. Most individuals think they're kinder, warmer, and more sincere than most other people. Research also shows that 94 percent of American professors rate themselves as above-average teachers, and two-thirds estimate they're among the top quarter. With amazing consistency, the great majority of us see ourselves as belonging to a superior minority.

You don't have to be a genius to do the math. It just doesn't add up. Granted, maybe you already knew that most people fooled themselves. But did you realize that nearly all of us believe it's *other* people who do so, while we, personally, remain realistic? Hmm.

But let's not start feeling bad about being conceited. Because scientists have also discovered that it's good for us to be slightly delusional. It's the sign of a healthy mind, even an ingredient of success. If people realistically gauged their own abilities, "they would rarely fail but they would not mount the extra effort needed to surpass their ordinary performances," write researchers Shelley E. Taylor and Jonathon D. Brown, in one of their investigations of this issue. Our self-delusions embolden us to take those risks that lead to achievement. (Though as for your driving, you may want to aim for more realism. Just sayin'.)

Other studies indicate that depressed people do the opposite, judging themselves negatively or perhaps too accurately. Whether that's a cause or a consequence of depression remains undetermined. What's clear is that we're better off avoiding self-stories that make us feel bad, and instead choosing tales that, within reason, lift us up, creating confidence to learn and grow.

The Inescapable Pull of Story

Because stories are inherently revisable, they allow us to be shape-shifters. Though Miriam had been making progress in my office, she achieved full transformation only by adopting a new self-story. Why was that the magic bullet? Because our brains are *designed* to respond to stories. New research shows that yarns—our own and those of others—influence our brains far more deeply than do mere ideas, data, or abstractions. Brain-imaging studies confirm that while isolated information may engage the mind, narrative stories set off neural fireworks.

Scientists have measured the brain activity of people watching movies, reading short stories, or listening to someone share a personal tale. The results show that, regardless of whether the stories are factual or fictional, our brains automatically create mental simulations. This holds true even, or perhaps especially, for stories about ourselves, which helps explain why children love to hear tales in which they are the heroes. Our visual cortex lights up when we read or hear visual details; the auditory cortex sparks at the mention of specific sounds, and so on.

Our brains turn yarns into virtual experience. This in turn activates strong emotions, which are dictated less by our particular personalities than by the story we're experiencing. Multiple studies show that disparate individuals' limbic systems react in roughly the same way to the same narrative. For example, one experiment found that people watching a James Bond thriller all ride the same basic emotional roller coaster, as mapped out by their brain patterns.

That's because, at a subconscious level, we each "become" James Bond. Stories can lead us to identify self-to-self with someone else, whether that's Bond or Bambi or Blade. Universal story structure—which we'll explore in a moment—requires that the protagonist (real or imaginary) be someone specific. That specificity helps us to enter the subconscious portal of emotional identification, bypassing intellect, and automatically causing us to *care*.

This is one reason that dry data about abstract entities cannot tap into our brains as deeply as do stories. One Carnegie Mellon study tested whether people would be more moved to donate money to charity if (a) they learned dramatic facts about hunger in Africa, or (b) they were given a brief story about a specific African girl on the verge of starvation. Sure enough, those who read the story donated *more than twice as much* as those given abstract facts.

Then researchers wondered whether donations would rise further if people read both story and facts. So they paired the story of the girl, named Rokia, with statistics about food shortages in Malawi, drought in Zambia, and the dislocation of millions in Angola. Would you guess that the added understanding boosted donations? Well no, they plummeted. Once abstract data were introduced, analytical thinking kicked in, flattening people's emotions and reducing their impulse to help. Additional research has confirmed this flattening effect of abstract information.

Why Stories Evoke and We Emote

Rokia's story is compelling but it also consisted of facts (or, as a politician might say, of "true facts"). So what is it that turns dry data into juicy story? Scholars from Aristotle on have identified the universal structure of narrative, one which we are often unconscious of yet are wired to respond to. This structure rests on three pillars:

1. **Character**, i.e., a specific protagonist whose fate we can care about.

2. **Conflict or challenge** the character faces.

3. **Cause-and-effect** route to resolution (or sometimes, as in tragedy, to ruin).

Story structure is wired into our brains, says neuroscientist Antonio Damasio. It "is something brains do, naturally and implicitly. Implicit storytelling has created our selves, and it should be no surprise that it pervades the entire fabric of human societies and cultures," he writes in *Self Comes to Mind*. And because our brains know this structure inside-out (even when we're not conscious of it), we don't need much to fill it in. For example, here is how even Rokia's very brief story fits the bill, as it was told in a note to potential donors:

1. **Character:** "Any money you donate will go to *Rokia, a seven-year-old girl* who lives in Mali, Africa."

2. **Conflict or Challenge:** "Rokia is desperately poor and *faces a threat of severe hunger, even starvation.*"

3. **Cause-and-effect resolution:** "*Her life will be changed for the better as a result of your financial gift* . . . to help feed and educate her, and provide her with basic medical care . . . ."

This simple one-two-three structure makes our brain cells perk up, especially our mirror neurons. We'll learn in chapter 10's sidebar, *The Mirroring Mind*, how mirror neurons inwardly simulate the actions and emotions we witness in others, helping us to "get" them at a deep level. This empathic engagement leads us to want to help Rokia. By the same token, our best *self*-stories allow us to see ourselves from the outside, with a broader perspective, yet also from the inside, with increased empathy—allowing us to better care about, and for, ourselves.

Moreover, by triggering emotion, stories stimulate the hippocampus to lock them into memory, so that we remember them better than other sorts of information. This gives them strong long-term influence.

TRUE STORIES ABOUT STORIES

Science confirms that we're deeply influenced by narratives, both when we believe they're true and often when we know they're false. Research aside, real life offers up plenty of proof. For example:

- In 1774, German writer Johann Wolfgang von Goethe published *The Sorrows of Young Werther*, a novel about a sensitive youth who wears a yellow vest and falls in love with a woman already engaged to someone else. After she marries the other man, the heartbroken protagonist kills himself. The book became so terribly popular that young men throughout Europe began wearing yellow vests and committing suicide. The phenomenon was called Werther Fever.

- Published in 1852, *Uncle Tom's Cabin* was the century's biggest best seller. Harriet Beecher Stowe dramatized the cruelty of American slavery, igniting public fervor over the issue. Historians credit the book with helping fuel the Civil War.

- Steven Spielberg's 1975 blockbuster *Jaws* featured a vicious shark out to kill as many humans as possible. Though it was a highly unrealistic depiction of sharks, the story scared people away from beaches. Coastal towns took a big economic hit.

So what's the moral? Recognize that narratives enchant our brains. Resist falling under their spell if doing so doesn't truly serve you—but on the other hand, don't fret too much about their undue influence. As scholar Jonathan Gottschall has documented, the great majority of fictional tales, across every culture ever known, promote good over evil. (See his charming book, *The Storytelling Animal*.) In general, the stories we consume make us better people. My hope is that, once you fathom the power of yarns, you'll be motivated to take command of your own self-story to positively influence yourself. May the Force be with you.

Stanford professor Chip Heath tests this strength every year. He gives his students some crime data, then asks them each to craft a one-minute talk on the subject. The students divide into small groups to rate one another's presentations. Usually, only one in ten speakers happens to use a story in their talk. Doing so doesn't boost rankings; students' highest votes typically go to the most polished, charismatic speakers. Before class ends, Heath gives the students a surprise quiz to find out what they remember from the talks. Alas, they recall very little, drawing a complete blank on many—including those they rated most highly—and remembering few ideas or statistics in general. Yet most of them—more than 60 percent—remember the stories.

Heath describes this experiment in *Made to Stick*, one of several nonfiction bestsellers coauthored with his brother Dan. The Heath brothers' books are all big hits, and deservedly so, largely because they illustrate their arguments with dramatic true tales.

Plato wanted storytellers banned from his ideal Republic because he believed they wielded too much influence. He thought, for example, that by describing sinners, they provoked sin. Was he right? Today some studies find that shoot-'em-up TV shows spawn real-world violence. Yet, at the same time, other research indicates that reading stories develops our social intelligence. In any case, we can't ban storytellers, because we'd be banning ourselves! Plato didn't know what science has since revealed: all humans are storytellers.

And for better or worse, what's undebatable is that narratives—fictional or factual— shape our behavior. Beyond the fledgling research, real-life evidence abounds. Did you see the 2004 film *Sideways*? The main character, a wine connoisseur, loved pinot noir and loathed merlot. When the film grew popular, it directly impacted the wine industry: merlot sales dropped; pinot noir took off. For other real-life examples of how stories pull our strings, see the sidebar, "True Stories About Stories."

Crafting Our Tales to Form Our Selves

Yarns make proverbial puppets of us because they hook into our brain's operating system. That is why the tales we believe about ourselves have the potential to make or break us. Based on this new understanding, a field of psychology has emerged focusing specifically on our self-stories. The *narrative psychologists* contend that our happiness hinges on our inner autobiographies. When those veer off course, so do we. When those take a positive direction, so do we.

"Your story and your self are so tightly intertwined that while you can reshape one in order to reshape the other, you can never fully disentangle the two.

"Life stories do not simply *reflect* personality. They *are* personality," write psychologists Dan McAdams and Erika Manczak in the American Psychological Association's 2015 *Handbook of Personality and Social Psychology*. Your story and your *self* are so tightly intertwined that while you can reshape one in order to reshape the other, you can never fully disentangle the two.

This lifelong connection was dramatically illustrated in a study by University of Kentucky scientists, led by Deborah D. Danner. Researchers looked at one-page autobiographies written many decades earlier by 180 women, then young, who were about to take their commitment vows at School Sisters of Notre Dame. Scientists rated the self-stories according to emotional positivity. They categorized them into four groups, the lowest quartile being the least positive, the highest quartile being most cheerful. Danner wondered whether an autobiography's happy-factor might predict its author's overall healthiness and therefore longevity. Would the nuns who told the most joyful self-stories early on end up living the longest?

You betcha. Of those ranked in the lowest quartile, 66 percent had passed away by age 85; a meager 34 percent still hung on. In contrast, how many nuns in the top quartile lived to that age? A whopping 90 percent survived to at least 85. (We'll explore more in chapter 8 about how positivity boosts health).

But this raises a chicken-or-egg question of which comes first, a healthier story or a healthier being. What we know is that each influences the other. "It's a Möbius strip: Stories are life, life is stories," concludes Julie Beck, science editor for *The Atlantic* magazine.

Whether or not we've written out our autobiographies, we're all spinning tales, and consciously or not, we're living out whatever scripts we've chosen. Given what science now says about the sway of stories, don't you think you should take charge of your own? Keep in mind that your story's not over, and that current setbacks can still lead to positive outcomes.

You may want to begin with an old-school exercise: First, write a one-page *negative* autobiography of your existence so far. Throw in self-pity, bad luck, regrets, what-have-you. Next, write your short autobiography with a *positive* spin, emphasizing happy events, your good fortune, your wonderfulness, gratitude and a sense of good things to come. Your own words will convince you, better than mine can, just how much capacity you have to weave your own yarn and hence, your life.

Use Your Self-Intelligence

Oh, the stories we tell ourselves! Regularly review your own to see if they're serving you. Sometimes the tales we hold onto most dearly—especially those of self-shame or self-pity—are the ones we most need to let go of to create greater happiness and success.

Studies find that workers who see themselves as cogs in the machine end up unhealthy and unhappy. People who see themselves as making a positive difference end up better off mentally and financially. But it's not necessarily the job itself that determines the outcome: two people with identical jobs may have opposite experiences, depending on the stories they believe. What story are you telling yourself about your job or career right now? Who are you in this tale, and what is your challenge? Your goal? Can you do a rewrite to make your work more satisfying?

Two of my acquaintances have survived stage-one breast cancer. One believes a story of unfair victimization, of *Why me?* This fails to inspire healthy habits, so she continues to smoke and drink excessively, which increases her chances of cancer recurring. The other woman thanks her lucky stars that doctors found her tumor when they did. This motivates her to embrace a healthy lifestyle, including exercise and a vegetarian diet, which increases her chances of remaining cancer-free. What yarn do you spin about your health? If need be, rewrite it so that it influences you to keep fit.

My favorite relationship scientist, John Gottman, has found that the stories couples tell about their past together (first date, wedding, honeymoon, etc.) correlate to how well they get along in later life. Positive stories foretell a positive future. Are the stories shared by you and your darling mostly happy? If you're single and looking, are the stories you believe about couples, in general, encouraging you to find your mate? Improve your relationships by improving your stories.

Many self-help gurus will advise you to embrace a "wealth mindset" in order to amass a fortune. So allow me to mention something else. We humans have the tendency to be dissatisfied with whatever we have and to always want more. Once we get more, we want . . . even more. Economists call this the "hedonistic treadmill." I suggest shaping your self-story to both support your ambition *and* to be happy with whatever you've got right now. Enjoy being you!

Quiz answer: Recent studies of how our minds process stories show that . . .

b. our opinions and actions are deeply influenced even by stories we know to be untrue.

In a Nutshell

Every human culture ever known has told tales, and now research confirms that they influence our brains far more deeply than do dry facts. This is why our inner autobiographies greatly affect our confidence and well-being. So consider what yarn you're currently spinning about yourself. Is your self-story sabotaging or serving you? Most likely, you can revise and improve your story, so that your story improves *you*.

I do not know what I do not know.

—SAINT AUGUSTINE

CHAPTER 6

QUANTUM PHYSICS

What It Is, What It's Not, and What About Negative Thoughts?

Prime-your-mind Quiz

Research says you'll remember this chapter better if you test yourself now. How will the answer affect *you*?

It is true that . . .

a. believing in good luck can produce measurable positive effects.

b. to be happy and successful, you must learn to control all your thoughts.

c. the subconscious mind doesn't understand negatives.

H as anything bad ever happened to you? It has? You must have attracted that misfortune by having negative thoughts. Admit it, you've sometimes entertained negative thoughts, haven't you? *Aha!*

These days, every self-help guru from Oprah to Deepak Chopra tells you to think positive. Me too. In chapter 8, I'll share the science on why you should aim for optimism. But meanwhile, a certain confusion about quantum physics has led some people to try to suppress their negative thoughts. Those attempts at suppression do harm—and *that's* the scientific truth.

Rigorous studies show that attempting to quash negative thoughts actually generates more negative thoughts. So if you have chastised yourself for negative thinking, I invite you to be much, much nicer to yourself from now on. There is a better, more Self-Intelligent way to be, which we will explore shortly.

Messing Around with Quantum Mechanics

Elizabeth, a sixty-two-year-old Canadian retiree, contacted me in a miserable state. During our first online video session, she told me, "I'm ruining my life and I don't know how to stop." Seeing a well-manicured silver-haired woman wearing an elegant scarf, I thought to myself that she didn't *look* self-destructive.

She said that, upon entering menopause, she'd begun having hot flashes throughout the day. One moment she'd be fine but the next she'd be sweating and panicky, shedding clothes, and running to open her freezer door to feel cool air on her face. Then, just as quickly, the flash would subside, leaving a chill in its wake, and she'd need to reach for a sweater. "It's driving me crazy, and it's my own fault," she said, striking the air with her hand as if to admonish herself.

Puzzled, I asked her to explain how menopause could be her own fault. She was worried, she said, that it must be her own negativity that was attracting such torturous hot flashes. Her friend Cindy had warned her against negative thinking. Cindy felt sure that Elizabeth's resentment about becoming an older woman had sent energy vibrations out into the universe, attracting trouble. "Cindy never suffered hot flashes, you see, because she has a better attitude about menopause." And, if that weren't proof in itself, Elizabeth now added: "Cindy says it's not just her opinion. It's a law of quantum physics that my thoughts are creating reality."

Then I understood what she was talking about. You've probably heard of it too. This century's first decade saw the release of two documentary-style films—*What the Bleep Do We Know* and *The Secret*—that espoused a so-called "law of attraction," an old idea (and one that predates quantum physics) that our thoughts send out energy waves that directly influence the physical world. So, the logic goes, negative thoughts will "attract" negative events into your life.

Of course, that also means that good thoughts should attract good events. As many of its followers will attest, when the "law of attraction" instills positive beliefs, it can be a wonderful influence, motivating folks to shift their focus away from what they *don't* want, in order to follow their dreams. But it has virtually nothing to do with our current science of quantum physics. (If you're curious about the films' references to science, see the sidebar "Talk About Mad Scientists!") And it can inadvertently do damage when it leads people to feel badly about themselves, or to try too hard to control their thoughts.

"Elizabeth, hot flashes are mostly hereditary, just the result of your DNA. But stress can intensify them. And by trying so hard to be positive, you may be adding unnecessary stress."

It was her turn to look confused, so I went on: "Okay, please tell me if this describes your experience: The harder you try to block your negative thoughts, the more they occur. The more they occur, the worse you feel. Is that right?"

TALK ABOUT MAD SCIENTISTS!

This is a true story. David Albert, an esteemed philosopher of physics at Columbia University, spent several hours being interviewed on camera. The filmmakers wanted to know how quantum mechanics might inform human consciousness. The patient professor good-naturedly explained why the current science of quantum physics had virtually nothing to say about consciousness, or spirituality, or the notion that thoughts might affect anything in the external world. The filmmakers seemed happy with his interview, and all was good.

Until the film appeared. There, Albert's careful explanation had been drastically edited, hacked up, and very cleverly rearranged to make it sound as if he'd said the opposite of what he did. Partly based on his own scientific credibility, the film, entitled *What the #$*! Do We Know?*, did quite well. The professor was, understandably, "outraged," by its dishonesty, as *Popular Science* reports. "I was taken," Albert said. "I was really gullible, but I learned my lesson."

Scientists all over the world have objected to the movie's slick pseudoscientific chicanery. (Harvard physics and cosmology professor Lisa Randall calls the film "the bane of scientists.") The movie *The Secret* elicited less rancor, but it likewise annoyed serious scholars by misrepresenting current research on quantum physics.

If you liked either of these movies and are wondering what to think, you might enjoy the book *War of the Worldviews: Where Science and Spirituality Meet— and Do Not*, written half by theoretical physicist Leonard Mlodinow and half by spiritual guru Deepak Chopra. Here, two good men agree to disagree. You might find yourself, paradoxically, siding with both.

And if you do, then good for you! As the American novelist F. Scott Fitzgerald put it, "The test of a first-rate intelligence is the ability to hold two opposed ideas in mind at the same time and still retain the ability to function."

On one point, the greatest scientists and spiritualists have always agreed: What we "know" at any given time is simply miniscule compared to all that remains a mystery.

She nodded, then said in a small voice, "I feel ashamed."

The pointlessness of her shame just about broke my heart. (Self-shame is destructive, as we'll discuss in chapter 20.) We did some hypnosis to reduce her stress levels immediately, then I taught her a self-hypnotic technique involving snow imagery that she could use to cool down her hot flashes somewhat. Finally, I suggested she talk to her doctor, because low-dose hormone therapy is typically the most effective treatment for hot flashes.

"You're a hypnotist and you're not against drugs?" She seemed startled.

"As a last resort, if they're safe and they work, why not?" I said. Honestly, we cannot control everything with our minds. Nor can we completely control the mind itself. Much of this book teaches you how to rewire your brain. Part One focused on directly programming your subconscious self, and *all* of the strategies shared in that section are highly effective. Yet you cannot, at any given moment, utterly control your subconscious self. Nor should you try.

> Is it, as some self-help gurus proclaim, that the subconscious doesn't understand negatives? No, that's another myth without scientific basis.

The Pitfalls of Trying to Ban Bad Thoughts

Scientists have discovered that the harder a person struggles to suppress negative thoughts, the more those thoughts will occur. It's called *ironic rebound*, a term coined by Harvard psychology professor Daniel Wegner. His and others' studies show that:

- Attempts to block your thoughts will backfire. Subjects who were instructed to not think about white elephants thought about them obsessively. In another study, some people were told to please *do* think about white elephants. They tried their best—but those other people who'd been asked to *not* think about them thought about them even more.

- Individuals who attempt to simply suppress fear or anxiety—for example, before undergoing a painful medical procedure or giving a public speech—tend to end up more fearful and anxious, with higher heart rates and other physiological stress symptoms to show for it.

- Likewise, when people try to suppress sad or self-critical notions (such as "I'm a loser"), their self-esteem falls faster than when they're encouraged to grapple openly with such ideas. (In just a moment, we'll discuss a technique for successfully combatting such thoughts. And for further support, see chapter 8.)

So what exactly produces this mental weirdness? Is it, as some self-help gurus proclaim, that the subconscious doesn't understand negatives? No, that's another myth without scientific basis. In fact, when we hypnotists help clients to stop smoking, we typically train their subconscious minds to hear a big fat *No!* anytime they think about cigarettes. We know the person is going to think about cigarettes. So we don't endeavor to make clients not-think about cigarettes—only to not-smoke them. You can successfully train yourself to *not do* things, because the subconscious understands negatives perfectly well.

You might even say it understands them too well. Because apparently, here is what happens when we humans try to *not think* about something. It seems that we activate two separate brain functions, which Wegner calls the operator and the monitor. The operator involves self-control in the frontal lobe—"I will *avoid* thoughts about the forbidden subject"—which greatly taxes mental energy. Imagine a race car driver who must concentrate extremely hard to navigate an obstacle course. In contrast, the monitor relies on a subconscious, lower-brain function, related to threat-detection, which runs almost effortlessly once we set it in motion with our negative *don't-think* command. It continually scans our brain activity for the outlawed idea, while inadvertently cluttering the course with more obstacles. "Remember, *no* white bears. Are you thinking about white bears yet? White bears are *not* allowed. How about now—any white bears? We *don't* want white bears. Uh-oh, that wasn't a white-bear thought, was it?" The operator quickly tires out, leaving the monitor still automatically scanning for—and thereby conjuring up—white bears.

Well then, what *can* you do about your own white bears? Here are Seven Self-Intelligent Solutions to Big Bad Thoughts:

1. Stop trying to suppress them, as doing so only invites more. Give that up. But . . .

2. As best you can, avoid *dwelling* on negative thoughts, chewing on them stubbornly like a dog relishing a bone. If you catch yourself brooding, it may work to simply shift your attention to something better. Admire a view, or watch an inspiring video. Also . . .

3. Notice that you don't need to *believe* your own negative thinking. Just because an idea occurs to you doesn't mean it's true. Studies show that you can dispute unhelpful notions. Try using the technique more fully described in chapter 8. Then again . . .

4. Another science-tested option is to visualize the negative thought as a cloud in the sky or a ripple in a pond, initially disturbing the calm but then quieting and dissipating. This imaging technique may more gently ease the offender from your mind. Meanwhile . . .

5. Remember that you can control your *actions*. Talking is an action. Talking too much about negative thoughts will bring you—and other people—down. No one wants to hang out with a complainer. So strive to be good company. Just remember . . .

6. At least some negative thoughts will always occur to us (chapter 8 explains our natural "negativity bias"), and some are necessary for survival, so never feel guilty when they do. Rather, train your brain for more positivity—for example, by doing a daily gratitude exercise. Finally . . .

7. Play rather than proselytize. Elizabeth's friend Cindy probably meant to help. But unsolicited advice often comes off as criticism, which makes people feel bad about themselves. If someone close to you is droning too loud and long on the negative, it's best to avoid preaching and, if appropriate, deploy humor instead. Being playful can work wonders. (See chapter 15.)

Once Elizabeth gave up trying to quash her troubling thoughts, they significantly abated. By allowing herself to non-judgmentally address negative beliefs that remained, she was able to think and to feel better about aging. Meanwhile, hypnosis and hormone therapy combined curbed her hot flashes. That in turn helped her to sleep better. As she began to feel more energized in general, she realized that retirement bored her. Reactivating a childhood dream, she launched a dog-training business. Perhaps most importantly, she let go of shame.

"But there's still something I'm wondering about," she told me as we wrapped up one of our last sessions on a winter afternoon. Through the window behind her could be seen a large spruce tree, its whorled branches gleaming with snow, as lovely as a fairytale. Then one of her two dogs, a gallant mastiff mix named Jake, sat down beside her. (I confess that, as an animal fanatic, I love to meet my clients' pets, even virtually.) Being highly trained, Jake sat politely still and silent, as if he were a butler waiting to take orders. Elizabeth continued, "Everything's going so well now. I feel twenty years younger. I love my new life. You're always telling me to expect the best, and the more I do that, the more I feel like it's having a magical effect."

"Yes!" I said.

"But if you know it works, then why are you against the law of attraction?"

"Ah, but I never said that." I lifted my hands. "Only, it's a spiritual belief, not a scientific law. Someday it could turn out to be scientifically provable. Who knows?" Then Jake suddenly spoke up. It wasn't merely a bark, but a long, meandering yodel. "See? He agrees with me."

"Well," she cracked a smile. "He's also saying, *Let's go outdoors*, because it's ten minutes past their regular walk time, and he loves to chase snowballs." With that, we ended our call.

The Magic or Science of Lucky Charms

Does the universe respond to our thoughts? There is no scientific evidence that it does. There are, however, plenty of anecdotal reports that it might. Here's one of mine:

My father died in early 2008, not long after being diagnosed with lung cancer. Dad once told me that, although he'd finally been able to quit drinking, he could not stop smoking, despite the cancer and having had two heart attacks. A few months after his passing, I learned that hypnosis can help people kick cigarettes; this became one of my motives for mastering hypnosis.

That same year I began to practice subconscious programming of various sorts, all designed to put myself on a positive track. In late summer, I opened my hypnosis practice in San Francisco. Shortly after, I was walking my big red hound dog, May, in Golden Gate Park on a Sunday morning. A silvery fog hung in the air. I was admiring sparkling droplets on the grass when I spotted a four-leaf clover, only the second one I'd ever found in my life. Later that afternoon, I realized it was September 14, my father's birthday. "Hmm. Maybe Dad or the universe sent me that lucky clover." I didn't exactly believe the idea—but didn't disbelieve it either.

From that day forth, I found four-leaf clovers regularly—hundreds upon hundreds of them. I did not spend time looking, but walked my dog as usual and kept my eyes open. I felt delighted by so much good luck. (The estimated ratio of regular three-leaf to rare four-leaf clovers is 10,000 to one.) I gave lucky clovers to friends, arranged them in picture frames, or stuck them inside books. Sometimes I knew from my mood that I was going to find a lot. One morning I was not surprised at all to come across twenty-eight four-leaf clovers in a patch that I had passed often, but without seeing any there before. After about three years of finding lucky clovers, I stopped feeling excited about the phe-nomenon. Quite abruptly, it stopped too. I haven't found many four-leaf clovers since, not even when I look.

What could explain my lucky-charm mystery? Did I "manifest" or "attract" those clo-vers? Or is there a more scientific explanation? Or maybe both?

Experimental psychologist Richard Wiseman has conducted studies to determine whether people who consider themselves lucky attract good luck. The answer is no . . . and yes. People who are twice as confident about winning the lottery are no more likely to win. But people who think of themselves as lucky *are* more likely to experience fortu-nate events by spotting opportunities.

For example, Wiseman had volunteers rate themselves as "lucky" or "unlucky," then gave each a newspaper, asking them to count how many photos it contained. The lucky people took mere seconds to finish the task. The unlucky subjects slogged along much more slowly, needing an average of two minutes. That's because they failed to see what the lucky ones spotted immediately: a big page-two ad, sporting bold type: STOP COUNTING—THERE ARE 43 PHOTOGRAPHS IN THIS NEWSPAPER.

Other studies, too, show that when we hold positive beliefs, our subconscious mind auto-scans for supporting evidence. Maybe that's why, as Wiseman also found, people who believe themselves lucky report greater life satisfaction than most. And maybe it likewise explains my encounters of the four-leaf kind.

Choosing the Best Beliefs for Yourself

Maybe the full explanation for luck lies beyond science. Who knows what's possible?

After all, we're still guessing at what the universe is made of. Scientists hypothesize that it's mostly dark energy and dark matter . . . but what do *they* supposedly consist of? No one knows. Is the universe ultimately analog or digital, continuous or grainy? Is it all essentially energy . . . or discrete bits of information, ones and zeroes? Or something we haven't yet imagined? Take a bet.

Nor has anyone yet figured out how to reconcile quantum mechanics and general relativity. Both seem to be true, but they contradict each other. There are many competing Theories of Everything attempting to solve this quandary—including several variations of string theory—but no last word in sight.

It's easy to make fun of the so-called law of attraction for being unscientific—which it is—but that doesn't prove that it's wrong. Not long ago, people who believed that "aliens" lived on other planets were dismissed as loony. Well, new evidence gathered from high-tech space telescopes now shows that our Milky Way galaxy alone contains billions of potentially habitable planets. Nearly every respectable scientist on planet Earth now agrees it is virtually certain that our universe contains other life-forms. What kind? We have no idea.

One of my heroes is Nobel laureate Niels Bohr, a founder of quantum theory, whose success sprang largely from his ability to embrace contradictory truths. His open-mindedness extended beyond physics to include various forms of wisdom, from biology to literature to sermons, though he rejected anything dogmatic. "It's something I feel very strongly about," he wrote to his fiancée, " . . . that I think that everything that is of value is true."

You cannot completely control your own moment-to-moment thoughts, nor should you try, because doing so causes *ironic rebound*. But over time, you can choose your own beliefs. What do you choose to believe? What is of value to you?

Use Your Self-Intelligence

Whether you're a die-hard skeptic, a woo-woo spiritualist, or something in between, science offers proven tools to help you navigate your personal path to a better life.

At the office, go beyond being either a Negative Ned or Positive Pollyanna. Embrace both optimism and fearless truth. Tackle problems head-on, confident that you've got the ability—and the good luck—needed to slay those dragons and create success.

Lower your stress by ending self-criticism. Want to "attract" positive energy? Give yourself a big hug (figuratively or literally, whichever suits you.) and let go of guilt. You'll feel better and do better too. (For the science on this, please see chapter 20.)

If you notice a friend or loved one being too "negative," resist the temptation to criticize. Can you make them laugh, or even entice them to go to a fun weekend workshop with you, to set them on a more positive track?

Remember, science shows it's beneficial to believe in good luck, but it won't help you win the lottery. Honestly appraise your own relation to money. Have you been too risk-averse or the opposite, too financially frisky? Without shame or blame, self-adjust accordingly.

Quiz answer: It is true that . . .

a.   believing in good luck can produce measurable positive effects.

In a Nutshell

Because of how the brain works, attempting to suppress negative thoughts tends to create more of them, due to what scientists call *ironic rebound*. So it doesn't help to berate yourself (or anyone else) for negative thinking. On the other hand, we can direct our minds toward more positivity. In fact, by reading this book you're doing just that—congratulations! The so-called law of attraction, which holds that the universe directly responds to our thoughts, is a spiritual belief, without scientific basis in quantum physics . . . but, hey, it could turn out to be true. The mere fact of our existence offers innumerable grand mysteries that science has yet to solve.

Every time you make a choice, you are turning the central part of you, the part of you that chooses, into something a little different from what it was before.

—C. S. LEWIS

CHAPTER 7

CHOICE

Choose to Use Yours

Prime-your-mind Quiz

Research says you'll remember this chapter better if you test yourself now. How will the answer affect *you*?

Consciously exercising your power of personal choice . . .

a. may help you live longer.

b. is beneficial only if you choose something different from what others would have chosen for you.

c. can cause migraines due to overuse of the brain's frontal lobe.

Fred seemed resentful when he arrived at my office. "It wasn't my decision to be here. My wife, Irene, made me call you. She was disappointed when you said I couldn't have her with me during the session. She probably knew I'd tell you the truth."

"What's the truth?" I asked.

Fred squinted at me through his bifocals. "Why, what I just told you. That this isn't my decision. She said to give you this." He handed me a piece of paper on which was written: *Fred is a sad sack ever since retirement a year past. No interest in anything. He won't DO anything!*

After reading her note out loud, I asked, "What's your own opinion, Fred?"

"I'm retired. It's my time to relax."

Irene had booked his appointment for him. She'd told me by phone that Fred had worked forty years as a supervisor for a residential-lighting manufacturer. She told me that although the job title might not sound impressive, "He basically ran the show. He called the shots. The owners completely depended on him." Now, he sat hunched over with arms tightly crossed.

"Fred, you don't *look* relaxed. I believe I can help you. But it's your decision. You can leave now if that's what you really would prefer. Of course, you're also welcome to stay."

For a moment he appeared nonplussed. Then he sat up, uncrossed his arms, and cupped his hands over his knees. "Well, I'm already here, so I'll stay."

As we talked, it grew clear that Fred was suffering from a malaise rather uncommon for a retiree. The challenges of retirement catch many people off guard, but one perk most folks can count on is that they enjoy greater choice in their lives; they make more of their own day-to-day decisions. Sometimes this even can lead to *choice overload*, a condition we'll explore in a moment—but Fred was experiencing the opposite problem.

After decades of daily decision-making at work, Fred had stopped exercising his power of choice when he left his job. Irene continued to decide which social activities they engaged in, what new appliances they bought, and which restaurants they frequented. For forty years, she had even picked out Fred's clothes. As Fred saw it, all of this was *her job*. What he didn't yet see was that his retirement changed things. Expecting Irene to continue her duties full time while he did nothing struck me as perhaps unfair. But more important for Fred's own well-being, he'd become a "sad sack" because he had stopped using his ability to choose.

Why We Live in a Choose-or-Lose World

Scientists have long known that experiencing choice can make a life-or-death difference. This was famously discovered by Harvard psychologist Ellen Langer. In her 1976 study, nursing-home residents were divided into two groups of the same average age and health. Those in one group were given a few seemingly mundane choices. Each picked out a plant to put in their room, decided how they'd care for their plant, and selected which night—Thursday or Friday—to watch movies on a big screen. In addition, the home's social coordinator emphasized their freedom to choose, noting that it was up to each individual to decide when and whether to read, watch TV, listen to the radio, or visit with others.

The control group got all the same perks *except* the power to choose or even the *perception* of choice. Each individual was handed a plant and told the staff would care for it. Each person was assigned a night to watch movies on the big screen. This group had the same actual freedoms in terms of how to spend the rest of their time, but to them the coordinator emphasized only that they were *permitted* to engage in various activities. Thus, they had a little bit less actual choice, along with a *much smaller sense* of choice, than the first group.

You may be wondering what difference this could possibly make. Well, a year and a half later, standardized tests found members of the choice-making group to be more cheerful, active, and alert, as well as *physically healthier* than before the experiment started. (And remember, these were all senior citizens to begin with.) Even more astounding, fewer than half as many of the choice-makers had died as had those in the control group. Consciously exercising your ability to choose, even regarding quotidian details, can literally extend your life.

This is because evolution has wired into us an innate need to choose, says world-renowned choice expert Sheena Iyengar. Studies show that all animals share this need to some extent, which is why choice-deprived zoo captives die young. And just as with humans, other animals prefer having choices about even minor matters. For example, when monkeys or pigeons are given a reward for pushing one button, or are given the exact same reward for pushing either one of two available buttons, the creatures consistently prefer the environment that offers them a choice.

While working with me, Fred came to realize that it was time for him to begin making some decisions at home. Soon, instead of Irene planning their weekly schedule, they began sitting down together to brainstorm. Eventually, Fred suggested they take daily walks; Irene was happy to follow his lead. Fred announced he wanted to buy a king-size bed to replace the queen-size one they'd had for decades; and so he did.

Too Much of a Good Thing: Choice Overload

When I suggested to Fred that he might do his own clothes shopping, he balked. "Irene knows all my sizes. She knows what socks are comfortable, what pants will look best on me. I feel dizzy when we go to Macy's together at Christmastime. Have you seen the number of hats—just hats alone!—that they have on display?"

Fred had come up against *choice overload*, a phenomenon that Iyengar discovered when doing experiments with kids. Her team invited three-year-olds to each spend a play session in a room filled with toys. Half the children were asked to choose a toy to play with; the other half were each assigned a toy, specifically whichever one the previous child had picked. Thus, overall the children played with exactly the same toys, but only half got to choose. Because of a history of research proving the benefits of choice, Iyengar fully expected that the kids who selected toys would show more enthusiasm during playtime. To her amazement, it was the non-choosing children who played happily, while those who chose their toys were "disengaged, listless."

This sent Iyengar back to pore over the previous data. She discovered a startling fact: all those key studies shared a common factor. Each had offered participants no more than six options to choose from. Her subsequent research confirmed that having up to six choices is indeed motivating, and far superior to having no choice at all; *however*, confronting too many choices (especially, say, twenty or more) brings on choice overload.

It was Iyengar who, along with colleague Mark Lepper, conducted the now-famous "jam study." This involved setting up a free tasting display in a San Francisco grocery store. Shoppers were offered either six or twenty-four jars of jam to sample from. Although the bigger selection attracted more people, shoppers who were confronted with only half a dozen alternatives turned out to be *six times more likely* to buy jam than those who got to choose from among twenty-four. (For an overview of Iyengar's groundbreaking research, see her book *The Art of Choosing*.)

Working with Fred, I followed Iyengar's cue to bypass choice overload by reducing his options, because he clearly did not want to pick out *all* of his own clothes. I asked, "Is there any element of your wardrobe that you would like more control over?"

Fred visually body-scanned himself from toes to chest. "Irene has her own opinions about shirts. But I'm going nowhere near that shirts department! And if I have to wear a suit and tie, she probably is the better judge."

"What about when you don't have to be so formal? Is there any particular kind of casual shirt you might enjoy buying for yourself, if we could make shopping easy?"

Fred shifted in his seat, as though he were feeling slightly embarrassed. "Our neighbor Arnold wears Hawaiian shirts. I like them, but Irene won't buy those. She says they're tacky."

"Any particular type of Hawaiian shirt you might prefer? Any particular color?"

"Arnold swears by those Tommy Bahamas. But no pink for me. Only green or blue."

Thus we managed to narrow down Fred's options. He realized he could go to Macy's, ask to see only one brand of Hawaiian shirt, in only two colors, and of course only in his size. My office was just a few blocks from the store, so he headed there right after his session. The next week, he strutted in, sporting an aquamarine Hawaiian silk shirt. I asked whether his wife objected. "Hunh!" he shook his head vigorously. "Irene says she finds me more attractive now that I'm getting off my duff."

I could see it too: choice had revitalized Fred. Perhaps none of his recent decisions had been monumental, but Fred's new awareness of his power to choose had restored his sense of agency in the world. What mattered most was that he had shifted his way of thinking.

As Iyengar puts it, "Unlike captive animals, people's perceptions of control or helplessness aren't entirely dictated by outside forces. We have the ability to *create* choice by altering our interpretations of the world."

Is there any area of your life in which you feel trapped? A shift in attitude can save the day.

For example, some of my clients complain they lack control over their time. They remark, "I *have to* spend the holidays with my in-laws." Or, "I *have to* go to a wedding next month." Or, "I *have to* work late every night this week." I help them to see that these are all choices. To maintain a happy marriage, one client decides to visit her in-laws. To honor a friendship, another chooses to attend a wedding. To vie for a promotion, a third is willing to work overtime. By rephrasing their situations, my clients recover their sense of freedom and command over their own lives.

How about you? Is there some way you spend your time that up until now left you feeling disempowered or resentful?

> **Is there any area of your life in which you feel trapped? A shift in attitude can save the day.**

Exchanging Self-Pity for Self-Pride

Maybe it will help you gain clarity on your own situation if I share some of my story. As a teen I lived with my father and my older brother Tobey, after my mom and oldest brother Farley had both left. Tobey already showed serious mental illness but had not yet received help nor been diagnosed as a severe paranoid schizophrenic. In those days, before he was medicated, Tobey could not control his hostile and sometimes violent urges. One afternoon he attempted to rape me. Because he had with him a coil of heavy rope and a roll of duct tape, I feared that he planned also to kill me. I managed to escape, but it was a very close call.

From then on, I strategized my safety. Our house stood on a forested hillside, so after school, rather than risk him finding me alone, I'd hide out in the woods, sometimes for several hours, until my dad's car pulled up the drive. Later, after dinner, Dad typically drank until he passed out. Knowing he could not protect me, I'd barricade myself in my room with furniture pushed up against the door. For me, those were painful times.

The lesson of *choice* came home to me following my father's death in 2008. Tobey had been living with Dad many years, but now it fell to me and Farley to take care for our brother.

We already had been managing many aspects of their Indiana household long-distance, working by phone and internet, plus visiting occasionally to deal with medical emergencies. This was all made easier because Dad had freely cooperated with us. But after Dad's passing, Tobey posed a challenge. He desperately wished to stay on in the house because, after having spent some years off and on in mental hospitals, he was terrified of being reinstitutionalized. Yet we knew that helping him would be difficult because Tobey can be unpredictable, unpleasant, and uncooperative.

Neuro-imaging studies show schizophrenia to be a brain disease, involving loss of gray matter in several key areas. Popular belief casts schizophrenia as denoting "split personality," but that's wrong. Rather, schizophrenics cannot distinguish reality from fantasy. This is why many of them harbor grand delusions. Tobey's own "proof" that he is "God of the Universe," as he puts it, runs several thousand handwritten pages, which he keeps in locked storage. In Tobey's belief system, his "god powers" are being blocked by evil enemies. Sometimes he believes those enemies include both Farley and me. You can imagine how hard it is to help someone who views you as working for Satan.

I confess that my first response to my new caretaker role was secret resentment. Here I was, poor me, "forced" to spend considerable time and energy seeing to the welfare of my sexual attacker. I still suffer reoccurring nightmares about his violence against me. That this burden should fall on me just seemed so unfair. Poor, poor me.

But what's the truth? The truth is, no one is forcing me to take care of Tobey. Moreover, after thinking it through, it's my honest opinion that I am under no moral obligation to help him. I *choose* to help him.

It's an ongoing, conscious choice. Indeed, I am always free to change my mind. Once I fully acknowledged this truth, my experience changed drastically. The resentment melted away. It's been replaced by gratitude for the opportunity to help. Instead of *poor me*, it's *proud me*, as I pat myself on the back for taking the road of compassion—for *choosing* to do so.

"And that," as the poet Robert Frost once wrote, "has made all the difference."

Use Your Self-Intelligence

Step up and choose what's right for you. Studies reveal that this is especially important for those of us who are American. The United States boasts the most individualistic population on Earth—followed closely by Australia and the United Kingdom. The more independent-minded you are, the more crucial it is to your well-being that you consciously exercise choice.

If you're an American, an Aussie, or a Brit, you'll likely work better if you increase your sense of autonomy. For example, a 2010 study from the University of Exeter found that simply adding wall art and potted plants to an office led employees to work 15 percent faster (revisit chapter 3 to understand why). And when workers were given the *choice* of how to customize their own space, their productivity shot up by twice as much again. In what ways might you exercise more of your own preferences at work?

Choose to make your fitness regimen more convenient and fun, so that you will feel more like exercising. Set up your home exercise area so you can watch your favorite shows while working out. Or, if you prefer to go to a health club, switch gyms for somewhere closer and nicer, or to be with your buddies. The more you choose what you like to do, the easier it becomes to follow through.

Have you and your sweetie begun to take each other for granted? Pause a moment to consciously own your choice to be together. How often can you renew this decision? Daily!

Finances is one area in which many people experience *choice overload*. For example, if you've neglected to save for retirement because you felt too intimidated to pick from dozens of 401(k) options, then ask your human resources department to help you narrow down your alternatives. Ask them to help you enroll now, so that you don't miss out—especially if your company provides matching funds.

Quiz answer: Consciously exercising your power of personal choice . . .

    a.   may help you live longer.

In a Nutshell

All animals have an innate need to make choices. Research shows that being robbed of choice thus typically leads to an earlier death. Among humans, the act of choosing tends to uplift and invigorate us. Look for opportunities to make your own decisions about things that matter to you, big or small. Also, practice recognizing the choices you *already* are making. And, if ever you feel overwhelmed by too many options (*choice overload*), first narrow their number—six or fewer is a good bet—before making your selection. In the end, whether you feel out of control or in command of your own life is up to you. So choose!

No pessimist ever discovered the secret of the stars,
or sailed to an uncharted land, or opened a new
doorway for the human spirit.

—HELEN KELLER

CHAPTER 8

UP

A Mental Direction Worth Aiming For

Prime-your-mind Quiz

Research says you'll remember this chapter better if you test yourself now. How will the answer affect *you*?

Because positivity plays a role in our social connections, scientific research has found that for a romantic partnership to last, the couple must engage in more positive than negative interactions—specifically, by a ratio of at least . . .

a. two to one.

b. three to one.

c. five to one.

Some clients reveal quite a bit about themselves right from the start. Procrastinators email me their background questionnaires ten minutes before the first session. A compulsive shopper once came in carrying three big bags straight from Nordstrom. One man, suffering from a social phobia, called and hung up several times before speaking. Sometimes such issues are not the same ones for which the client is seeking help. But often, they end up being related.

Roberta introduced herself by email:

> Ms. Ransom:
>
> I will forego your preliminary phone consultation. My friends recommend you, therefore no sales pitch is necessary, and I am too busy to waste time. I will describe my circumstance here, then you can state whether or not you are qualified.
>
> I anticipate an imminent breakup with my partner of two years. I know from past experience that I am likely to suffer lack of sleep, loss of appetite, and crying spells. I accept that grieving is natural, but I wish to finish the process as quickly as possible. Your website fails to make clear whether you can address this issue. Please state whether you are competent to help me or not. Please reply within 24 hours.

To me, she sounded awfully demanding; I considered turning her down as a client. But she was a referral, so I just emailed her back my standard questionnaire, along with a note that whether or not I could help would depend as much on her as on me. Three weeks passed before she emailed me her completed form. From it I learned, among other things, that Roberta was a corporate tax attorney.

When we met by Skype, she appeared sitting in an office full of overflowing bookcases. She began by telling me that my client information form was too long: "Most of the questions are irrelevant. I didn't contact you to help me with my family history or my professional goals. I just want to get through a breakup." I thanked her for her feedback (noting to myself that she seemed quick to criticize), then asked her to tell me more about her romantic relationship.

"What do you want to know?"

"You've indicated that the relationship isn't going well. Is your partner an attorney also?"

Roberta seemed to squint at the question. "God, no," she said. "Greg is an actor. He earns money temping as an IT expert, but most of his time and energy go into acting. Greg is at an acting workshop right now, which apparently is part of the problem." She glowered.

"Yes?" I prompted.

"There's a woman in the workshop. *Sandra*. He mentions her all the time. Last week I saw them at a Starbucks together and they were sitting very close together at a table. I don't know if they're getting ready to have an affair or if they're already having one. He even wants the four of us to go out to dinner: me, him, Sandra, and her partner Chris." Roberta ran a hand across her forehead. She had short black hair and rather dramatic dark eyes.

"I don't know if Greg is conscious of his feelings or not," she continued, "but they're quite evident to me. I feel like I'm in a Woody Allen movie—you know what I mean— where people are falling out of love with their partners, and into love with somebody they're not supposed to be in love with, and it takes them the whole damn movie to figure things out."

This struck me as funny, but Roberta wasn't smiling. "Are you also saying you're falling out of love with Greg?"

"I'm *not* saying that." She exhaled loudly. "*Please* pay attention. I am *saying* I think he's in love with someone else. We haven't been happy for at least a year. That's what happened in my last relationship before *it* imploded. Maybe men just lose interest in monogamous sex. Or maybe I'm just not that sexy or interesting."

After a moment, I ventured, "Is that what Greg thinks?"

"I have no idea what he thinks," Roberta glared. "He's an actor, for god's sake! He could be thinking anything without my knowing it. Who knows what his motives are? I make a lot more money than he does, and I pay most of the rent. In my experience, men either can't handle that or they want to take advantage of it."

"Roberta, please bear with me. I'm trying to understand the situation. Do you *want* to break up?"

She sat back. Her eyes grew sad. "No. I love Greg."

Then we began to talk, and Roberta told me her story. Two years earlier she and Greg had fallen madly in love. They moved in together after only three months. At first, they'd been happy, but then something shifted. They began to argue a lot. Initially, this led to make-up sex, but soon Greg had declared a moratorium on make-up sex, saying that what he really wanted was for them to stop arguing. However, they continued to argue, only now they weren't having *any* sex, which made Roberta feel hurt and rejected. And that, in turn, made her angrier. It sounded as though every day their interactions were becoming more negative.

"I know from previous relationships that when it gets to this point, it means we're breaking up," she concluded. "I want to get through it as painlessly as possible."

Roberta had stated on her questionnaire that her parents divorced when she was eleven, that her father was now in his third marriage, and that her mother, who never remarried, was struggling financially. I asked Roberta about all of that now. She acknowledged that while growing up, she'd never had high relationship expectations. While other girls had fantasized about Prince Charming, she'd dreamt of making enough money to be financially independent. "I just wanted not to need anybody—you know what I mean? And I don't *need* Greg, not really."

"My opinion is that if you give up on your relationship, it will definitely end," I said. "The more pessimistic you are, the faster it's likely to end. I guess if your goal is to get it over with as quickly as possible, then that makes sense."

" Scientists have found that we can countermand the downward pull of the negativity bias by purposefully embracing the positive, by aiming up.

"But . . . ?" Roberta narrowed her eyes. "You're hinting at something."

"Well, on the other hand, maybe you could still save the relationship. No guarantee, but from your description, it sounds as though you and Greg have fallen into a cycle of negativity. Both of you feel hurt, and both of you keep on hurting each other."

"It doesn't take a genius to see that. So what's *your* brilliant solution?" Roberta asked.

What I told her—and want to tell everyone—is that although this may sound simplistic, the surest antidote to negativity is . . . positivity. I suggested to Roberta that if she could consistently behave toward Greg in a more positive manner, it might change everything.

"It can't be that easy," she said.

"You're right." In fact, we were both right. Positivity can cause great change—yet for most of us, it also takes great effort, especially at first, until we've established a positivity habit.

Negating the Negativity Bias

Research shows that evolution has made it innately difficult for humans to focus on the positive. Imagine a gravitylike force constantly pulling our emotions downward, urging us to pay more attention to negative events and to spend more time dwelling on negative thoughts. This force exists within our brains. Scientists call it *the negativity bias*.

To help us survive many millennia ago, evolution constructed our brains to notice and focus on the negative far more than on the positive. This made sense when we were living in constant danger, fending off saber-toothed tigers, catastrophic weather, and hostile neighbors. To avoid early death, we needed to be on high alert for the various threats surrounding us and indeed for anything even remotely suspicious.

Various studies show that this old wiring still directs the brain. But today, for those of us in the civilized world, such relentless negativity is a vestigial handicap. It makes us fearful, insecure, and sometimes even paranoid. Instead of helping us to survive, it undercuts our ability to bond with others . . . and in modern times, those bonds are exactly what we need to live well and long (which we'll talk about in chapter 13).

So what can we do? Scientists have found that we can countermand the downward pull of the negativity bias by purposefully embracing the positive, by aiming *up*. This means consciously adopting constructive thoughts. And it means interacting with others in a more uplifting manner than might come naturally at first. Initially a challenge, this all becomes easier with practice. Then the force of habit prevails.

Roberta heard me out, then said, "You sound like one of those smiley-face people who believes that everything happens for the best." She appeared genuinely disappointed.

"Not at all," I said. "History proves that's not true. But sometimes we can *cause* the best to happen, by being positive. For example, try to remember exactly how you and Greg interacted during your happy first year, when you had high hopes about your future together. If, from now on, you began behaving toward him like that again, it's possible he would follow suit. If you felt optimistic about him now, what would you do differently?"

She said she would think about it.

Quitters versus Strivers (and Who Has More Fun)

In 1998, Martin Seligman, then-president of the American Psychological Association, officially ushered in the field of positive psychology. He called for scientists to stop concentrating on what's broken (up until then, most research had focused on mental illness)—and instead to explore what works: What exactly do happy, healthy, successful people *do* in order to thrive?

Ironically, this new field began with the discovery of *learned helplessness*. Seligman found that most dogs who were repeatedly exposed to mildly painful shocks, with no way to escape, eventually stopped trying to flee *any* such shocks, even ones that would have been easy to avoid. Similar experiments with humans, exposing them to unpleasant noise, likewise engendered learned helplessness.

But one very promising fact stood out: A third of the people tested never succumbed to learned helplessness. Despite repeated initial failures, they never gave up trying to fix the problem. Seligman realized that if he could discover their secret, maybe he could help the rest of us become more resilient.

Clearly, most of us could use the help. No doubt you have witnessed many cases of learned helplessness. One person wants to be a professional singer, but after several unsuccessful auditions simply gives up. Someone else wants to lose weight but after a series of unsuccessful diets, loses hope. Either could achieve their goal with additional effort (and perhaps better strategies), but because they feel helpless, they stop trying.

What makes some people quit while others strive? Seligman's research revealed the answer: In general, quitters are pessimists; strivers are optimists. But here let's head off any misunderstanding. Sometimes people think of *optimism* as a kind of Pollyannaism, an absurd denial of reality. This is the mindless happy-face attitude wrongly associated with "positive thinking." Instead, Seligman's definition has to do with "explanatory styles," particularly what we tell ourselves when things go wrong.

He has found that optimists view trouble as temporary and limited, while pessimists experience adversity as being permanent and widespread. For example, after being turned down for a job, a pessimist might decide, "*No* one will *ever* hire me for *any*thing." An optimist's reaction to the same event might be, "That company turned me down, but there are plenty of other companies out there; eventually, I'll get hired."

One attitude leads a person to quit. The other spurs them to keep going.

Optimists also tend to be easier on themselves: "My interview went poorly because they asked bad questions." Pessimists are harder on themselves: "I screwed up that interview because I have no social skills." Perhaps neither perspective is ever 100 percent accurate, but one is clearly more self-encouraging. And *both* tend to be self-fulfilling.

In most fields, optimists far outperform pessimists. Seligman's decades of research have determined that optimism measurably boosts success among U.S. military recruits, professional athletes, salespeople, students, service professionals, and presidential candidates. Optimists tend to achieve more because they set bigger goals, brave more risks, believe in themselves, and plain stick with it. Their optimism offsets their negativity bias and immunizes them against learned helplessness.

There are, however, a few exceptions. For some jobs, pessimism and the negativity bias actually serve as strengths. We hire certain professionals to be on high alert for mistakes—detectives looking for lies, auditors trained to catch errors . . . and *lawyers*, conditioned to spot flaws in other people's versions of events.

Unfortunately, this professional asset can become a personal liability. Many expert fault-finders begin to find fault everywhere, including in themselves and the people closest to them. Psychologists say that this propensity to criticize—which is drilled into law students from day one—explains why lawyers are 3.6 times more likely than the rest of us to suffer from depression. And so, following our first Skype call, I found myself worrying some about Roberta.

But then she showed up for her second session in a remarkably good mood.

"I decided to take your dare," she smiled. "You asked me what I would do differently if I felt optimistic about me and Greg. All right, I decided that in that case, having dinner with Sandra and her partner Chris would be no problem. I took Greg up on his suggestion of a double date. But to tell the truth, I expected to discover I was right after all, and to find Greg guilty."

I thanked Roberta for her honesty.

"You're welcome," she said. "It did turn out like a Woody Allen movie, but not in the way I expected. *Chris* is short for *Christine*. Sandra is gay. I mean lifelong, one-hundred-percent lesbian. At first, I wondered why Greg never told me, but then realized it's because it doesn't matter to him. They're buddies. It was the best night out that we've enjoyed together in a very long while. We're getting along great now."

Arguing Yourself into Better Beliefs

Roberta's news made me ecstatic. (See "Good news? Effuse!") After congratulating her, I shared with her a strategy that Seligman developed and has tested, called "disputation." In this way, Roberta could benefit by using her lawyerly skills to win arguments against . . . herself.

You can deploy this tool, too, to combat unhelpful beliefs. In most adverse circumstances, what causes us emotional pain isn't the situation per se, but rather our belief about its cause. For example, imagine that your best friend, Jenny, used to phone you every week and now she hardly ever calls. What hurts is that you find yourself obsessing, "Jenny doesn't like me anymore." Here's how disputation works, in four steps:

1. **Evidence.** Look for evidence to disprove your belief. Does Jenny still sometimes call? (If she really didn't like you, she'd never call.) Does she answer the phone when you call her? When you get together, does she seem to enjoy your company?

2. **Alternatives.** Consider alternative causes for the situation. Is it possible that Jenny's work schedule changed, making it difficult for her to call you so often? Could she be busy with a new project? A new relationship? Or maybe she's going through some personal crisis. Often, those first two steps will be all you need to demolish the old belief. But if it persists, proceed to step 3.

GOOD NEWS? EFFUSE!

Scientists have discovered that one great way to strengthen our relationships is to celebrate one another's good news. Researchers even have a name for it: *capitalization*. They've found that capitalization may be more important to a good relationship than giving support in hard times. But they've also determined that there's *only one* beneficial way to respond to others' good news.

University of California, Santa Barbara, psychologist Shelly Gable found that the only helpful response is to show enthusiasm, make supportive comments, and ask questions. "That's terrific that you got a promotion! Your boss must realize what a fantastic job you did on that last project. When did you find out?"

In contrast, here are the three losing responses, *all* of which tend to do emotional harm:

- Being passive. ("Oh, how nice.")

- Being negative. ("You're kidding. *You* got a raise—really?")

- Worst of all, ignoring their good news. ("Huh. Did you see the game last night?")

By responding enthusiastically, you will connect better with others and spur them on to even greater accomplishment. But I also want you to notice what sort of responses *others give to you*. If your partner, for example, tends to react passively to your good news (say, with a mild, "Congratulations, dear," a warm smile, and nothing more), then please educate your mate on this issue. Research indicates that a passive "positive" response can be almost as demoralizing as an openly hostile one.

If some friends or family members refuse to welcome your wins with interest and excitement, then it may be wise to stop sharing your good news with them. Why expose yourself to disappointment? Instead, seek out supporters who you know will cheer you on wholeheartedly.

3. **Implications.** Suppose your belief turns out to be true. Are the implications really so terrible? Okay, Jenny doesn't like you anymore. So darn what? Other people like you. You can always make new friends. Your happiness doesn't depend on Jenny.

4. **Usefulness.** Even if your belief were correct, is it useful to dwell on it? If Jenny no longer likes you, then it's time to let go. Glean whatever learning you can from the situation: maybe you realize you haven't been supportive of Jenny's goals, or fun to be around; with your new insight, you can decide to conduct your future friendships better. And so you move on.

Take a moment right now to consider whether you've been harboring any beliefs that cause you pain or hold you back. Do you imagine your coworkers or family members are sabotaging you? Do you tell yourself you'll never be able to write that book, lose that weight, or meet the mate of your dreams? Nonsense! Deactivate that belief with disputation.

You may recall Roberta's initial conviction that if a woman earns more money than a man, "men either can't handle that or they want to take advantage of it." Here's how she used the first two disputation steps:

1. **Evidence.** When she put her mind to it, Roberta was able to come up with several examples of happy couples where the woman brings home a bigger paycheck. (For example, Oprah.) Next, she also found evidence—right at home, in fact—that Greg in particular was neither threatened by her income nor attached to it. She had to admit that he showed no real interest in money or material possessions. As she put it, "He lives for his art." True, she paid most of their rent but then it had been her decision that they live in a luxury apartment.

2. **Alternatives.** She acknowledged that there might be other, nonfinancial reasons for him to remain in their rocky relationship—such as that he loved her. And she confessed that there could be other causes for their relationship troubles, including her own habit of finding flaws. She now saw that she had been constantly criticizing Greg at every turn, from correcting his grammar to pointing out his clothes didn't quite match to critiquing his choices of wine at dinner.

Those first two steps of disputation allowed Roberta to let go of her paranoid belief that Greg might be in it for the money. Her improved perspective would of course be crucial to their long-term success. But I felt certain that she also needed to address her fault-finding habit.

During our fourth session, we discussed it directly: "If you want to stay together, I believe you must curb your tendency to criticize. Save your critical skills for the office. Don't bring them home. It makes no difference whether you're wrong or right. Criticism kills relationships."

Swapping Critiques for Compliments

My favorite couples researcher, John Gottman, has found that in an intimate relationship, "despite what countless people believe, *there is no such thing as constructive criticism.*" When a difficult issue must be broached, Gottman advises us to frame it as a desire or a need. For example, instead of criticizing your mate with, "You're such a cold person, you never hug me," tell your partner, "I love it when you hug me. Can I have a hug?"

The main problem with criticism ("You never hug me,") is that it puts the other person on the defensive and thus makes change even less likely. Moreover, it causes *hurt*, which may trigger your partner to strike back, setting off a self-perpetuating cycle of negativity.

I suggested to Roberta that she start looking for ways to praise and support Greg, to create positive interactions. Tell him he's handsome! Thank him for being a good lover! (Because yes, they had resumed their sex life.) Acknowledge his acting art, his kindness, his loyalty, his thoughtfulness. I warned her that regularly appreciating him might feel artificial and forced at first, because any new habit does—and because she'd be defying her own negativity bias.

"But it will be worth it," I promised, because it might just save their relationship.

Gottman is known around the globe for proving that successful couples must maintain at least a 5-to-1 ratio of positive to negative interactions. That's a *minimum* requirement. To make sure his ratio was correct, Gottman videotaped 700 soon-to-be-wed couples having 15-minute conversations. His team counted the positive versus negative interactions for each couple. Based on the 5-to-1 ratio, they then predicted which couples would succeed in marriage, and which would eventually divorce. Any couple who conducted fewer than five times as many positive to negative interactions was predicted to fail. Ten years later, Gottman followed up. His predictions turned out to be 94 percent accurate. Wow.

This doesn't mean that you should keep score of your relationship interactions. Instead, just aim for maximum positivity while remaining genuine. And, as you learn to aim up, be kind to yourself. When unhelpful thoughts or feelings do occur (such as envy, insecurity, resentment, etc.), never self-condemn. Simply step back for a bigger view, then steer yourself in a better direction, using disputation when needed.

And, as best you can, surround yourself with positive people. Due to the subconscious process scientists call *emotional contagion*, we humans deeply influence one another's moods. When you're in a positive state, you buoy up others. So why not choose to be around others who buoy up you? Start noticing how others affect your energy. Those who complain, drain you. Those who sincerely praise you, raise you up.

Pointing Yourself in the Right Direction

Psychologists differentiate between *approach goals* versus *avoidance goals*. Roberta had first contacted me with an avoidance goal: to avoid the emotional suffering of an inevitable breakup. As her situation changed, she could have shifted to another avoidance goal—to avoid ending the relationship—but I helped her to reframe it as an approach goal: To build a stronger relationship.

"That makes me a little nervous," she said during our last session. "I set high professional goals because I know I can achieve them. If I set a high relationship goal, I might fail."

"That's true. But what's worse is that if you set a low relationship goal, you might succeed. How scary is that?!"

Researchers have found that couples who are most ambitious about the quality of their relationships end up the happiest. Those who aim low get what they settle for. In the end, I was optimistic about Roberta's future with Greg. She had the alacrity and the courage for genuine success—and now she had the map.

How about you? Think about your own goals. Do you tend to focus on what you don't want or what you *do*? Studies from the universities of Rochester and Missouri have found that avoidance goals may actually do harm. They can breed anxiety and rob us of a sense of control. Approach goals, on the other hand, will energize you.

As you develop a habit of aiming for what you desire, you'll become less fearful and more cheerful. However, before you jump in, you may be wondering: Aren't there exceptions? Aren't there times when too much positivity might be ill advised? Yes. We'll see in the very next chapter why financial decisions are best made in a neutral, or even skeptical, state. Recent history reminds us how overoptimism can lead to lost money:

the dot-com bust, the housing bubble, the Bernie Madoff debacle. In general, any very high-risk decision—including whom to marry—should be carefully considered rather than rushed into with headlong abandon.

There may also be smaller, more everyday challenges where negative worrying will help. This depends partly on your personality. For natural worriers like me, Wellesley College psychology professor Julie Norem recommends "defensive pessimism." It means thinking through what might go wrong, in order to get things right. For example, when creating a seminar, I'll come up with potential problems in order to solve them beforehand: Participants could get hungry, so let's have snacks on hand. The room might be cold, so let's ask people to bring sweaters. What if my slide show malfunctions? Let's have a backup plan.

As you continue building your Self-Intelligence, you will recognize those times when it helps to welcome a bit of worry or a dose of skepticism. But, in general, you'll find that optimism furthers both your happiness and your success. And as you raise your standards—of what your relationships, your work, and your life *can be*—you will encourage others to follow suit. You will become a leader in positivity. You will lift yourself and others *up*.

Use Your Self-Intelligence

It's time to up-level all areas of your life by embracing positivity.

Become the person your colleagues look up to, by generating positive energy. Whenever the opportunity arises to appreciate others' good work, take a moment to give genuine praise—and make it specific. This small act can have a huge effect. If you don't believe me, read Tom Rath's classic, *How Full Is Your Bucket?*

If you're already physically fit, know that studies show optimism increases longevity and helps prevent disease. (See Martin Seligman's book *Flourish* for details.) If you're not yet fit, decide now to get in shape, then cultivate optimism so that you stick with it. Refuse to give in to learned helplessness. *You can do it*, and that's a fact.

Play a game with yourself. When you interact with anyone close to you (friends, family, or lover), look for openings to help that person—not by telling them what they should do but by applauding something they're already doing. What do you respect/appreciate/admire about that individual? Make it sincere and say it out loud. (For extra credit, give hugs.)

$ This is the one area of your life where it literally won't pay to be too optimistic, especially when it comes to big risks, such as buying pricey real estate or overvalued stocks. The best way to implement positivity here is to plan to live a wonderfully long life—so start earning, saving, and investing accordingly.

Quiz answer: Because positivity plays a role in our social connections, scientific research has found that for a romantic partnership to last, the couple must engage in more positive than negative interactions—specifically, by a ratio of at least . . .

    c.   five to one.

In a Nutshell

To help us survive in the wild, our brains evolved a tendency to focus on the negative. But this *negativity bias* no longer serves us—especially when research shows that optimists outperform pessimists, and that successful romantic relationships require at least five times as many positive to negative interactions. The solution? Consciously commit to positivity. Aim *up*. This means disputing your own overly negative beliefs, and it also means buoying up other people. Stop criticizing and start encouraging! Aim your goals *up* as well. Focus on what you *do* desire, and set the bar high.

PART THREE

THINKING THROUGH YOUR EMBODIED SELF

To build our Self-Intelligence model from the inside out, we began in the hidden depths of your *subconscious self*, then progressed a bit outward to your *conscious self*. Ultimately, we will work our way to your *striving self*, the one who takes action out in the external world.

But first, let's pause at that miraculous intersection of inner and outer, mental and physical, intangible and tangible: your *embodied self*. Although it may sometimes seem as though your thoughts are one thing and your body quite another thing, recent research proves otherwise. Much of what you experience in your body—and therefore, also what you *do* with your body—significantly shapes your brain processes. In a very real sense, *you think through your body*, and indeed, you need your body in order to think at all. As neuroscientist Antonio Damasio quips, "No body, never mind."

Four centuries ago, French philosopher René Descartes declared the creation of his *self* through pure thought: "I think, therefore I am." He believed in a strict divide between mind and body, postulating that the mind did its thinking independently of the body, and that the body did not think, period. Today we know better. Science shows the mind to be inseparable from the body; the two are cozy as clams. As Frank Sinatra might have sung it, "You can't have one without the other." As neuroscientist Damasio declares, "There is no such thing as a disembodied mind."

Therefore, in this part we'll continue to follow our primary thread of *interconnection*, which creates cohesion and flexibility not only between brain and body but also, as you recall, among all five sub-selves of the Self-Intelligence model. Remember, this empowers you to mix and match positive-change strategies in whatever way serves you best.

For example, in the next chapter, you'll hear how my client employed hypnosis to establish new subconscious brain maps while he also addressed his body—or perhaps I should say, *dressed* his body, in the form of wearing certain shoes!—in order to reinforce those same neural maps. In the chapter after that, we'll dive deeper into the brain-body loop by exploring some exciting research on *embodied cognition*. The other two chapters here tackle topics that have long been associated with physical self-care, but which scientists now recognize as essential for brain strength: physical exercise and sleep—a mysterious body-mind event during which your brain does some extraordinary things.

Never ignore a gut feeling,
but never believe that it's enough.

—MANAGEMENT EXPERT ROBERT HELLER

CHAPTER 9

JUDGMENT

Know When (And When Not) to Trust Your Gut

Prime-your-mind Quiz

Research says you'll remember this chapter better if you test yourself now. How will the answer affect *you*?

When buying real estate or stocks, it's a good idea to . . .

a. be optimistic.

b. beware of euphoric emotions.

c. just trust your gut.

Joshua is an online day trader who sometimes makes more money in a day than many of us make in a year. Joshua also plays video games, flies helicopters, and drives race cars for fun. He lives in Connecticut with his wife, Emma, and their dog, Clancy. He called me because one small thing about his work was bugging him.

"Every now and then I screw up my trading, and I don't know why," he said. "I've practiced this game and know how to play it. I've got two computers and four monitors and I'm watching the charts and data change second by second. My reaction times are phenomenal. If I want to, I can get in and out of a stock before you can blink. I trade on margin, meaning I can make or lose huge amounts of money in a short time. Here's what I don't understand. When I have a phenomenal morning, I mean really great, almost without exception I will screw it up before the day's over. Basically, I'll buy crappy stocks I shouldn't buy, totally convinced whatever I touch is on the way up. What creeps me out is that while I'm doing it, I have no awareness that my game is off."

We made a video-session appointment for the following Sunday afternoon. When we met webcam to webcam, he was sitting in an office much larger and nicer than mine, with plateglass windows and a view of white poplar trees behind him. Soon we were interrupted by a dog, a Boxer-ish mutt with adorably droopy jowls, who put his chin on Joshua's arm in a clear bid for attention. "He's kind of ugly, isn't he?" Joshua laughed. "We went to the pound thinking we were going to find some handsome lab, but we met him first and after ten minutes looking around the shelter we decided to take him home."

I asked Joshua to tell me more about his day-trading problem. "Some days my focus gets foggy but when that happens, I don't fight it," he said. "I respect my own stop-loss limit and take the rest of the day off. The problem happens on those mornings when I'm so totally in the zone it's like I can't lose. I can make more than a hundred thousand dollars very fast. But at some point it's like I lose touch with reality. I feel great, like I'm still in the zone, but in fact I'm in la-la land. I buy crap I shouldn't. Then more crap . . . bam, bam, bam, and lose a fortune. In hindsight, it's just plain stupid but at the time it's like some altered reality. I don't take drugs. I have to be able to trust myself."

I asked if it hurt to lose all that cash. He waved his hand dismissively. "At this point, money's a game. Trading gives me the same kind of thrill I get from racing cars or playing *World of Warcraft*. It's the sport that matters. I watch my trading monitors the same way I watch the racetrack. It's about self-control, staying calm and alert no matter what happens. It's about trusting my gut in order to act fast—way too fast to think about it."

Given that money to him was no big deal, I asked how his big winning streaks affected him. His face lit up. "It's an incredible feeling. I like money, don't get me wrong. But I *love* winning." Then he shook his head. "It's my loss of judgment that kills me. Afterward I'm so furious at myself for the next few days that Emma worries about me." Joshua sat up straighter and leaned in. "See, there's an example of how I operate. First time we went out, I knew she was the one, and I told her so right then and there. I like to move fast without overthinking. That's why I can't have this weirdness keep happening."

A possible solution was taking shape in my mind. I inquired, "Do you ever lose your sense of judgment, or lose your sense of reality in that same way, when you're racing cars?"

He pulled back. "Of course not. I'd be dead."

"You know," I told him, "it sounds as if those big winning streaks give you an individual case of what economists call *animal spirits*. It's a specific emotional state that leads people to buy like maniacs, whether it's tulips, houses, or stocks. Usually the term refers to mass misjudgment by a large population, a sort of contagious overoptimism. It's what caused the dot-com bubble and the real estate debacle as well. But you, you're so self-reliant, it's as though you bring it on yourself when you win really big. Those big wins cause neurochemical reactions in the brain, including the release of dopamine. That's the neurotransmitter behind most addictions. So you're right on target when you compare your loss of judgment to someone on drugs."

"Uh-hunnh," Joshua took this in. "So then what's the solution?"

Taming Those Animal Spirits

We needed to inoculate Joshua against animal spirits. The people who never succumb to animal spirits are those spoilsports who stay in touch with actual risk. They were the ones who shunned adjustable rate mortgages because they remembered what many people forgot: that interest rates could rise and send their payments sky-high. Even though Joshua was one cool-headed trader in general, the fact that he had money to burn weakened his subconscious sense of risk. Especially after winning big, he could easily afford to lose big, too. The reason his judgment stayed sound on the racetrack was that there, the risk of death remained close-up and personal. I wondered if maybe we could bring some symbol of that very real risk into his trading practice, to put his subconscious mind on alert against animal spirits.

Then I thought of the real-life animal on hand. "Does Clancy hang out with you while you're trading?" I asked.

"Yeah, right at my feet," he grinned. "Why?"

"My apologies to Clancy because I adore dogs. But in this case his presence may be too comforting to your subconscious. Let's try banning him from your workday for a while. That's still not enough, though. We need something more. Do you wear some kind of protective gear while you're racing? Something that you associate with danger? A helmet or something you could put on while trading?"

Joshua thought for a moment, then said, "There's just no way I would wear the helmet. I could wear my shoes. They're flame-resistant. When you have to worry about your feet catching fire—to me, that signals danger."

"That's it," I agreed.

It was time to do some hypnosis. I asked Joshua to send Clancy out of the office, and to get his racing shoes ready to put on. (He held them up to the camera; they looked like red leather sneakers.) It was always easy for Joshua to enter a hypnotic trance, probably due to his power of focus; high-performing athletes are the same. While he was hypnotized, I helped him draw on his own memory of "being in the zone" to access his best trading state of mind. Then I suggested he put on his fireproof shoes and while lacing them, silently say to himself his own words: "Calm and alert." This created what we hypnotists call an *anchor*, which he would use in the future to quickly access that same physiological state. Next, I had him visualize a terrific morning of trading—winning *big*—while maintaining that state. Then he visualized finishing out the rest of the trading day remaining *calm and alert*.

Following hypnosis, we went over our plan. Joshua agreed that at least for a while, he would ban Clancy from the office during trading hours. More importantly, as soon as Joshua sat down to work, he would put on his racing shoes. As he tied the laces, he would say to himself, "Calm and alert," anchoring himself into his optimal mindset. He couldn't predict when the next big win would be (it depended on market opportunities), so we agreed to do reinforcement sessions until the time came.

Over the next two months, he told me that his performance was improving, that he felt steadier and more focused, and that the anchor was "kicking in" faster each time. This good news meant that his new subconscious neural connections were growing stronger, and thus more likely to withstand animal spirits. Finally, one morning arrived when a company he'd been tracking released a piece of news that he pounced on; then he rode the waves, swiftly making a small fortune. Almost immediately, he became aware that the old euphoria was creeping back in. But he glanced down at his shoes, heard himself saying inwardly, "Calm and alert," recovered his cool-headedness and quickly decided to call it a day.

"I almost miss that high feeling," he told me, "but not much. Emma says I seem more relaxed lately, and when she's happy, I'm happy. We're flying to France next week to celebrate." As far as I know, Joshua never again suffered animal spirits.

Betting on Our Emotions

Jolted by the dot-com and real-estate bubbles earlier this century—and persuaded by new scientific insights into the subconscious mind—economists have abandoned their long-standing belief in *Homo economicus*, the idea that humans are reliably motivated by self-interest to make logically sound financial choices.

High-tech studies have found that various brain areas go more or less haywire at the prospect of making lots of cash, while other areas go off-kilter with the fear of losing money. The ventromedial prefrontal cortex tricks us into believing something is a better bet than it is. The nucleus accumbens ramps up greed and excessive positivity, while the amygdala can warp our logic with fear. Experiments by behavioral economists, neuroscientists, and a whole new breed called neuro-economists, confirm that the ultimate effect of all this is poor judgment. One of the greatest dangers occurs when a heady rush of positivity blinds investors to real risk.

"High-tech studies have found that various brain areas go more or less haywire at the prospect of making lots of cash, while other areas go off-kilter with the fear of losing money.

It's frighteningly easy for this to happen. Scientists have found that merely looking at photos of smiling faces can trigger brain reward centers and lead investors to place overly risky bets. In chapter 3, I encouraged you to surround yourself with images that make you happy. But when playing the market, you don't want to feel overjoyed.

Here's Judgment Rule Number One: When it comes to financial decisions, be on guard against the effect of euphoria. Crunch numbers, deal with hard data, and watch out for the sway of optimistic feelings, particularly the "high" brought on by good news. Right now, consider what big wins might befall you in the future—a promotion? a sweet contract? a generous inheritance?—and start planning what you will and won't do. Mentally rehearse your response, so that when the time comes, you'll easily access the emotions and decisions that serve you.

Scientists now know that we are neurologically designed to heed our feelings. It's useless to deny the subconscious, so we must learn to influence it instead. Recall that to be a better trader, Joshua didn't banish his emotions. Rather, he programmed his subconscious to create a particular emotional state. He learned how to temper his winner's high with the fear of risk.

The scientist who discovered that we actually *need* our emotions in order to make decisions is University of Southern California neurologist Antonio Damasio. He also found that while emotions may originate in the mind, we feel them in our bodies, and in turn, those physical feelings help us to think better, creating a continuous brain-body loop. See the sidebar "Head vs. Heart? Don't Take Them Apart." Quite often, it is wise to trust our so-called gut instinct.

When to Follow Your Feelings

If studies on animal spirits warn us that we should *not* always lead with our viscera (such as by playing stocks while euphoric), then when *should* we follow our proverbial hearts? The answer is social situations, especially when choosing friends or mates. Here, feelings are often better judges than thoughts.

For example, perhaps you've heard of a Duchenne smile (named for its discoverer, the 19th century French neurologist Guillaume Duchenne). When you feel a burst of joy or hear a good joke, your cingulate cortex triggers a sincere smile that affects your mouth, eyes, and eyelids in very specific ways. That's a Duchenne. In comparison, when you force an insincere smile, you use your motor cortex only to move your mouth, in which

HEAD VS. HEART?
DON'T TAKE THEM APART

In the 1980s, neurobiologist Antonio Damasio began working with patients who, because of brain damage, had lost their ability to emote. While these patients scored high on tests of logic and intelligence, Damasio was initially shocked to find that their lack of emotions left them in a nearly helpless state, incapable of making commonsense decisions. In an oft-quoted passage from his book *Descartes' Error*, Damasio tells what happened when he asked one such emotionless patient to pick an appointment time:

> I suggested two alternative dates . . . . The patient pulled out his appointment book and began consulting the calendar. The behavior that ensued, which was witnessed by several investigators, was remarkable. For the better part of a half hour, the patient enumerated reasons for and against each of the two dates: previous engagements, proximity to other engagements, possible meteorological conditions . . . . walking us through a tiresome cost-benefit analysis, an endless outlining and fruitless comparison of options and possible consequences . . . .

Finally the staff on hand could stand it no longer and suggested he take the later date, to which the patient blandly responded, "That's fine."

Damasio's research has helped dispel the traditional dichotomy of head versus heart. To think and behave rationally, we *must* draw on our feelings. Because this occurs for the most part subconsciously, it's easy to delude ourselves that we're "above" emotional influence—but we very rarely are, nor should we want to be.

And, while emotions are key to decision-making, it turns out the body is key to emotion-making. New studies show that emotions begun in the brain create feelings in the body, and these sensations in turn influence the brain. This nonstop loop has led Damasio and others to recognize the body as part of the brain. If this seems odd, it may help to remember that neurons are the basic brain cells of thinking, yet neurons extend throughout your physique, communicating back and forth with brain headquarters via the spinal cord. Indeed, a single neuron can extend up to three feet long in a tall person, reaching from the tip of the big toe to the base of the spine. (We'll go deeper into how what you do with your body affects your thoughts, in the next chapter on Kinesthesia.)

Recent research into the brain-body loop explains why people around the world refer to parts of the body as though they had thoughts of their own: "Trust your gut," or "Follow your heart." The new science reveals why those phrases make sense. Many studies point, in particular, to the vagus nerve, which creates feelings in both the gut and heart areas.

The vagus nerve is a bundle of neurons that originates in the brain stem, at the top of the spinal cord, and connects to the neck, chest, and abdomen. The vagus nerve regulates the heart, lungs, liver, and digestive organs, and it orchestrates many emotional sensations. For example, during stress, the brain's anterior cingulate cortex stimulates the vagus nerve to cause negative "gut" feelings of physical pain and nausea. It's also the vagus nerve that produces visceral "heart" feelings of compassion, gratitude, love, or happiness.

The next time you face a difficult decision and feel pressured to choose between either using your brain or following your feelings, remember that in fact you're bound to do both. Your best bet is to mindfully direct each to influence the other.

case you create a qualitatively different, non-Duchenne expression. And an observer will likely sense the difference, subconsciously.

Research shows that our brains are equipped, via mirror neurons (more about those in the next chapter) and other intricate mechanisms, to correctly assess other people's feelings, including whether their smiles are Duchennes. But research also shows that we often override these accurate emotional readouts with our thoughts, and therefore misjudge. So here's Judgment Rule Number Two: Heed your emotions in social situations. All things being equal, if you *think* you *should* like that person you just met, but have bad feelings about her or him, please trust your gut. And, on the other hand, if you feel a big rush of warmth toward your new acquaintance—as Joshua did for Emma on their very first date—then I'd advise you (within reason) to follow your heart.

In my personal opinion, this goes for choosing pets, as well. Perhaps you, too, have fallen in love with a dog or cat at first sight. Have you ever experienced that delightful sense of cross-species mutual recognition? Since such critters don't tend to overthink things, they can be very good judges of us humans. Recent studies have found that dogs are particularly adept at reading people's emotions. By paying close attention to our facial expressions, body language, and voice tones, dogs often know how we feel before we know ourselves. Hmm. While Joshua and Emma may have thought they spent ten minutes making their decision at the pound, maybe Clancy knew as soon as he met them that they'd be taking him home.

Use Your Self-Intelligence

We all rely on both our heads and our hearts to make decisions, so make a note of when it's wise to mostly follow feelings, and when it's best to respect your intellect.

Be cautious about making risky business decisions when feeling great. Maintaining a warm mood when working with your team can be good—but in tough negotiations with vendors, it may behoove you to be cool.

A common mistake for someone in poor shape is to get overexcited by the prospect of instant change, and to adopt a fitness plan that involves too much too fast (for example, going from zero exercise to running four miles a day, starting tomorrow). That overconfidence leads to crash-and-burn. Use good judgment: Ramp up your routine gradually, step by step, building change that's sustainable.

When choosing a mate, it's fine to have a list of top qualities you're seeking. And it's good to be level-headed (for example, requiring your prospects to be financially solvent). But no list can predict emotional connection. Look into your potential mate's eyes while paying close attention to your heart (or perhaps more accurately, your vagus nerve).

Keep an emotional distance from crowd behavior. If everyone and their brother thinks they've found an easy way to get rich quick . . . sorry, it just ain't so. Likewise, don't panic when the herd does—for example by selling a falling stock that is likely, in the long run, to go back up.

Quiz answer: When buying real estate or stocks, it's a good idea to . . .

b.   beware of euphoric emotions.

In a Nutshell

Economists used to believe that we human consumers were rational beings who could be counted on to act in our own best interest. But now, neuroscience shows that almost no one makes purely logical judgments. Subconsciously, our thoughts and feelings remain interdependent, each influencing the other. While it may be wise to "simply follow your heart" or "just trust your gut" in some social situations, don't let your euphoria buy real estate or play the stock market. Financial decisions, in particular, call for a calm, risk-conscious mindset.

Our bodies change our minds, and our minds can change our behavior, and our behavior can change our outcomes.

—HARVARD SOCIAL PSYCHOLOGIST AMY CUDDY

CHAPTER 10

KINESTHESIA

The Inner Influence of Your Body-Talk

Prime-your-mind Quiz

Research says you'll remember this chapter better if you test yourself now. How will the answer affect *you*?

Please nod and smile while reading this, because if you do, then scientific studies predict that . . .

a. you will experience a mood boost.

b. you will think more highly of the book.

c. both a and b.

When Angie, a recently divorced certified public accountant came in one October afternoon seeking more self-confidence in order to start dating again, I told her to go take a walk—*literally.*

If that sounds rude, please allow me to explain:

Angie arrived wearing an anxious expression and her shoulders slumped. Upon sitting down, she covered her midsection with her hands as if in abdominal pain. Staring at the floor, she described her difficult divorce and her experience living alone for the first time in her life. She brightened up only when mentioning her four-year-old nephew, Bo. Angie told me she was not a depressive person in general; she wanted to feel better.

We spent some time cognitively reframing her situation, including making a list of her core values and strengths. Then, I worked with her in hypnosis for half an hour. While she was still hypnotized, I sent her out the door and down the hall, with specific walking instructions:

- To carry herself well. To walk tall, spine erect, chin up, shoulders back, swinging her arms in comfortable sync with her steps.

- To allow a genuine smile to transform her mouth and eyes. If at any time her smile felt forced, she was to think of four-year-old Bo singing *Itsy Bitsy Spider*, something which she had confessed always made her grin.

- If anyone walking toward her seemed friendly, she should feel free to say hello and, ideally, while doing so, to also nod.

There was no danger of her getting lost, because my office was in San Francisco's historic flatiron Phelan Building, whose long hallways follow the building's triangular circumference. Thus, she simply kept walking and within two minutes arrived right back at my door.

The hallway stroll had seemed strange to her, she said. Laughing with apparent delight, she added that she now felt good. After I brought her out of hypnosis, we discussed how she could make the effect last. More sessions would help, but I suggested that she also take daily walks while maintaining the upbeat physical attitude she had just practiced.

In this way, her body would continue to positively influence her mind via *kinesthesia*, which the *American Heritage® Medical Dictionary* defines as, "The sense that detects bodily position, weight, or movement of the muscles, tendons, and joints." In other words, kinesthesia is our own *inner* awareness of what others perceive as our body language.

Moving the Body to Improve the Mind

Recent research confirms something that many parents and schoolteachers already knew: Our body language not only expresses our emotions, it can *create* them. Kids often resist adults' admonitions to, "Put on a smile" or "Sit up straight." But once you understand the latest science related to kinesthesia, you may choose to never slouch again.

You already know from the previous chapter that the body and the subconscious are in constant cahoots. But what makes kinesthesia so remarkably useful is that you can *consciously* move or position your body in order to influence your *subconscious* mind. You may sculpt the emotions and self-image of your choice. Adding hypnosis helps, but that's just frosting; kinesthesia is the cake!

And, like the cakes Alice ate in Wonderland, which made her shrink or grow . . . kinesthesia can either hinder or help you. Recent studies show that slumping tends to lower self-esteem. Frowning and closed posture invite negative emotions. So do shaking your head or physically pushing something away. In contrast, sitting up straight and walking tall increase pride and self-confidence. Smiling boosts your positive affect, improves your sense of humor, and helps you recall happy memories. Expansive positions (uncross those arms!) also induce positive feelings, as does nodding your head or pulling objects toward you.

> **Recent research confirms something that many parents and schoolteachers already knew: Our body language not only expresses our emotions, it can create them.**

Is this good news? Is it even true? Can it make a real difference in your life? Nod your head several times, pull this book closer in, smile like a toddler being served ice cream . . . And now you're more likely to agree when I insist that yes, this kinesthesia's powerful stuff.

The scientific term for such body-mind correspondence is *embodied cognition*. Current research indicates that even abstract ideas, such as time and morality, are grounded in the body's neural circuitry. For example, a 2010 experiment using motion sensors found that when thinking about the past, people tend to sway two millimeters backward; when pondering the future, they lean forward. Recent studies indicate that such tiny physical movements are not mere by-products of thought, but often are actually necessary neural components for all sorts of thinking, from learning, to conceptualizing, to the very formation of language.

Brain-imaging studies show that a key player in all this may be the insula, a small area near the ears that boasts a remarkable number of connections with other parts of the brain—a true networker. The insula combines information about external and internal body awareness and passes it along to our brain's emotional engine, the limbic system. The idea that how you hold yourself can affect your mood is not new, and indeed was proposed in the 1800s by both Charles Darwin and William James. But the theory was long dismissed for lack of an explanation as to *how* the body could so influence the brain. Now, neuro-imaging studies are uncovering the secrets of our brain-body circuitry. In this area, there will be much more research and many revelations to come.

Ways That Your Body Sways Your Thoughts

Let's check out the science to explore how you can use kinesthesia, in particular, to improve your life. (I also recommend Amy Cuddy's TED talk, "Your Body Language Shapes Who You Are," and her book, *Presence*.) These are a few of my favorite experiments:

Good posture strengthens self-worth and motivation. In one study, scientists had subjects take an "achievement test" while either slumping or sitting up straight, under the ruse that what was being studied were ergonomic conditions. Afterward, all the subjects were told they did well on the test—but only those who had sat up straight enjoyed significant self-pride at this news. The slumpers were unable to feel as good about themselves. In another experiment, subjects were led to adopt either upright or slouched positions and afterward were given puzzles to solve. Those who'd practiced the better posture persisted longer on the puzzles, indicating a boost to their confidence and motivation. *To increase self-esteem and follow-through, sit up straight and walk tall.*

The brain associates pulling-toward with positivity, and pushing-away with negativity. Researchers had subjects view neutral Chinese ideograms while either pressing upward on the tabletop (i.e., pulling toward themselves) or pressing downward (i.e., pushing away). Then the subjects rated the ideograms. Those who had pulled-toward generally liked the symbols. Those who had pushed-away tended to dislike them. In a second study using the same push-versus-pull technique, subjects were asked to remember the names of people they liked or disliked. Those who had pulled-toward remembered more people they liked; those who had pushed-away remembered more they disliked. *If you want to like something less—say, a bowl of potato chips—literally push it away. To feel more positive about someone, step a little closer, assuming it's appropriate, or even pull them in for a hug.*

Head-nodding creates positive feelings, while head-shaking does the opposite. In two separate studies, people were induced to either nod or shake their heads, under the guise of testing headphones. During one experiment, subjects "just happened" to hear a message about a university issue. Later, those who had nodded reported more favorable opinions of the message than those who'd shaken their heads. In the second experiment, subjects "tested" the headphones while a pen lay on the table before them. Later they were offered either the same pen or a different one. The head-nodders preferred the original pen. The head-shakers felt more negatively toward the same pen; they tended to choose the other. *Decide whether it serves you to like something less or more, then use your head! For example, to steel yourself against an unwanted sales pitch, while listening to it, shake your head. To better appreciate a coworker's new idea, keep nodding.*

Smiling makes the funnies funnier. In a now classic study, scientists either forced people to smile or kept them from smiling while looking at *Far Side* cartoons. How did they do that? Researchers told subjects that the experiment was to test ways for paraplegics to write by holding pens in their mouths. Some subjects were directed to hold a pen in their teeth, in a position that forced smiling. Others held a pen with their lips, in a way that made smiling impossible. While viewing the same cartoons, subjects used the pens in their mouths to write down their ratings of funniness. As you can by now guess, smiling affected the participants' sense of humor: The smilers found the cartoons significantly more amusing than the non-smilers. (Just picturing this zany study makes me smile.)

More recently, other scientists sought to determine whether controlling for the *type* of smile would make a difference. As mentioned in chapter 9, our most heartfelt smiles are so-called Duchennes, which not only affect the mouth but also raise the cheeks and

“
Smiling makes the funnies funnier.

wrinkle the outside corners of the eyes. In this study, researchers used a similar pen-in-mouth approach but altered it slightly to compare the impact of non-Duchenne versus Duchenne smiles. The results indicated that only the real Duchennes exerted a powerful effect. *To more deeply enjoy life's laughs, smile more and smile better—with your mouth, your cheeks, and your eyes.*

Research shows that smiling does more than prime your funny bone. Smiling produces all sorts of happy effects and can be combined with a positive posture for a double win. One experiment had subjects adopt either an expansive posture with a smile—or a slump with a frown. Then all subjects were asked to remember personal experiences. The expansive smilers speedily retrieved happy memories; the slouching frowners were quick to recall bad times.

Research shows that the adoption of poses or facial expressions associated with fear, anger, sadness, or happiness can induce the actual emotions, without any external stimuli. This is why, when Angie assumed positive body language, her subconscious automatically rewarded her with positive feelings.

Within six weeks, her confident carriage had become habitual; she moved far more gracefully than when we'd begun. It was our last session. She had noticed something she wanted to tell me. "When I prepare my clients' taxes, I save them as much money as I legally can, but it's all got to add up in a way that feels right. Sometimes someone will come in wanting me to cheat. They don't say it, but they hand me numbers that don't make sense. I politely ask them to find another CPA because of my feeling that some-thing's off. The first few times that you sent me home wearing a big grin and holding my shoulders back, it felt fine when I left your office. But then, during the week, making myself smile and sit up felt weird, like something was off."

"Learning anything new can seem awkward," I said.

Angie reached over to pat my arm. "Relax. Here's what's important to me. For this last week, everything has been matching up. It's all finally coming together. I can feel it."

"Ah. And I can see it," I said.

She told me she was ready to start dating again, and asked for suggestions about how to maintain her newfound confidence when meeting single men. We talked about mirror neurons, and the recently discovered fact that emotional cognition is contagious. For example, if I see your authentic smile, it triggers a subconscious smile response in me,

THE MIRRORING MIND

If I reach for a glass of water, certain of my brain cells fire. What's astonishing is that many of those same cells fire if I see *you* reach for a glass of water.

When I watch another person cry, or jump for joy, or bite an apple, special neurons in my brain are activated as though I myself were performing those very actions.

Scientists have named them mirror neurons, and many now believe it's these recently discovered cells that allow us to empathize with other people—to literally feel what they are feeling—and to understand others' intentions with laserlike accuracy. In his captivating book *Mirroring People*, neuroscientist Marco Iacoboni describes a study showing that our mirror neurons can discern whether someone lifting a teacup is planning to sip from it or merely clear the table. Mirror neurons guide us to "just know" all sorts of things about others without conscious pondering.

Because of mirror neurons, humans from infancy onward automatically imitate others, and in doing so, learn by imitation. Studies also show that in social situations we unconsciously mimic one another, both revealing and creating a sense of connection.

But mirroring also can be conscious. Practitioners of Neuro-Linguistic Programming have long used it to create rapport with clients (and now the science backs us up). To relate better to someone during conversation, try emulating their body language—crossing your arms when they cross theirs, leaning in when they do, laughing when they laugh and so on. Don't be robotic about it. To mirror well, you must perform an emotional leap of faith and be willing to *feel*, at least for a moment, what the other person *feels*. Genuine mirroring is a way of respecting another person's attitude by experiencing it yourself.

Here's some mirror magic that may sound bizarre but can work wonders. When an individual is angry and belligerent, if you wish to calm that person down, don't immediately act calm. Instead, match their state (as least somewhat) to create subconscious rapport. One February night I left my office around 10 p.m. to find the street outside my building dark and deserted. A very unkempt man came out of the nearby subway station punching the air. He placed himself in front of me, blocking my way, shook his fist and yelled, "They should do something about it, those goddamn bastards!" It seemed doubtful that he wanted to slug a petite, middle-aged woman, but still it was clear he wanted to hit *someone*, and there was nobody else on hand.

I matched his angry squint, bent my knees like his, clenched my fists, put my heart into it, and yelled back, *"Those bastards!"* This seemed to both startle and calm him. He drew back his head, perplexed, and I did the same, being very careful not to appear mocking. He stepped slightly away, and I took that as my permission to also step away, then quickly strode around him and down into the train station to go safely home.

so that *I* end up receiving positive neurological rewards from *your* smile. (See the sidebar "The Mirroring Mind.") Best dating advice ever: Smile sincerely and often.

Of course this gives us even more reason to adopt positive body language in general. We're not only boosting our own emotions, we're contagiously improving how others feel too. Consider your kinesthetic experience at this very moment. Are you sitting up straight? Are your arms comfortably relaxed rather than folded tight? Are you smiling with your mouth, cheeks, and eyes? If not, try it now . . . Doesn't that feel nice? Feel free to nod: *Yes.*

Use Your Self-Intelligence

Knowing that the way you move impacts the way you think and feel, how will you employ kinesthesia to best serve your thoughts and emotions?

To be authentically friendly and confident in a job interview and on the job: straighten your spine, uncross those arms, allow your eyes to soften, and when it's your turn to listen, genuinely nod your head. One study indicates that job candidates do better if they *mirror* their interviewers by laughing when they laugh. More on *mirroring* in the sidebar, and more on laughter in chapter 14.

Research shows that in general, the more you smile, the longer you live. If you're not yet used to smiling often, compose a list of people or things (kids, pets, movie scenes, whatever!) that elicit your grin, and draw on it to keep smiling.

Hmm, did I just mention smiling? That's because it's good stuff. Follow Angie's example by sharing a genuine smile to strengthen all your relationships. And enhance your romantic connection by *mirroring* your partner more often (see the sidebar). You'll feel more empathy, and your honey will feel more loved.

The next time you want to get a good deal on a big purchase, here's a tip from recent research: Sitting on a hard chair rather than a cushion will make you a tougher negotiator. Sit tall, but lean back a little and position your elbows slightly behind you. You rule!

Quiz answer: If you nod and smile while reading this book, then studies indicate you will . . .

    c.   Both *a* and *b*: experience a mood boost *and* think more highly of the book.

In a Nutshell

Recent studies prove that neurologically, your body language doesn't merely reveal thoughts and emotions, it also *creates* them. Good posture increases self-esteem. Smiling boosts your sense of humor and emotional well-being. Nodding your head leads to liking. Don't let a difficult day impair how you carry yourself. Instead, adjust your body to improve your mood. (P.S. Having trouble understanding how someone else feels? Adopt their body language to instantly "get" it.)

The mechanisms by which exercise changes
how we think and feel are so much more effective
than donuts, medicines, and wine. When you say you
feel less stressed out after you go for a swim,
or even a fast walk, you are.

–JOHN J. RATEY, M.D.

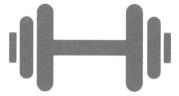

CHAPTER 11

EXERCISE

Of the Physical Kind—
One Great Way to Build Your Mind

Prime-your-mind Quiz

Research says you'll remember this chapter better if you test yourself now. How will the answer affect *you*?

The latest and most extensive research on physical exercise shows that it . . .

a. becomes less important with age, as the elderly have less need to burn off energy.

b. primarily strengthens the heart, lungs, and body, though it may provide mild mental benefits.

c. is essential to build and maintain a high-performing brain.

S ometimes you have to look for silver linings, and other times they appear by surprise.

In 1993 my father passed out drunk with a cigarette in his hand and burned down the house. Because he and my brother Tobey had piled the halls high with newspapers, unopened mail, and empty cereal boxes, and because it was a wooden house, it went up lightning-fast. Dad and Tobey were lucky to get out alive. There was no insurance. Yet this seeming tragedy brought positive change.

I flew out to Indiana for a couple of months to oversee construction of a new home on the same property. The old dwelling had crawled with cockroaches. I mean that if you had looked at the oven door it appeared to be moving because bugs continuously swarmed over its surface. The cobwebs had been so huge and thick in that house they looked like fake Halloween decorations. The toilets were black with filth. All of this went up in flames. The new house, though it was prefabricated and a bit tacky, was functional and *clean*. My oldest brother, Farley, and I immediately hired a cleaning service to come by regularly. Can you imagine the difference?

But the full silver lining spread even further. My father had failed several dry-out programs over the years before being fired from his professorship. With each program, he'd stop drinking for a while but soon start up again. Watching the house burn down motivated him to sober up for good. He never drank again.

My father, a lifelong depressive, was not one to look for silver linings. But perhaps he attracted them, for an even more dramatic twist of fate occurred before he died, briefly illuminating the sort of man he might have been had he lived his life a little differently.

For decades, there had been something off about Dad. At the grocery store, wearing his favorite clothes covered with cigarette burns and coffee stains, he might begin randomly lecturing the cashier on Plato's *Republic*, oblivious to the people waiting in line behind him. Although he'd once been a brilliant man, alcohol and loneliness had gradually unwired much of his brain, as well as robbed him of motivation to *do* anything; he spent his days lying in bed.

Then, in 1995 at age seventy-two, he had a minor heart attack—and afterward was told by his doctor to exercise. He had long avoided exercise, declining even to walk to the mailbox. But now, thrice a week, he shared a ride to the senior center where he joined other old folks working out on treadmills or weight machines under the eye of a friendly staff. This social interaction had to be healthy for him (as we'll see in chapter 13). But it could not fully account for the stunning transformation that followed.

Over the next several months, my father gradually turned into a younger, smarter, more functional man. He became more cheerful, engaged, quick on the uptake, energized, confident. He sent me a personal note in the mail eloquently elaborating on a conversation we'd had. He visited an old friend in the hospital, the first self-initiated socializing he'd done in more than thirty years. He began taking real interest in staying healthy. On the phone, he sounded to me like the dad I had always wished for. Tobey told me the other day he still remembers "those months when Dad really perked up."

Alas, the change was short-lived. All my life I've had psoriasis, and suddenly, my father became afflicted too, only far more severely. The palms of his hands and the bottoms of his feet erupted with scaly, itchy, painful sores. He could barely limp to the kitchen or claw open a carton of milk. He stopped going to the gym or getting any exercise. Very quickly, the new man vanished. Eventually medication made the psoriasis manageable, but Dad had lost his momentum. He never resumed exercising. The old sedentary habits returned, along with his depressive, antisocial personality and confusing conversation.

At the time, it seemed natural that he should revert to his old self, since that was the long-established norm. What remained mysterious was why he had changed at all. What could explain his astonishing transformation, his brief dip into the fountain of youth?

The answer is physical exercise.

Working Your Body to Sharpen Your Brain

The emerging research on the benefits of exercise may astonish you. If exercise once struck you as an inconvenient chore, let me assure you that it offers enough silver linings to wrap ourselves in from childhood to old age. Of course, you already know that exercise helps stave off diabetes, strokes, and heart attacks. But neuroscientists now tout even richer benefits.

In short, working out makes you *smart*. For young and old, in study after study, being a couch potato leads to low cognitive performance, while habitual exercise boosts mental focus, reasoning power, long-term memory, problem-solving flexibility, and general intelligence.

Rigorous exercise also wards off depression, stress, and anxiety. It rebuilds the alcohol-impaired brain, and it slows—and sometimes reverses—neural aging.

The dumbest thing you can do to your brain is to avoid physical exercise.

Remember that old stereotype pitting dumb jocks against wimpy geeks? Throw that out. After reading this chapter, I invite you to go deeper into the research, because it will help motivate you to stay fit. I frequently prescribe to my clients, and wholeheartedly recommend to you, a terrific book by medical doctor and Harvard professor John Ratey, *Spark: The Revolutionary New Science of Exercise and the Brain*.

So why is physical activity so nice for your noggin? For one thing, unlike your other organs, your brain has no energy reserves of its own. All it has to go on is the fuel (mostly glucose and oxygen) carried in your blood. Regular exercise expands and vastly improves your circulatory system so that more blood makes it to and from the brain. Maybe you're musing that the brain shouldn't require much energy; after all, it's just hanging out in your head. But while it weighs only about three pounds, or about 2 percent of your body weight, your brain typically uses 20 percent of the energy you burn. Your brain guzzles energy, even when you sleep. (Your brain works hard while you snooze. Remember chapter 1 and see the upcoming chapter 12.) So a better blood supply means more brain fuel.

Furthermore, as a glutton of glucose, your brain generates loads of toxic waste, especially those free radicals that, if left unchecked, can really mess you up, even mutating your DNA. Exercise produces antioxidants that turn that waste into disposable forms such as carbon dioxide, which your blood carts off to the lungs to be exhaled. Exercise takes out the garbage.

But that's not all. Scientists have also learned that exercise fuels production of what Ratey calls "the master molecule of the learning process"—brain-derived neurotrophic factor, or BDNF. We now know that the adult human brain sprouts new neurons, particularly in our center of learning and memory, the hippocampus. BDNF plays a crucial role in neurogenesis, plus it helps those baby brain cells to survive. It also enables existing neurons to grow new dendrites, and to create bigger neural maps through stronger, better connections with one another—that is, *to learn*. Besides boosting BDNF, exercise produces insulinlike growth factor 1 (IFG-1), which likewise stimulates cell growth, neuroplasticity, and learning. Research shows that exercise improves brain power in people of all ages. Here are just three examples:

- In a 2007 experiment, German scientists found that people learned new words 20 percent faster following exercise, and that their learning speed corresponded directly with levels of BDNF.

- Repeated studies by the California Department of Education show that kids who pass a general fitness test achieve much higher SAT scores than their unfit peers, even when taking socioeconomic status into account.

- In a landmark survey of more than 18,000 elderly women, those who exercised achieved better cognition, memory, and intelligence. Meanwhile, several studies show that exercise slows down neurodegenerative diseases such as Alzheimer's and Parkinson's.

Maybe you're beginning to wonder why brain health doesn't depend on more, well, *brainy* activities, like doing crossword puzzles. Blame evolution. Homo sapiens go back millions of years. Until very recently in our long history, we had to walk or run many miles every day to get food. Our brains evolved primarily to help us move in order to feed ourselves without becoming someone else's lunch. Today's sedentary lifestyle—sitting at computers, in classrooms, or facing TVs—is woefully out of sync with our physiology. We simply aren't designed to sit around. In general, research shows that the more sedentary we are, the more stupid we become.

Why Exercise Can Exorcise Depression and Stress

To add injury to insult, lack of exercise also correlates with depression. And depression makes us even dumber, because it overgenerates cortisol, which shreds our neural maps. Brain-imaging studies show that depression actually shrinks the hippocampus. What a depressing thought!

But therein lies the next silver lining: Exercise combats depression.

Exercise produces—and *balances*—the Big Three neurotransmitters targeted by most antidepressants: norepinephrine, dopamine, and serotonin. The Big Three together regulate virtually all brain activity. While most antidepressant drugs target one or more of these three, the drugs cause side effects because their sledgehammer approach throws off the brain's delicate biochemical balance. Regular cardio exercise restores and maintains the Big Three in beautiful harmony. New research indicates that habitual exercise works as well as—or better than—drugs to fend off depression. Moreover, it reduces anxiety and stress. Here are just three examples:

- A 2006 Dutch study of more than 19,000 twins found exercisers to be less anxious, less depressed, less neurotic, and more socially outgoing than their couch-potato counterparts.

- A Finnish study of more than 3,400 subjects revealed that people who exercise at least two to three times a week experience lower stress, anger, or depression than people who are sedentary.

- A 2005 experiment determined that a mere half hour of treadmill running significantly reduced panic attacks.

So now we know that exercise not only makes you healthier, smarter, and happier, it also makes you less anxious or stressed. One way that exercise lowers stress is by releasing gamma-aminobutryic acid (GABA), the brain's main calming-down neurotransmitter and primary target of anti-anxiety medication. Research comparing exercise to drugs has found exercise can be just as effective to lower anxiety. Cardio exercise in particular also spurs production of another calming agent, a hormone called atrial natriuretic peptide (ANP).

And as if all that's not enough, rigorous strength training unleashes the nearly miraculous human growth hormone (HGH), which helps keep you young—melting belly fat, building muscle fiber, and boosting brain volume.

" Exercise produces—and balances—the Big Three neurotransmitters targeted by most antidepressants: norepinephrine, dopamine, and serotonin.

Even in this quick synopsis, you can see that the more research we have, the bigger and brighter those silver linings of exercise shine. If you weren't exercising regularly before now, set yourself up for success by beginning modestly and making it as fun as possible. Find a buddy to take walk-and-talks with. Install a video screen in your fitness room, or even get a motion-sensor video game that compels you to move vigorously to win. What's most important? Commitment.

For that brief period when my elderly father got fit, it seemed as if everything about him changed, from his mental clarity and new sociability to his stronger physique and more confident carriage. But having grown up with the jock-versus-geek stereotype, he could not have understood his own transformation. Perhaps if he'd learned back then what scientists now know about exercise, he would have committed to staying in shape.

Our public schools are getting rid of physical education even as research mounts that kids who exercise regularly perform far better academically. What can we do? Get in shape. Lead by example. Others will follow. No more excuses. *Do it.*

Use Your Self-Intelligence

Give yourself a leg up in life. Get smarter by getting fitter.

 Exercise provides one of the few actually smart ways to multitask. You think better when you're in motion. So walk while conducting business on the phone. Consider answering emails on the treadmill. Step away from your desk every hour to do a few squats or dance to a video.

It's not about losing weight; it's about working out. Science shows it's better to be 200 pounds of muscle than a slender reed of ennui. Start exercising!

Build your relationship while building your bods. What better way to bond than to hike together, climb together, or go kayaking? Or try something more intimate. I asked my friend Jack, who's eighty-nine, spry of mind, and happens to have a girlfriend, whether he was getting enough exercise. He responded, "Absolutely. I'm having a lot of sex." Good thinking.

($) Most personal bankruptcies are driven by medical bills. By keeping fit, you will save on health care. And you don't *need* to spend money on trainers or gyms to exercise. As author and entrepreneur Jim Rohn once said, "You can't hire someone else to do your push-ups for you."

Quiz answer: The latest and most extensive research on physical exercise shows that it . . .

    c.   is essential to build and maintain a high-performing brain.

In a Nutshell

From boosting student test scores to creating healthy new brain cells in old age, physical exercise strengthens neural connectivity. It's a scientific fact: Exercise makes you smarter. Working out also harmonizes the Big Three neurotransmitters targeted by most antidepressants—norepinephrine, dopamine, and serotonin—meaning exercise makes you happier, as well. To be truly Self-Intelligent, get your body moving.

I had dinner recently with a guy who bragged that he had only gotten four hours of sleep that night. I didn't say it, but I thought to myself, "If you had gotten five, this dinner would have been a lot more interesting."

—ARIANNA HUFFINGTON

CHAPTER 12

SLEEP

The Natural Makeover, from a Brain Shampoo to a Slimmer You

Prime-your-mind Quiz

Research says you'll remember this chapter better if you test yourself now. How will the answer affect *you*?

One thing scientists have learned about sleep is that . . .

a. people who regularly sleep six hours or less tend to suffer brain dysfunction without realizing it.

b. while asleep, your brain is mostly at rest, and consumes far less energy than when awake.

c. because people who sleep less spend more time in motion, sleep loss is correlated with weight loss.

F iguratively speaking, this chapter includes my confession of having been caught asleep on the job.

I felt impressed by Holly before we even met. Her online intake form stated that, at age twenty-seven, she was already a division manager of a large accounting firm. She planned to take the Graduate Management Admissions Test (GMAT) in order to pursue a master's degree so that she could advance even further and faster in her career. She sought my help for a common complaint: study-and-exam anxiety.

Holly had written: "My friend Jonah told me he struggled with this problem until you hypnotized him. Afterward he aced his GMAT. He got into Stanford's MBA (Master of Business Administration) program and is there now."

A glance at old files reminded me that Jonah had been highly hypnotizable. In just a few sessions, we dispelled his severe study-and-exam anxiety. At my urging, he had also begun exercising regularly because, as you may remember from chapter 11, physical fitness promotes brain fitness. Jonah was so career-oriented that he had never bothered working out, until he knew it affected his mental performance. I was thinking about his story when I met Holly.

Tuesday morning she arrived in my office at nine on the dot, looking corporate in a navy suit and pearls, and carrying a Burberry briefcase. I wondered if it might be the attire that made her seem older than her years, or maybe it was the heavy makeup. She looked to be in good physical shape, although as she settled into my recliner, her movements seemed heavy—and, again, like those of someone older.

She told me that a month earlier, she'd begun her GMAT prep by taking a practice test to establish her baseline scores. Since then, she'd been studying two hours a night Monday through Thursday, plus five hours on weekends. Every Sunday she took another practice exam. Wow—this was one self-disciplined young woman.

When I complimented her on that fact, she said, "I keep a Teddy Roosevelt quote over my desk: *With self-discipline, most anything is possible.* But my practice test scores have been plateauing or going down instead of up. This anxiety ruins my concentration. Jonah says it was exactly the same with him. I researched hypnosis online to confirm it's legit, so I'm trusting you can help me too."

Remembering Jonah's experience, I asked Holly about physical exercise. She said, "I work out five mornings a week."

I asked about her diet. "Complex carbs, lots of vegetables, eggs, fish, organic poultry."

I asked whether she had sleep issues. "None. Regular sleep, no problem sleeping."

Wow again! This all sounded exemplary. I inquired whether test-taking had ever caused her trauma in the past. She said no; she'd never procrastinated about studying, and often even *enjoyed* her exams. This, too, boded well. I thought she'd be easy to treat—as, indeed, she was.

Only, in the end, it would turn out that I had failed to pose *the* million-dollar question up front, one that I now make sure to ask every new client. (We'll come to it in a moment.)

Next, I wanted to know how Holly was physically experiencing her anxiety. Had she noticed a pounding heart, for example, or an upset stomach, or excess sweating? She gazed down at herself as if checking for symptoms. "Maybe I've gained a few pounds, but I don't care about that. What I care about is test scores. Let's hope you can hypnotize me."

Holly turned out to be highly suggestible—so much so that when I intoned, *"deep sleep,"* she didn't just go into a trance; she fell literally asleep. I had learned during my professional training to let such clients benefit from a three-minute "hypno-nap," after which

I gently rouse them into a trance state (rather than bringing them fully awake). Then we proceed with the hypnosis part of the session, which in Holly's case centered on anxiety relief. Afterward, she reported feeling wonderfully calm. "Excellent," I said, glad it had been so easy.

For her second session, Holly again arrived punctually on a Tuesday morning, although this time she wore sweatpants and a hoodie. She carried her briefcase in one hand, a Starbucks thermos mug in the other, and a garment bag draped over her arm. "Long work day already," she said, leaning back in my recliner while half-stifling a yawn. This time she wore no makeup; I saw circles under her eyes.

She explained that she'd needed to file a company report from home that morning before eight o'clock. "My alarm went off as usual at five, but normally I go to the gym first thing to wake myself up. Today I had to crunch numbers instead. I'll head to the gym after this, and shower there. Anyway . . . " She snapped open her thermos. "The hypnosis hasn't helped yet. That night, I even fell asleep while studying. On Sunday, as usual, I bombed my practice test."

Registering this news while watching her sip coffee, I at last woke up to the likelihood— which should have occurred to me a week earlier—that she wasn't suffering from study-and-exam anxiety at all. She was *tired*.

At last I posed the million-dollar question: "How many *hours* a night do you sleep?"

She peered at me over her thermos mug. "Five. I used to get more, but studying adds two hours to my day. I remember reading that President Clinton slept five hours a night. If he did it, I can too."

The Deceptive Nature of Sleep Deprivation

Dear reader, please beware of *sleep macho*—the myth that if we just try hard enough, we can function perfectly well on less than seven or eight hours of shut-eye per night. During the twentieth century, even some scientists believed this tall tale (although not Albert Einstein, who preferred to sleep at least ten hours). Recent studies show that, for the grand majority, it's a big fat lie. Not only do most people who regularly sleep less than seven or eight hours suffer significant brain dysfunction, scientists say, but experiments also show that those very same people remain blithely unaware of their own poor mental performance.

Some of the most thorough sleep experiments to date have been led by David Dinges, chief of the University of Pennsylvania's Division of Sleep and Chronobiology. In one study, dozens of healthy adults were randomly assigned to sleep four, six, or eight hours per night for two weeks, during which time they lived in the lab and were continuously monitored. While awake, they were tested every two hours for cognitive performance.

The eight-hour group showed healthy brain function throughout the two weeks, as expected. In contrast, those who slept only four or six hours declined steadily on all their tests. These included working-memory tests, speed-and-accuracy tests, and the "psycho-motor vigilance task," or P.V.T., a standard measure of mental alertness.

A few days into the experiment, the four-hour and six-hour groups said they felt a little sleepy, but did not think they were suffering cognitive impairment. After fourteen days, their test results showed that their brains were so compromised, they might as well have been legally drunk. Yet the subjects continued to rate themselves as fully functioning.

This type of self-delusion helps explain why sleep-deprived people brag about their sleep habits, thereby luring others to follow suit, without anyone catching on that they're sacrificing their own brainpower. It's like zombies who don't know that they're zombies mindlessly indoctrinating others to become zombies! Okay, that's a bit melodramatic, but Dinges and other sleep experts do believe that very few people—5 percent of the population at most—can truly perform well on as little as five hours of nightly sleep, and that's only because they have unusual genes. Likewise, up to 5 percent of people require 10 or more hours of sleep. The rest of us need between seven and nine hours, depending on the individual.

It's true that President Clinton used to boast about sleeping five hours a night; he caught the sleep macho fever in college after hearing a professor declare that great men sleep very little. But since leaving the White House, Clinton has concluded that "Every important mistake I've made in my life, I've made because I was too tired." Now, the former president gets a full night's sleep and rails against the competitive culture of sleep macho. He told one television host, "You have no idea how many Republican and Democratic members of the House and Senate are chronically sleep deprived because of this system."

What Your Brain's Up To While You Snooze

Why does sleep deprivation muddy your mind? For one thing, it sets off biochemical reactions that reduce your ability—by up to a whopping 30 percent—to metabolize glucose. That's the fuel that powers your brain. Your brain is an energy hog. As we discussed in chapter 11, your brain constitutes only 2 percent of your total weight but it typically burns 20 percent of the calories you use. Getting too little sleep puts your brain on a dangerously low energy supply.

I wasn't at all confident about persuading Holly of what I now believed to be the real problem. I had already screwed up by failing to recognize her exhausted state sooner. (Yes, *I* had been asleep on the job.) As she set her thermos on my desk and proceeded to rub her eyes, I began to describe recent research. I told her about Bill Clinton's turnaround. I suggested that for the rest of the week Holly continue studying the same amount but adjust her schedule to get a minimum seven hours' nightly sleep, and then see how she did on her practice exam.

She listened to all this with such a controlled, blank expression that it was easy for me to imagine her negotiating a corporate contract. At last she said, "I'll look into the information. If it checks out online, I'll try it." She stood and began to gather her things. "Let's not do hypnosis today," she said. "Let's try one thing at a time."

As she left, I sensed that Holly was annoyed with me, but I believed her to be the kind of top performer who keeps her word. No matter how inconvenient the arrangement was, once the research checked out for her, she would begin sleeping at least seven hours a night, because we had a deal. I also believed that her study results would improve very fast.

My confidence that sleep would cure Holly's problem arose from the fact that it plays a *primary* role in learning and memory. Scientists long suspected as much, but only recently have they made startling discoveries about what your sleeping brain is really up to:

1. **Your sleeping brain thinks like a genius.** During sleep, your brain does not rest. Sure, you lose consciousness, but your brain continues working so hard and fast that it consumes nearly the same energy as when awake. It's as if your sleeping brain is an ultra-speedy thought-processor that, in many ways, outperforms your waking brain.

   Research now shows that your sleeping brain actively *sorts through and judges information* received during the day. Your brain then *erases* those memories it deems unimportant and strengthens new knowledge it decides is worth keeping, by routing it into long-term memory and by reinforcing neural connections. Meanwhile, other studies reveal that if earlier in the day you struggled with a problem (a math problem, for example), your sleeping brain will not only strive to solve that problem, it will also *develop faster strategies* for you to solve similar problems in the future. All told, your sleeping brain does massive amounts of thinking. This may be why, whenever Einstein was tackling a particularly difficult quandary in physics, he reportedly increased his nightly sleep from ten hours to eleven.

2. **What a pro! Your sleeping brain always shows up for practice.** You can rely on your sleeping brain to practice the piano for you, or do dance moves, or play tennis, or rehearse whatever other new skills you may have learned during the day. Evidence of this first emerged in the 1990s, when researchers recorded the brain activity of rats being taught to run a maze. When those rats fell asleep with wires still stuck in their heads, scientists saw that they were mentally running the maze in their sleep. Since then, a variety of experiments confirm that humans, too, practice and improve new skills while snoozing. This is one reason that many professional sports teams now hire sleep coaches to help athletes get eight or nine hours every night. "It's all about investing in our players and investing in them reaching their full potential," former University of Tennessee head football coach Butch Jones once explained.

3. **Your sleeping brain washes its hair.** That is to say, it sends cerebrospinal fluid sluicing through the spaces between your stringlike neurons (unlike body cells, your 100 billion neurons are stringy in structure), in order to shampoo out the brain dandruff. This sounds funny, but it's serious stuff: toxic buildup includes pieces of beta-amyloid, a protein linked to Alzheimer's disease. If you don't sleep, your mind grows dull with brain-waste products. When you do sleep, ultimately the dirty residue gets flushed into the liver for disposal, leaving your neurons fresh and clean. Danish biologist Maiken Nedergaard discovered this cerebral salon system in 2012. Scientists now hypothesize that getting more sleep might help prevent Alzheimer's.

Why Scientists Say Sleep Is Lookin' So Good

Holly phoned me the morning before her third appointment. She said that she'd slept seven-and-a-half hours every night since her last visit. Her practice scores were up by fifty points already. With a smile in her voice, she said, "Of course keep the money, but let's please cancel our session tomorrow because there's no more need."

I asked if she were experiencing any other benefits. She said, "Jonah stopped by yesterday and the first thing out of his mouth was that I looked gorgeous. I explained to him that yes, sleep had done that. We geeked out discussing the science of it."

The research that Holly was referring to shows that if you are currently stinting on sleep, then getting more of it will indeed make you better looking. It will slow your aging process, causing you to appear younger. It will improve your complexion. If you are overweight, getting more sleep will slim your physique even if you don't change your eating or exercise habits. In contrast, of course, sleep loss lowers your attraction factor. (For details, check out "Why Better Sleep Makes You Sexier" on page 162.)

Before we said good-bye, I asked Holly what advice she'd offer to people who think they can't fit more sleep into their busy schedules.

She recited her Teddy Roosevelt quote: "With self-discipline, most anything is possible."

My experience with clients bears this out: whoever makes sleep a top priority can find a way. For some, this means reducing time spent on TV, social media, or browsing online. For others, it means learning to work more efficiently for fewer hours. Yet others must conquer insomnia. (See "Nine Proven Ways to Get More Sleep" on page 163.)

Despite the thousands of sleep studies conducted so far, a million-dollar question remains: *Why did we evolve to need sleep in the first place?* Spending a third of our time unconscious doesn't make obvious survival sense, especially given that we were once in danger of becoming a saber-toothed tiger's midnight snack.

And it's not just us. Tigers, too, and apparently *all* animals, from birds to bees to jellyfish, must sleep or die. If *you* find it challenging to get more sleep, consider how hard it is for those who have no safe place to rest. Dolphins, who must surface regularly in order to breathe, sleep with half of their brain at a time, swimming with only one eye open while they snooze. Likewise, migrating birds that are airborne for days on end sometimes fly with half-sleeping brains. (How do we know? Scientists recently outfitted Ecuadorian frigatebirds with monitoring devices, sort of like little hats and backpacks.)

Why is sleep as necessary to our lives as water and air? Researchers still don't know, but in their ongoing quest, they continue to discover more and more benefits to getting your Z's. Evidence now indicates that sleep strengthens your immune system, reduces inflammation, wards off heart disease, and helps prevent depression. Exactly what causes these effects, at a molecular level, isn't fully understood, but it may be

WHY BETTER SLEEP MAKES YOU SEXIER

A full night's sleep makes you more attractive, whereas sleep deprivation robs you of your good looks, due to a triad of scientific factors.

Getting good sleep smooths your complexion. Experiments confirm that skipping sleep leads directly to droopy skin, uneven pigmentation, and fine lines, as well as circles under the eyes. This is partly because sleep deprivation *increases* the release of cortisol—a stress hormone that breaks down collagen, a protein needed to keep skin supple—while it *decreases* the release of human growth hormone, needed for daily skin repair.

Plentiful sleep keeps you young. As we age, certain genes get switched on while others get switched off. Scientists have found that a lack of sleep speeds up this gene-switching process, ultimately leading to an earlier death. For example, one British study of 10,000 people found that over a period of twenty years, those who reduced their sleep from seven to five hours or less per night nearly doubled their risk of death from all causes.

Increasing your Zs helps fight flab. Numerous studies confirm that sleep loss contributes to weight gain. Why? First, sleepy people are hungry people. That extra cortisol makes us crave carbs. Also, sleep loss boosts our levels of the *hunger-inducing* hormone ghrelin. Meanwhile, it lowers our levels of the *hunger-curbing* hormone leptin. But second—and here's the kicker—even if you muster up superhuman willpower and refuse to overeat when tired, your sleep-deprived body will still pack on more flab.

It's not fair, but it's true. Studies show that even if you eat and exercise the same, if you skip sleep, you'll get fatter. Why? Because two sleep-loss effects we've mentioned before—your lack of growth hormone and your excess cortisol—both screw up your ability to process fuel, prompting your cells to store more fat while burning through your other soft tissue, such as muscle, for energy.

All of this means that regularly getting a full night's sleep will help firm up your skin and slim down your figure.

I love rigorous science, but one of my favorite experiments showing the weight-loss effect was a nonscientific, do-it-yourselfer carried out by *Glamour* magazine. *Glamour* directed seven women to begin getting a full night's sleep without changing their diet or exercise habits. After ten weeks, all seven women ended up significantly thinner. (For a fun read, check out "Lose Weight While You Sleep" by Jenny Stamos Kovacs at glamour.com.)

Are you packing extra fat? If you're still wondering whether weight loss really could be that easy, why not conduct your own personal experiment? Start getting more sleep, record your weight each day, and watch those pounds melt away.

NINE PROVEN WAYS TO GET MORE SLEEP

I've conquered insomnia, and you can too. But there is no one-size-fits-all cure, so your winning strategy may differ from mine. Make it a top priority, refuse to give up, and you *will* find a way.

Now I use self-hypnosis to go to sleep, and to fall back asleep when I wake in the night. For me, that's a great solution. (You can download my free get-to-sleep MP3 at self-intelligence.com.)

Below is a list of proven drug-free remedies for people who face sleep difficulty. None of these works for everybody, but each does work for some—and you may want to combine several. A little trial-and-error experimentation will produce the solution that's right for *you*.

1. Keep regular hours, going to bed at the same time each night and getting up at the same time every day, including on weekends. This programs your body and mind to sleep, and to wake, on cue.

2. Practice saying *no*. No caffeine in the evening and no alcohol within two hours of bedtime, because those chemicals mess with your autonomic nervous system.

3. Also no looking at electronics—from TV to laptop to cell phone—close to bedtime, as the blue light that these devices emit can confuse your circadian rhythm and disrupt melatonin production.

4. Experiment to see how eating before bed affects your sleep. For many, it's wise to forgo late-night snacking, because food can signal to your physiology that it's time to start the day. (But personally, I like to ingest some protein and fat—for example, scrambled eggs with plenty of butter—just before bed, to avoid waking up hungry in the night.)

5. Spend at least a half hour before bedtime relaxing. This does not mean watching your favorite shows or hanging out online, as both those activities stimulate the release of dopamine, and neither actually relaxes your physiology. Instead, listen to soothing music or read something calming, meditate, or cuddle with someone you love.

6. Practice abdominal breathing for several minutes before bed. That means breathing all the way down, as if right into your belly, while keeping your shoulders almost perfectly still. Too boring? Then get a bubble blower (the bottle-and-stick sort), and blow some bubbles. That will regulate your breathing while taking your mind off adult anxieties.

7. Check your sleeping environment. Is it dark all night? If not, consider getting blackout curtains or an eye mask.

8. Is it quiet? If not, wear ear plugs or try a white- or pink-noise machine or phone app.

9. Got stuff on your mind at bedtime? Write out a to-do list for the next day. This reassures your subconscious that you can "let go" and nothing important will be forgotten.

Sweet dreams!

partly because sleep regulates gene activity. (We'll learn in chapter 13 that social connection does this as well; how our habits affect our genes is the focus of a fascinating new discipline called *epigenetics*.) In one study, when subjects reduced nightly sleep from eight hours to six, blood tests showed that within a week, the activity of 711 of their genes had been altered.

Scientists say that one sure sign of sleep deprivation is needing an alarm to wake up. Far too many people depend on a buzzer to wrench them from dreamland. How about you—are you smarter than them? That is, are you already getting the seven to nine hours of sleep required in order to be your best? If the answer is no, then I beg you to make sleep a top priority, starting tonight. On the other hand, if the answer is yes, please *rest* assured that it's time well spent.

Use Your Self-Intelligence

The more that scientists study sleep, the more benefits they discover to getting plenty of it. Make sure you're getting enough sleep to succeed in all areas of your life.

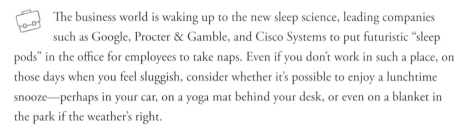

The business world is waking up to the new sleep science, leading companies such as Google, Procter & Gamble, and Cisco Systems to put futuristic "sleep pods" in the office for employees to take naps. Even if you don't work in such a place, on those days when you feel sluggish, consider whether it's possible to enjoy a lunchtime snooze—perhaps in your car, on a yoga mat behind your desk, or even on a blanket in the park if the weather's right.

Some scientists believe the obesity epidemic in this country is driven by sleep deprivation. One thing is certain: If you want to lose weight, the smartest first step you can take is to begin getting eight hours of nightly sleep. That alone will probably slim you up. It will also re-energize your brain, increasing whatever willpower you need to eat healthy foods and exercise regularly.

A well-rested couple is a happy couple. If you and your honey sleep soundly side by side, that's fabulous. But if not—say, if either of you snores or is jumpy, or if you keep very different hours—then there's no shame in choosing separate bedrooms. (By the way, sleep deprivation lowers men's testosterone. The better sleep you both get, the better your sex life.)

Bill Clinton isn't the only person who makes bad decisions when he's tired. We all do. For those of us who aren't heads of state, it's often our wallets that suffer.

Before finalizing an expensive purchase, from a new car to a time-share, please ignore any pushy sales pitch and be sure to sleep on it. One serious investment that might well pay off? A comfy mattress.

Quiz answer: One thing scientists have learned about sleep is that . . .

a. people who regularly sleep six hours or less tend to suffer brain dysfunction without realizing it.

In a Nutshell

While scientists still don't know exactly why we humans—and apparently all animals—must sleep to stay alive, they have determined that the great majority of us need at least seven or eight hours' nightly sleep to maintain optimal intelligence. When awake, your brain functions much better if you've gotten a good sleep, partly because when well rested, you metabolize more glucose. Perhaps more astounding, your sleeping brain does a whole lot of *thinking* that supports learning and memory. Recent research shows that getting ample sleep makes you smarter, healthier, younger-looking, and even slimmer. Say no to sleep macho! Make a self-commitment to get the rest you need to do and be your best.

PART FOUR

INTEGRATING YOUR SOCIAL SELF

N ow that we've got our minds and our bodies playing nicely together, it's time to go out and make new friends. Seriously! It also would behoove us to deepen our ties with old friends, build stronger bonds with coworkers, connect with our communities, improve our romantic relationships, and study up on the other gender.

But why, if we're concerned primarily with our *selves* in this book, should we bother worrying about other people at all? Because scientists have discovered that none of us can thrive on our own. To lead long, happy, successful lives, we each need a robust network of interpersonal relationships. Therefore, as we move from inner to outer while constructing our model, we'll focus here on *Integrating Your Social Self.*

Fortunately, today's researchers have been finding wonderful ways to build and rebuild your relationships; you'll learn many surprising strategies throughout this section. Sometimes it's wise to laugh at the unfunny. Sometimes it's smart to refrain from trying to fix an inter-gender conflict by "talking things over" (at least until you've had a chance to study the other's language). And sometimes it's right to relinquish your adult inhibitions to just play.

Much of the science here will be as beneficial to you individually as it is helpful to your relationships—because you'll be gaining self-insight while building your Self-Intelligence. So again, please feel free to mix and match your use of the tools in this book. For example, while two of the chapters here share couples' stories, you can apply the same science to improve platonic friendships, business alliances, and family attachments as well.

We won't leave anyone behind—and of course, we'll bring the rest of our *selves* along too. The *subconscious, conscious,* and *embodied selves* will continue to play their parts. It's no accident that scientists now refer to the totality of our neural wiring as *the connectome.* So, let's all stick together, eh?

Since we are social creatures, a need to belong is as basic to our survival as our need for food and oxygen.

—NEUROSCIENTIST RICHARD RESTAK

CHAPTER 13

REACHING OUT

How to Roll the Social Snowball

Prime-your-mind Quiz

Research says you'll remember this chapter better if you test yourself now. How will the answer affect *you*?

Recent studies reveal that being chronically lonely and socially isolated . . .

a. might be unpleasant but won't affect your physical health.

b. can increase brain function and lead to genius-level creativity.

c. can be as harmful to your physical health as smoking and can also impair brain function.

E ven over Skype, Kevin looked terrible. His eyes were bloodshot. His shoulders sagged inward as though the stuffing had been removed. He sounded awful too, sniffling and clearing his throat.

We had just finished introducing ourselves and going over his personal information. He was a twenty-eight-year-old software engineer who currently had a cold. "I don't Skype very often," he said. "Tom once told me that he and Linda sometimes Skyped even when they could have just walked down the hall. Well, I guess if it was the middle of the night or something."

"Kevin, may we back up a second? Who are Tom and Linda?"

"They had the apartments on either side of me. The three of us used to hang out together all the time. Then they fell in love with each other and moved to the West Coast six months ago."

"Ah. Are you still friends?"

"They're pretty wrapped up in their romance right now. I'm not calling them because I'm pretty sure they don't want me to intrude." Kevin sneezed into a crumpled handkerchief. "Tom asked me to be best man in the wedding next year. I won't know anyone there and I'm already dreading it. But the issue we should talk about right now is my trouble focusing at work. It's not like me. I've been snacking a lot to help myself concentrate. Yesterday my boss made fun of my desk being covered in candy-bar wrappers. Maybe she was joking, but I felt humiliated. I've been sick a lot lately, which is really unusual, but maybe she's secretly angry at me for that. It seems like everybody's being rude to me lately. I feel like when I talk with people at the office, they sort of withdraw, like they're suddenly allergic to me. I have this weird feeling . . . "

"Yes?"

"That nobody likes me. As if people are avoiding me. They suddenly stop talking when I walk up, as if they were gossiping about *me*. When I ask, they deny it, but it's still possible. I just feel sort of . . . mmm . . . " He gazed downward.

"Kevin, maybe since Tom and Linda left, you're feeling lonely? That would be perfectly natural. It sounds as though they were your best friends."

He wiped his nose with the handkerchief. "I haven't been this lonely since freshman year in college. But so what? I'm worried about my focus at work."

I suggested to him that loneliness might well be causing his lack of focus, and maybe even his cold.

"Seriously?" He appeared doubtful. But I was indeed serious.

The Ways Our Social Snowballs Roll

Loneliness is not a disease—we're all lonely sometimes—but if left unchecked, it can become far more dangerous than most people realize. Chronic loneliness attacks the brain, reducing focus, memory, and self-control. It also ravages the body on several fronts. A 2010 analysis of 148 studies found that social isolation increases your risk of death about as much as smoking fifteen daily cigarettes.

Are you as shocked as I was by that finding? In my thirties, I chose to be a loner. I'd hide out for days on end writing dark poetry or fiction, shunning human contact as an unnecessary intrusion. It never occurred to me that this wasn't brilliant behavior, or that it might be downright dumb.

To be honest, I didn't read much science back then, arrogantly assuming science itself must be rather dull. But coincidentally, around that same time in the early 90s, a new field was emerging—*social neuroscience*—focusing on the human need for connection.

It began with a few top researchers such as Chicago University psychologist John Cacioppo, and now includes hundreds from various disciplines who explore how social interactions (or lack of them) affect our mental and physical health.

Imagine this: Even a *fruit fly* will die early if cut off from the company of other fruit flies. The same has been proven true of mice, rats, pigs, rabbits, and many of our closer-cousin primates. Consider that we humans are the most social of all species. If all those critters need it, then *of course* we too need social connection to thrive. This insight compelled Cacioppo to investigate and write the book on *Loneliness: Human Nature and the Need for Social Connection*, establishing him as the topic's leading expert.

He and others have discovered what I call the social snowballs, one good and one bad. The good snowball rolls like this:

Experiencing good relationships with other people makes you healthy and happy.

→ Being happy, you reach out to people in a positive manner.

→ This further increases the number and quality of your relationships.

→ And that, in turn, makes you even happier, healthier, and, apparently wealthier.

Wealthier? Cacioppo reports that "people who are less lonely tend to make more money. How is this possible? Relying on our data, we cannot say precisely. But we do know that happier, less lonely people form good relationships, including relationships in the workplace, and it may be that these good relationships, rather than happiness itself, improve job performance, increase the likelihood of receiving good performance reviews and promotions, and provide better networking opportunities for career growth."

Extensive business research confirms that strong relationships drive professional success. This is also borne out in my own clients' careers. Which brings us back to Kevin's feelings of disconnection at the office. The bad snowball was gaining ground. His example was typical of how that snowball rolls:

Kevin had lost the company of his two close friends, which left him feeling lonely.

→ Months of loneliness had put him in a negative mindset, suspicious that his peers disliked him.

→ At the office, his negativity led to off-putting behavior (for example, accusing coworkers of gossiping about him).

➤ Picking up on, and overreacting to, their response (perhaps even imagining some of it), he was growing even more lonely and negative.

Studies show that loneliness puts most people in a terrible mindset, tending toward depressive self-absorption and paranoia. Their confidence plummets. When the bad snowball builds too much momentum, the sufferer may feel helpless to stop its progress. That is why loneliness is a leading cause of suicide.

Maybe you're thinking: *But wait: Tom and Linda are still Kevin's friends.* True, yet Kevin believes they don't want to hear from him. He feels shut out—first by them, and now also by his colleagues. Is it all in his head? In a profound sense—*yes*. In terms of affecting our physiology, what matters about our relationships is how we think and feel about them.

For example, Cacioppo's research reveals that a person with scores of acquaintances and a full social calendar can nevertheless be chronically lonely. Meanwhile, someone with few relationships might not be lonely at all, as long as that individual *feels* happily connected. These examples are atypical but demonstrate the primacy of our inner experience. Therefore, when working on your relationships, it's almost always best to start with yourself. (For a pleasant, quick exercise to strengthen your *self*-relationship, see the free video at self-intelligence.com.)

Connecting the Scientific Dots of Social Connection

Scientists now know some of the specific ways that an inner sense of social connection—or disconnection—directly shapes the brain, powering either the negative or positive snowball:

- People who feel connected to others get a bigger boost from positive input. For example, when these folks see pictures of smiling faces, their ventral striatum (part of the brain's reward circuitry) lights up. That feels nice! Lonely people—whose brains are wired toward the negative—don't get the same emotional lift.

- Socially disconnected people experience a deeper hurt from negative input. For example, they suffer an extra dose of negativity from seeing photos of angry or fearful faces. Non-lonely folks don't react strongly to these, but lonely people do. Their right amygdalae overrespond, creating an internal sense of being threatened.

- Feeling excluded is literally painful. When a person feels shut out or otherwise ostracized, the emotion activates the dorsal anterior cingulate cortex, a brain region normally sparked by physical pain. All personality types show the same *ouch!* response to rejection, even those who think they're "tough." Social exclusion *hurts*.

The pain serves an evolutionary purpose, scientists say. It's meant to be temporary, motivating us to reach out to establish the social connections that help us thrive. But it backfires when disconnection lasts too long, launching the bad snowball of fearfulness, negative thoughts, and unpleasant behavior.

To make matters worse, loneliness also impairs the very brain area we need most to turn ourselves around: the prefrontal cortex. That's our executive control center, the seat of decision-making, intentional focus, and willpower. Its impairment explains why, as research shows, lonely people tend to eat poorly, drink too much, and exercise too little.

Kevin's prefrontal cortex already appeared to be somewhat offline, judging from his weak mental focus and excessive snacking. I asked him if he had experienced those same problems when he'd previously felt isolated, during his freshman year.

He cocked an eyebrow. "Mmm . . . actually, my first semester was terrible. Not to brag about my IQ? But that was the only time school was ever a problem. I snacked my way through that time too. Guys in the dorm called me 'the junk food junkie.' But by the end of the year, it was okay. I had friends and was acing my classes as usual. Actually, do you think my current situation might improve on its own?"

"Maybe, but let's not leave it to chance," I suggested.

Freshman-year alienation tends to self-repair because college students begin as strangers in the same boat, who naturally make friends with one another. Adulthood's different. The lonely adult is surrounded by cliques and communities whose doors may appear closed. Reaching out can require a big effort, which can be especially tough for a person who already feels down.

My job was to help Kevin shift his internal perspective—so that he would *feel* more con-nected and positive—and then help him successfully reach out to other people, so that he would *be* more connected. We needed to get the good snowball rolling.

Over several sessions, we used hypnosis to reduce his loneliness. While hypnotized, he re-experienced times when he'd felt close to other people. He thought of Tom and Linda and of other good relationships he'd had throughout his life, including with friends, mentors, and family members. But it wouldn't have helped him much to simply remem-ber those relationships. I had him practice deeply *feeling* the positive connections.

This restored positive social pathways in his brain. By our fourth session, he was emotionally back on track. "This voodoo works!" he chuckled. "I'm *me* again."

To safeguard Kevin's newly positive feelings, we used cognitive reframing to improve his thoughts. His homework assignments included contemplating questions such as: What if Tom and Linda *did* want to hear from him, and had just been too distracted to get in touch? What if his coworkers in general thought well of him, even though he might have startled them with his recent accusations of gossip? What if most people *respected and liked him?* These things weren't guaranteed—but were they *possible?* He began to see they were possible, even probable.

As his feelings and thoughts improved, Kevin's mental focus returned. So did his physical health. No more sneezing or sniffling. Problem solved, end of story? Not quite. It was time for him to begin creating a solid social network.

"So I'm not done yet, huh," Kevin said. "I think you like to give me homework." He wagged his finger at me. "Just don't tell me to go to singles clubs or join a drum circle."

"Neither of those will be necessary," I laughed. Luckily, the research tells us what *is* necessary for social fitness. Basically, just two factors:

- **Closeness.** We need intimate friendship, based on trust and appreciation. Ideally, and if we're lucky, our romantic partners and family members will be among our closest friends. Not all of our friendships need be so deep, but it's good to have at least a few.

- **A wide web.** Scientists prescribe a broad range of relationships, so that we're plugged into multiple groups and communities. They call this *social integration,* measured by the number of social "roles" that we play.

For example, if you're married, have kids, work in an office, sing in a choir, keep up with relatives, volunteer at a soup kitchen, maintain close pals, play soccer every weekend, and belong to a synagogue, then even if you lose one role, even a major role—say, by getting divorced—you've got the others to keep you connected.

By the same token, people with too few roles become vulnerable. A workaholic with a corporate job and no other social life might appear connected to scores of people professionally—but never get close to any. When the person retires, that role ends and so do the connections that went with it. The individual is left feeling utterly alone.

Kevin agreed to a multipronged plan that you, too, may want to follow:

- **Reach out to friends.** Kevin called Tom and Linda. Delighted, they Skyped him back ("We want to *see* you!") and kept him conversing for more than an hour. How about you? Are there friendships you'd like to rekindle or simply strengthen?

- **Get to know colleagues.** At the office, Kevin targeted two people he particularly respected. He began soliciting their advice on projects and offering help, having lunch with them and hanging out after work. "I've always liked programming, but now I actually like showing up for my job," he reported. Studies show that job satisfaction zooms skyward when colleagues become friends.

- **Connect with family.** Kevin decided to contact his older sister, with whom he'd once been close. "I hadn't even realized how much I missed her," he said.

- **Join a value-driven group.** This could be civic or spiritually based. Kevin signed up to help plant trees around town, because he cares about the environment. Common values provide fertile ground for friendship.

- **Take up some group fun.** This could range from knitting to stock-car racing. Kevin started a weekly poker game with a few friends. "It's easy. Provide beer and they will come."

How Stronger Bonds Make Stronger Bodies

Is putting all this effort into social connection worth it, for Kevin or for you? Yes, big-time. Scientists have discovered that our level of social integration reaches right down to our DNA, switching on—or off—genes meant to keep us healthy. For example, social isolation inhibits genes designed to defend against viruses. So among other things, lonely people catch colds. We know this from some mighty weird studies.

Carnegie Mellon scientist Sheldon Cohen sticks cotton swabs up the noses of healthy volunteers to expose them to common cold viruses, then quarantines them to see who gets sick. He's been doing this for decades. About a third of his subjects fall ill. In general, he has found, those are the people with three or fewer social roles. People with four or more social roles usually don't succumb to the virus. The more social roles, the better the body defends itself.

But colds are hardly the worst of it. Other studies now reveal that social isolation leads to an astonishing range of bad health effects. Here's a small sample of the research:

- A study of 665 stroke patients found that socially isolated people were nearly twice as likely as others to suffer another stroke within five years. Social isolation far outweighed other factors such as cardiovascular disease or lack of exercise.

- Another study tracked nearly 17,000 senior citizens over six years. In that time, those with low social integration showed weaker cognition and significantly more memory loss.

- Scientists followed almost 7,000 Californians for nine years. They found that socially isolated people were twice as likely during that time to die of all causes, including heart disease, cancer, stroke, accidents, or suicide. Having *close* relationships proved particularly helpful. A lack of social ties proved at least as harmful as a bad diet or smoking.

New research aims to pinpoint how loneliness and social isolation play out at a cellular level. So far, studies indicate that social disconnection:

- Constricts the arteries, increasing blood pressure and taxing the heart.

- Raises levels of the stress hormones cortisol and epinephrine.

- Locks a person's physiology in "alert" mode, preventing both the good sleep and the effective relaxation needed to stay healthy and energized.

- Overactivates genes that promote inflammation, while de-activating genes that would curb inflammation.

- Inhibits genes meant to protect us from viruses, including not only common cold viruses, but also flu and HIV.

By now, more than 100 studies show that people with strong relationships—with family, friends, and community—remain healthier and live longer. How about you? If you already enjoy numerous social roles and close connections, pat yourself on the back. But if you feel at all lonely, consider taking three simple steps:

1. Strengthen your sense of self-connection. For example, use my quick but powerful PACE exercise (view the free video at self-intelligence.com).

2. Practice reframing any negative thoughts about yourself and others so that you set your mind to the positive, to get that good snowball rolling.

3. Reach out to others in order to build meaningful connections and a wider network. This may take time, but once that good snowball gains momentum, it will energize you.

Kevin soon found himself comfortably connected to others, while playing many social roles. He thus averted any danger of sliding back into the bad snowball. As a bonus, now that he felt socially confident, he genuinely looked forward to serving as Tom's best man.

"And remember that by maintaining your friendships with Tom and Linda, you're helping them to stay happy and healthy too," I said. "Plus, you're probably strengthening *their* relationship."

People in romantic relationships often neglect to keep up with friends. It's a huge mistake. If either partner comes to depend solely on the other for companionship, such dependency fosters neediness. Neediness breeds boredom and resentment. Meanwhile, the low level of social integration can produce ill health and negativity, neither of which makes for a happy couple. To keep a romance strong, each partner should maintain other close connections.

At the same time, committed partners should put their friendship with each other above any other. This creates the trust that leads to lasting romance. Maybe you've heard that marriage promotes longevity. Not always. Studies show that a bad marriage can take years off your life. But if your partnership is based on being supportive best friends, then yes, you're likely to live longer.

What keeps us well is not any legal formality but rather intimate true friendship, whether with a spouse, relatives, or yes, "just friends." Historically, it was believed that friendship, while it might be nice, wasn't essential. Only last century, theologian C. S. Lewis wrote, "Friendship is unnecessary, like philosophy, like art . . . It has no survival value; rather it is one of those things that give value to survival."

Now we know better. Meaningful friendship not only adds value to our lives, it keeps us alive. Our relationships with other people matter more to us—physically, emotionally, and mentally—than even the greatest of thinkers in the past ever imagined.

Use Your Self-Intelligence

Build a better life by forging strong interpersonal connections.

One of the best ways to succeed at work is to strengthen your relationships by helping your colleagues. Check out the science in Adam Grant's well-researched book, *Give and Take*.

Since friendships help keep you healthy, why not deepen a friendship while getting fit? Find an exercise partner to jog or work out with. Or, ask a pal to be your "accountability partner." Share specific fitness goals with each other, then check in daily or weekly to report your progress and hold each other accountable. A fitness partnership will help you both stay on track while you become better friends.

It might seem obvious that successful partners must accept and appreciate each other. But if you are too *self*-critical, or lack *self*-respect, you will compulsively criticize and disrespect your mate. Build a strong *self*-relationship. Remember the power of positivity from chapter 8, and practice being kind to *you*. (For additional science on self-forgiveness, see chapter 20.)

As Cacioppo's research shows, people who enjoy plenty of positive relationships also make more money. Instead of focusing directly on the dollar, expand your social and professional network by being genuine, trustworthy, and compassionate. This will (literally) pay off.

Quiz answer: Recent research reveals that being chronically lonely and socially isolated . . .

    c.   can be as harmful to your physical health as smoking and can also impair brain function.

In a Nutshell

To thrive, you need other people. Chronic loneliness and social isolation can weaken your immune system, impair brain function, and shave years off your life. What matters most is how you feel and think about your relationships. At the same time, research shows that by expanding your network—that is, by playing more social roles— you can protect your inner sense of connection. Your inner and outer social experiences each reinforce the other, creating a snowball effect. So practice improving your social mindset, then use that positive attitude to reach out to good people to strengthen your circle. You'll be far better off—happier, healthier, and probably wealthier.

If you wish to glimpse inside a human soul and get to know a man, don't bother analyzing his ways of being silent, of talking, of weeping, of seeing how much he is moved by noble ideas; you will get better results if you just watch him laugh. If he laughs well, he's a good man.

—FYODOR DOSTOYEVSKY

CHAPTER 14

LAUGHTER

What's So Darn Funny About It

Prime-your-mind Quiz

Research says you'll remember this chapter better if you test yourself now. How will the answer affect *you*?

Which of the following is true?

a. Humans are the only species known to laugh.

b. Most laughter has little if anything to do with humor.

c. Humor is the key to laughter, so humor is the key to happiness.

Yvette presented an unusual personal challenge for me. On the phone, she had sounded slightly defensive, but that's not unusual for an initial client interview. She told me she had moved to San Francisco a year earlier for an information-technology job at a bank. Although she was a skilled employee, she felt subtly ostracized by colleagues. Her boss appreciated her good work, but when she'd asked him why others seemed to avoid her, he had replied, "Maybe you could be nicer to people."

"The problem isn't my being nice or not nice," she told me. "I don't criticize other people and I am perfectly polite. The reason I'm calling you is that I don't know whether I should look for another job. I want some help deciding."

That seemed reasonable. But within fifteen minutes after Yvette's arrival at my office, a peculiar problem arose: I found myself disliking her! It took me a moment to realize what I was feeling. The sensation resembled a mix of anxiety and impatience.

This was bad news, because for me to help clients, I must truly care about them, and to do that, it sure helps to like them. Usually that's easy, because the folks who seek me out tend to be decent people.

And Yvette too was quite decent. She spoke well. She dressed well. She had good manners. So what *was* it? The light coming in through my window was dim that day because outside, rain was steadily falling. I switched on my desk lamp but still saw nothing objectionable about my new client.

"Please tell me more about your interactions at work," I prompted.

Yvette inhaled sharply. "No one talks to me unless they have to. No one invites me to join them for lunch. I can't help noticing that people go out of their way to avoid me. It's almost as if everyone else knows something I don't. As if they have some private club, with a secret password, and they hold clandestine meetings each morning before I get there."

I laughed, but then saw that she was not laughing.

"That was a joke, right?" I asked sincerely.

"Yeah, I guess so."

We could hear rain pummeling the window glass. "Well, do you stop and chat with people when you arrive at the office?"

"About what?"

"Oh, I don't know, just *Hello, how was your weekend, how are the kids . . . ?* I nodded toward the window and laughed again, "Or just, *What a lot of rain we're having!*"

She winced. "I don't like small talk. It seems fake. I don't believe in playing games."

Her response gave me an idea. "No games ever? Not even Scrabble or twenty questions or pin-the-tail-on-the-donkey?" I laughed heartily to indicate the question was meant in fun.

She didn't crack a smile. "I enjoy chess. I play online."

With great relief, I felt a wave of empathy for her. She wasn't *trying* to act standoffish. It was almost the opposite, as though she were being too earnest. "Yvette, how long has it been since you *laughed*?"

She gave me a blank look. "What? Oh. Probably the last time I saw a funny movie, but I don't remember specifically."

That was it. For whatever reason, Yvette was inhibiting her natural laughter instinct.

"Before you moved here, when you felt more accepted at your previous job, do you think you laughed more—you know, at other people's silly comments, even when they weren't really funny?"

She took a while to answer. "I don't remember. Maybe I was more lighthearted. But the position I have now is with a bigger firm. They're not paying me to laugh."

"Well, this is probably going to sound odd," I said, "but your job entails working with other people, which means you need to get along with them, which may also mean you need to laugh."

The Surprising Stuff That Makes Us Laugh

Thank goodness I had recently read *Laughter* by neurobiologist Robert R. Provine. Until he came along, we remained in the dark about laughter. I had bought his book hoping to learn more about laughter's physical benefits—its ability to induce muscle relaxation, decrease physical pain, and possibly even combat heart disease—which have long been known. It's easy to get clients to laugh under hypnosis, plus it's fun for both them and me. I'd already been using laughter to help several clients control chronic pain and stress, and I had wanted more science to bolster my practice.

What I found out instead was a complete surprise to me, as it had been to Provine himself—evolution has programmed us to laugh with one another, and most often at nothing funny. Laughter aids our survival by creating social bonds. As the most socially evolved species of all, we laugh the most. But others laugh too, including chimps, gorillas, orangutans, dogs, and even rats!

Our triggers for laughter lie deep within ancient parts of the subconscious brain, where they long remained a mystery. For at least 2,000 years, thinkers from Plato to Freud had assumed that laughter resulted primarily from humor. Now, thanks in part to Provine's groundbreaking research, we know that's just not true.

Provine began in the 1980s as a neuroscientist hoping to study the brain on laughter. He brought people into his lab and subjected them to funny audio and video recordings, from Rodney Dangerfield to *Saturday Night Live*. The result? Barely a chuckle ensued. "I was surrounded by laughing people who would go stone sober when brought into the laboratory," wrote Provine. This was his first big clue that laughter depends far more on social context than it does on comedy.

So finally the scientist and three undergrad assistants set out to study human laughter in its natural habitat: shopping malls, city sidewalks, and the student union. Basically, they eavesdropped. They documented 1,200 *laugh episodes*, writing down the remarks that generated laughter, as well as who laughed more, speaker or listener.

The tallied results shocked everyone. Provine found that 80 percent to 90 percent of laughter came after phrases that weren't funny at all. These included such banalities as, "I'll see you guys later," or, "It was nice meeting you too."

The remaining 10 percent to 20 percent of laugh episodes followed any comments that the researchers deemed even remotely humorous. The best of these side-splitters included, "Look at that hunk of burning love," and "What did you do to your hair?"

Twelve-hundred laugh episodes and nary a good joke among them! So why were these people moved to laugh? Because evolution has wired our brains for laughter to create camaraderie, to help us survive. (Recall from the previous chapter the crucial role of social connection.) The subconscious mind already gets this, which is why we normally laugh at the proper social moments without making any conscious effort—often without being consciously aware of our own laughter. We are guided by our laugh instinct.

Scientists now believe that human laughter grew out of primate laughter, a special pant-pant that occurs when chimps play tag or tickle. (Indeed, *play* may be an even more primal bonding activity, as we'll explore in the next chapter.) Laughter signals friendship and nonaggression. After we humans took an evolutionary leap forward by developing speech, we incorporated laughter into it. How do we know that? Because laughter respects grammar: Both speakers and listeners laugh only at the end of full statements or questions, a phenomenon scientists call the *punctuation effect*.

Laughter's role in social communication is further borne out by Provine's discovery that usually it's the *speaker*, rather than the *listener*, who laughs the most. In everyday life, most laughter is not a *reaction* to humor, but an instinctive *action* to strengthen social bonds. This explains why, for 2,000 years, the great philosophers got it wrong. When pondering laughter, what came into their minds were memorable instances of laughing at wit or comedy. They thus supposed that laughter must be a rational, even conscious response to humor. As it turns out, the joke's on them.

Most laughter occurs during normal conversation, and it is so automatic as to go unnoticed by our conscious minds. But the subconscious *does* take note. We subconsciously pay attention to whether someone laughs or not—which is why, when Yvette inhibited her natural laugh instinct in an effort to seem more professional at her new job, other people became nonplussed. This also explained my own momentary feelings of dislike. By refusing to laugh with others, Yvette was violating subconscious social etiquette.

> **Most laughter occurs during normal conversation, and it is so automatic as to go unnoticed by our conscious minds.**

The Hidden Hierarchies of Laughter

Thinking back to my early twenties, it struck me that I had once faced a situation similar to Yvette's. I had moved to Puerto Rico for a job as assistant city editor of the English-language *San Juan Star*. Most of the reporters and photographers under my charge were Puerto Rican men much older than I. Many were not thrilled at being directed by a *gringa* in the first place, much less a novice so fresh out of college. Besides that, it was my first time on the island, where I knew little of the local history or culture. My Spanish was passable but imperfect. Feeling overwhelmed yet anxious to prove my competence, I strove to be hyper-professional, staying ultra-focused on work while avoiding small talk or horsing around.

After several months, I met up socially with one of the few other *gringas* on staff, a reporter named Karen. We hit it off over dinner, leading her to exclaim, "I had no idea you were this much fun. At the paper, you're *sooooo* serious that our nickname for you is *the robot*." Ouch! After that dinner, I loosened up. Close friends have always known me as someone who laughs loudly and a lot; now the staff began to experience that side too. My job became much easier after that.

Recent research bears out that laughter affects professional relations. But its role is trickier than one might think. Researcher Phillip Glenn found that people often subconsciously adjust their laugh habits to support the office hierarchy. Higher-ups tend to initiate laughter, to which underlings respond with reciprocal laughter. Rarely do those in lower posts laugh first—and if they do, their superiors may put them in place by maintaining silence or changing the subject. (For you serious science readers, check out Glenn's prizewinning book, *Laughter in Interaction*.) Looking back to my time at the *San Juan Star*, it's possible that my initial straight-faced countenance was a lucky accident, though it didn't make me any friends. Perhaps that early aloofness helped establish my authority among newsmen reluctant to grant it.

Laughing Her Way to Professional Success

Yvette faced a challenge quite different from mine, however. She was expected to be a team player among equals. By being too uptight to laugh when prompted, she was unwittingly offending her colleagues. It likely made things worse that she also refused small talk. Scientific studies show that, just like laughter, small talk serves as subconscious social glue. While its content may seem meaningless, its subtext of social connection means a great deal.

What would happen, I wondered, if Yvette began chatting and laughing normally with her peers at work? When we discussed it, she proved to be as open-minded as she was earnest. Her main concern was that it would seem forced. "If I'm just pretending to laugh, they'll really think I'm strange." She was right. But fortunately, she wouldn't need to learn any unnatural behavior. It was simply a matter of releasing the inhibitions she'd been imposing on herself—of relearning what she instinctively knew how to do. And so Yvette relearned to laugh.

At first, to pave the way, we resorted to humor. I led her during hypnosis to imagine funny scenarios (such as her entire department reporting to work in chicken suits). Under hypnosis, she also mentally replayed her favorite comedy scenes from film or TV, only made them more hilarious in her mind. She laughed and laughed and laughed, which made me laugh too. (Just how contagious can laughter be? See the sidebar "When Giggles Grow Out of Control.")

Once she'd reconnected with laughter in general, I led her to visualize herself laughing and chatting easily with others throughout the day. At first, I role-played for her such trivial lines as, "Hey, have fun this weekend! Ha-ha-ha!" It helped that she began to find it amusing that people laugh so often with no rational excuse. "It's completely crazy!" she said.

First with hypnosis, and then without needing it, Yvette shed her old self-imposed strictures. When back at the office, she quite naturally began laughing more—even about the weather. Now that she understood the function of small talk, her objections evaporated. "Did you know," she said, "that people will practically fall out of their chairs if you say, *The fog this morning is as thick as whipped cream.* But you have to sort of chortle when you say it."

Yvette began enjoying her job and decided to stay. She found herself easily chatting—and laughing—away from work as well. She consequently got asked out by a man she

WHEN GIGGLES GROW OUT OF CONTROL

Can you remember a time when you and a friend got carried away laughing? That's *laughter contagion*. Like other forms of *emotional contagion*, shared laughter is triggered by the brain's mirror-neuron system. (Remember those from chapter 10?) Neuro-imaging studies show that the mirror response to laughter is particularly strong.

It's so strong, in fact, that laughter once wreaked havoc in what is now Tanzania, Africa. In his book *Laughter: A Scientific Investigation*, Robert Provine recounts that, in 1962, three girls at a boarding school began laughing and couldn't completely stop. They'd quiet down a while but soon resume. Their out-of-control laughter spread to other students . . . then to neighboring schools . . . and then to entire villages. Before the epidemic ended *two and a half years later*, the outbreak had forced 14 schools to close and afflicted 1,000 people. No one was injured, but the contagion was so strong that authorities finally had to contain it through quarantine.

HOW GENDER IS A LAUGHING MATTER

When it comes to laughter, studies find that males and females subconsciously play out highly gender-specific roles. Beginning around age six, boys are the principle instigators of laughter, while girls do most of the laughing. Girls prefer to laugh with boys (more than with other girls), although boys do not return the favor. In adulthood, women tend to seek a man "who makes me laugh," while men prefer women who laugh easily.

Robert Provine's vast study of 1,200 laugh episodes reveals an even more dramatic gender gap. In general, speakers laugh far more than listeners, but one big exception stands out: When a man is talking to a woman, *she* laughs more.

Here are the stats: For all two-person pairs, speakers on average laugh 46 percent more than listeners. A woman talking to another woman laughs 73 percent more than her audience. A man addressing another man laughs 25 percent more than his listener. Gals speaking to guys laugh a whopping 126 percent more than their conversation partners.

But men talking to women laugh eight percent *less*!

Why? We don't know. Provine suggests that it may have to do with a male tendency to engage in one-upmanship and a female inclination to please. As much as we feminists may cringe at the idea, it does seem to fit in with scientifically established gender differences (due to a combo of nature and nurture), which we'll explore in chapter 16.

Ladies, if it's dismaying to know that most gentlemen won't deign to laugh as much as you do at either your wit or their own, take comfort in the fact that your laughter holds power. German psychologists conducted a study of mixed-sex pairs of young adults meeting for the first time. Researchers measured each individual's laughter, and later asked how much sexual attraction he or she had experienced. It turns out that a woman's laughter reliably predicts not only how attracted *she* feels, but how much *he* does, too. The man's laughter does not mean much either way. *Her* laughter signals the level of *mutual* attraction.

Apparently, this predictive power occurs because a woman laughs more both when she feels attracted to her partner and when she senses his interest. Other studies indicate that her laughter *makes her more enticing* to him, and that laughing boosts a woman's sexiness more that it does a man's. But gals, before you begin guffawing like mad to attract a mate, know that it won't increase your allure one bit if you grunt, snort, pant, or otherwise engage in so-called unvoiced laughter. A study done at Vanderbilt University found that what drives men most wild (in a good way) is a woman's singsong laugh, that which melodically travels the musical scale.

met in the tickets line at the de Young Museum. "He's taking me to Gary Danko for dinner. We'll laugh between bites," she reported. Research confirms that while everyday laughter serves as a social adhesive, it's downright Super Glue for sexual attraction. (And it differs dramatically by gender. See the sidebar "How Gender Is a Laughing Matter.")

As Yvette learned, the funny thing about laughter is that it's usually not very funny. It serves a serious purpose to create social bonds and, most often, follows straight lines such as, "See you later." Next time you're among other Homo sapiens, take note of your own laughter habits. If you join in easily, you deserve kudos for both your Self-Intelligence and your social intelligence. If, on the other hand, you've been repressing your laughter instinct, it's high time to lighten up.

Give yourself permission to laugh without needing any logical excuse, trusting your subconscious to follow social cues. Other people will appreciate it—consciously or not—so that in the end, everybody benefits. New research shows that laughter stimulates the brain's nucleus accumbens, a major reward center, while apparently also releasing endorphins, those natural opiates that make us all feel oh-so-good.

As philosopher and psychologist William James observed more than a century ago, "We don't laugh because we're happy—we are happy because we laugh." And, I might add, we're happy because by laughing we remain more deeply connected with others.

Use Your Self-Intelligence

All joking aside, tap into your natural instincts to laugh your way to a better life.

Laughing readily with colleagues will make teamwork flow more smoothly. Reciprocating your boss's laughter will subconsciously convey your good attitude. But if you need to wield authority over resistant subordinates, be careful not to overdo it.

For anyone seeking relief from stress or chronic pain, laughter is prescribed. (Check out Norman Cousins' classic memoir, *Anatomy of an Illness*, about curing himself through laughter.) Join a laughter-yoga club, go to comedy shows or rent funny videos—whatever you enjoy most!

Psychologists know that a telltale sign of couple trouble is when partners refuse to reciprocate each other's laughter or to laugh at each other's jokes. If that ever occurs between you and your mate, get some relationship help—and start laughing.

Which do you think is the best title for my next book: *Laughter for Millionaires* or *Laugh and Get Rich*? Just kidding . . . although Warren Buffet *does* have a famously great sense of humor and an easy laugh.

Quiz answer: Which of the following is true?

b.   Most laughter has little if anything to do with humor.

In a Nutshell

Laughter's primary purpose is social connection. Indeed, most of the time, what prompts laughter has nothing to do with humor, and all to do with bonding. The neurological mechanisms for this lie deep within the brain, indicating that laughter plays a part in our very survival. In this, we're not alone. Other critters laugh too, including our closest relatives, chimpanzees. So please don't make the understandable but misguided mistake of refusing to laugh at the unfunny. Be an easy laugh, and your life will be easier too.

It is a happy talent to know how to play.

–RALPH WALDO EMERSON

CHAPTER 15

PLAY

You Seriously Must, Scientists Say

Prime-your-mind Quiz

Research says you'll remember this chapter better if you test yourself now. How will the answer affect *you*?

Studies indicate that children who are prevented from playing freely may be more likely in adulthood to . . .

a. follow the rules and stay out of trouble.

b. become murderers.

c. keep their jobs.

At sixty-five, Larry was tall, blue-eyed, and fit. He invariably showed up to my office in jeans, an Italian linen shirt, and espadrilles. Prosperous as a general contractor, he nevertheless called himself a "certified beach bum" because he'd spent his childhood cavorting on the California shore, and still enjoyed living on the Pacific coast. Maybe that was why Larry, despite his fast-paced schedule, generally came across as easygoing. At this moment, however, he had a problem.

"Too many girlfriends. Sounds like a joke, but honestly, I'm exhausted," he said. It was the beginning of our session, which was my last session of the day. I, too, felt tired, although it was always pleasant to see Larry. Most people naturally resist change, but Larry tended to implement my coaching suggestions at lightning speed.

Over several months, I'd been helping him to, as he put it, "level-up life." He had kicked cigarettes, taken care of back taxes, learned to get more sleep, and strengthened his emotional sense of self-worth. But until now he had seemed content with his dating situation. Ever since a bitter divorce in his forties, he'd made a habit of dating several women concurrently. He was honest with all of them about this fact, and in the San Francisco Bay Area, his lifestyle wasn't too unusual.

"How many girlfriends is too many?" I asked now.

"I'm down to three—four if you count Alicia, but I generally don't count her as a girlfriend. Anyway, you know what? I'm ready to be in love with just one woman again. This week I realized something. Until my marriage fell apart, I used to feel quite happy being faithful to my wife. Don't look shocked—you're the one who's been helping me make changes. The problem is, I have fun with all my girlfriends but, to be honest, none of them cares very much about me."

He was right that I shouldn't have been surprised. Larry's decisions often seemed out of the blue, but they weren't, really. He just thought things out very fast, sometimes—although, not all of the time. "Remind me why you don't count Alicia?" I asked.

"Oh, she's more of a friend with benefits. I love her, but she's not all that exciting I don't think of her as a girlfriend, much less *the one*," Larry insisted. "There's something missing."

Alicia was his best friend, whom he'd known for fifteen years. They had dinner and a sleepover at least once a month, and every spring they shared a vacation. Just a week after Larry's session they'd be flying together to Spain's Costa del Sol. A health-services executive, Alicia was smart, dependable, and confident.

Larry didn't respect any of his three "official" girlfriends nearly as much as he did Alicia. Nor, apparently, did they revere him. Samantha regularly stood him up. Loraine borrowed money she never paid back. Christy got drunk and insulted him in public. However, all three were what he called "entertaining." He had described to me some good times: he and Samantha chased each other around the dining table; Loraine pushed him into her swimming pool fully clothed, then jumped in after before pulling clothes off; Christy instigated a naughty game of hide-and-seek.

It didn't make sense to me that Alicia wasn't in the running. I asked if sex might be the issue, or perhaps he didn't find her attractive. "Oh, no, she's beautiful! They all are. Sex is never a problem between me and women. No, it's something else." Larry waved his hand to indicate he was momentarily tabling the subject and asked for my help on other matters. He wanted to do some stress-relief hypnosis, plus he wanted a motivational boost to sort through boxes of memorabilia he'd inherited from his parents. The boxes had been in his garage for years, and he wished to finally dispatch this chore prior to leaving for Spain.

An hour later, before saying good-bye, he fished two pennies from his pocket and handed me one. "Let's make a bet," he said. "We'll stick these on our foreheads and see whose penny stays up the longest. Whoever wins gets to keep both pennies!" I was ready to go home, but his eyes sparkled with such delight that I obediently stuck my penny onto my face. We stared at one another, each determined to hold very still. Larry began energetically humming "Old MacDonald Had a Farm" in an effort to win by making me laugh.

Suddenly, I realized that this totally absurd moment was the most fun I'd had all day. "Larry!" I exclaimed. This caused my penny to pop off my forehead and clink onto the desk. "Do you *play* with Alicia?"

He raised his eyebrows, jarring his penny to fall, as well.

"You kid around a lot with your three official girlfriends," I went on. "What about Alicia? Do you and she *play* together?"

Larry lifted his chin in thought, then pocketed both pennies: "Victory is mine, hah! The thing is, Alicia's more emotionally mature than the others. The energy between us is different. Her schedule is as demanding as my own. We have lots to talk about, and better things to do than joke around."

I reached for my purse and pulled out a dollar bill. "Let's make a bet," I said. "Aim to be as playful as possible with Alicia on this trip. Do your best to get silly with her the way you do with the others. I'll bet you this whole dollar that it will change your relationship." Larry plucked the currency from my fingers, peered at it with feigned concern as if checking for counterfeit, then handed it back. "You're on," he said.

Falling In Sync and In Love Through Playing Together

Researchers have found that *playing* together vitalizes our relationships with others, especially when it is *free play*, that is, spontaneous rather than too strictly bound by rules. Our natural inclination to play appears soon after we're born. In every human culture ever studied, mother and infant gaze into each other's eyes, smiling, cooing, and babbling. Their exchange generates mutual joy and causes their brain waves to fall into sync, a state that scientists call *attunement*. "This experience is the most basic state of play and . . . becomes a foundation for the much more complex states of play that we engage in throughout life," says psychiatrist and researcher Stuart Brown in his delightful book, *Play: How It Shapes the Brain, Opens the Imagination, and Invigorates the Soul.*

While the ways we play change over time, playing together continues to forge our deepest interpersonal bonds, even in adulthood. Whether it's acting goofy to make one another laugh, waging a pillow fight, or inventing on-the-spot games, free play releases bonding chemicals such as oxytocin and natural opioids, and it activates joy. In fact, scientists say that just as we cannot tickle ourselves, we cannot experience true joy alone. Neurobiologist Jaak Panksepp has discovered that because playing and joy occupy the same primal brain circuitry, play provides our most direct access to joy.

Virtually all romances begin with some form of play, even if it's as subtle as a flirtatious exchange of eye contact. If partners stop being playful together, their brains cease to sync and they lose that primal bond of shared joy. It's as if their love battery drops its charge; the connection feels dead. "Sustained emotional intimacy is impossible without play," warns Brown. Fortunately, he says, research shows that relationships are rechargeable.

Larry's email from Spain offered four photos and the subject line, *Beach bum, then and now*. "I found old pics while emptying out those boxes," he wrote. "The other two were taken by a friendly expat here."

The black-and-whites were of a boy, around age five, presumably Larry, at the beach. In one, the child lay buried up to his chin in sand, laughing with apparent delight. In the other, he wore a man-sized T-shirt with the collar pulled up to hide his head. The boy's upraised arms held a beach ball on top—creating the effect of a beach-ball-headed monster, lurching menacingly toward the camera.

The new photos were each of Larry and a woman, presumably Alicia. In the first, she lay buried in sand up to her chin, mugging a panicked expression, while Larry stood with one foot propped on her midsection, his arms crossed in mock triumph. In the second, they both wore large T-shirts with the necklines tugged over their heads; the two headless creatures appeared to be wrestling over dibs to a beach chair. One might say that Larry and Alicia were acting like five-year-olds, which is also to say, they were having fun.

Neurobiologist Panksepp has discovered that the primal *impulse* to play resides in our most ancient, subcortical brain areas, while the *activity* of playing develops some of our highest brain regions—building cognitive function, creative keenness, and above all, social intelligence. This is true not only of us humans but of most mammals, and particularly the smartest ones; scientists have found that, in general, the more an animal plays, the larger its brain.

Because playing promotes healthy brains, researchers say it can make a long-term difference whether a preschool focuses more on academics or on playing. Forcing toddlers to sit and study at their desks all day might seem like a good idea, but it is not.

One study followed sixty-eight kids from poverty households over two decades. Scientists found a marked contrast at age twenty-three between those who'd attended heavily academic preschools versus those who'd gone to play-based schools. Almost half of those from the academic preschools later suffered emotional problems, compared to only 6 percent of those from the play-oriented schools. Those who attended play-based preschools also turned out far less likely to commit a felony and far more likely to keep their jobs.

How could playing more during childhood have the effect years later of deterring that person from committing a crime or screwing up at work? The answer is that play wires our brains for life-success skills such as how to recognize a bully from a friend; when to stand ground versus when to back down; how to regulate our own emotions; how to cooperate and compete at the same time; and how to create mutual trust. While historically play was not a classic topic of scientific study, research is now on the rise, partly due to concern over mounting evidence that depriving a child of free play can program that person for lifelong social alienation.

In 1966, early on in Brown's psychiatric career, a twenty-five-year-old named Charles Whitman climbed a University of Texas tower and shot forty-six people. Until then, Whitman, an engineering student and former Marine, had seemed like a disciplined and responsible young man, not the criminal type at all. Asked to investigate this mystery, Brown ended up interviewing twenty-six convicted Texas murderers for a pilot study.

Most of the killers, he found, had two things in common. They had grown up in abusive families, which hardly surprised him. What did startle Brown was his discovery that as children, these murderers *had not been allowed to play*. (An autopsy suggested that Whitman also may have suffered a brain tumor—but that possibility does not discount Brown's overall findings.)

Since then, over more than four decades, Brown has taken the "play histories" of 6,000 people. His studies confirm the primary importance of free play in childhood. Nevertheless, because of neuroplasticity—the fact that our brains continue rewiring throughout life—playing together as grown-ups also delivers strong brain benefits. Brown finds that playing together in adulthood both combats depression and dispels loneliness, enabling friends or family members to reconnect and helping couples to regain their romantic mojo.

The Three Un-Rules of Free Play

Are you ready to put "play" on your schedule? Experts say that, to give you the biggest brain-boost, your play should be social, rather than solo, and meet the following three criteria:

1. **It invites spontaneity.** While competitive play is great, avoid anything too rule-bound or cutthroat. How do you know? If everyone's having fun being creative, no matter whether they win or lose, then you're good.

2. **It demands active participation.** Watching a funny movie together might be nice, but it's too passive to constitute play. However, reenacting your favorite scenes later could qualify. Physical exertion is welcome but not required. Amusing word games will do.

3. **It induces joyful laughter.** If you're not letting go enough to laugh, then you're probably not full-out playing. Are you afraid to be, or to look, silly? Get over your silly fear by playing in a safe environment. Maybe take an improv class, teach a niece hopscotch, or ask friends over for a game of charades.

Research shows that even perfect strangers will quickly bond if led to play together in ways that make them laugh. In one 2004 study, pairs of same-sex adults were directed to play a game where one person spoke through a straw while directing the other, who was wearing a blindfold, to toss a Nerf ball back and forth. The pairs soon broke into laughter; after only a few minutes, they reported a strong sense of closeness. The unfortunate people in the control group, however, who had to do the same exercise without straw or blindfold, neither laughed nor bonded.

"Hold out your hands," Larry commanded. "Yep, like that." He had returned from Spain even more blond, more tan, and more cheerful than before. Now he pulled a coin roll from his pocket, ripped it open and emptied it into my cupped palms. "You won our bet!" he said with such relish it seemed as though *he* had won.

The pennies were new, shiny, and cumulatively heavy. I poured them onto my desk. "Okay, I'll bite: Why not just give me a dollar bill?"

"Becaauuuse," Larry said, looking extra pleased with himself, *"change is good."* I shook my head with amusement.

"Lucky I still have those boxes I emptied, because next month I'm moving in with Alicia. *What?* To you it seems sudden, but if you think about it, we've taken fifteen years.

As for our Spanish vacation, I hope you liked the photos. We got *much* crazier after that. She's *a lot wilder* than I'd realized. Then we ended up telling each other lots of things we'd never shared. She's the one. She was always the one. I just never saw what was right in front of me. We have agreed that from now on, we'll spend *more* time being *less* serious. Hah!"

I asked how his three other girlfriends felt about his decision.

"None of them got upset. It helped that I sent them all flowers. Alicia says they'll miss me but I doubt it. Who cares? We're on cloud nine." And indeed, that was where Larry and Alicia seemed likely to live from then on, as long as they continued to play freely together.

"The true object of human life is play," theologian and literary giant G. K. Chesterton wrote in 1908. "Earth is a task garden; heaven is a playground. To be at last in such secure innocence that one can juggle with the universe and the stars, to be so good that one can treat everything as a joke—that may be, perhaps, the real end and final holiday of human souls." Therefore, unless you're reading in the middle of the night, or on an airplane, or secretly during a corporate meeting, I invite you to put down this book a while, round up a playmate, and go have some fun.

Use Your Self-Intelligence

It may sound like a silly idea, and that's the beauty of it: We really can improve our relationships, and thus our lives, by playing more together at work and home.

A *Harvard Business Review* study found that the most successful executives tend to be playful types who purposefully provoke laughter. (Remember from chapter 14 that laughter isn't as much about funniness as it is about bonding.) Step up your leadership by being more playful.

"Trick" yourself and your friends or loved ones into getting some healthy exercise by playing. Whether it's tag, touch football, or some crazy stuff made up on the spot, it's all good. As long as it's fun and sparks joyful laughter, you'll get fitter, and emotionally closer.

We've talked about long-term couples, but what if you're single? Studies show that, among humans and many other smart mammals too, playfulness is an attractive trait. Consider turning your next romantic evening into a spontaneous playdate.

Liquidate your investments, stack the mountain of cash in your living room and invite friends over to fold all the bills into tiny origami animals. Just playin' with ya! Some things NOT to play with: fire, money, and other people's hearts.

Quiz answer: Research indicates that people who are prevented from playing freely as children may be more likely as adults to . . .

    b.   become murderers.

In a Nutshell

Playing is how we most joyfully bond with others. This begins in infancy, when mother and baby spontaneously interact, syncing their brain waves in emotional *attunement*. Later, as youngsters, playing freely with peers builds healthy brains, fostering both Self-Intelligence and social intelligence. Kids who are forbidden to play likely will develop interpersonal problems later on, possibly leading to criminal behavior, including murder. For families, friends, or couples to maintain joyful closeness, they must find ways to play together. So practice letting go of old inhibitions in order to rediscover your innate playfulness. Invite others to play along with you. Share the joy!

Many men honestly do not know what women want, and women honestly do not know why men find what they want so hard to comprehend and deliver.

–DEBORAH TANNEN

CHAPTER 16

XX AND XY

Girls and Boys and Stress, Oh My!

Prime-your-mind Quiz

Research says you'll remember this chapter better if you test yourself now. How will the answer affect *you*?

It has been confirmed by science that . . .

a.   men are far better than women at math.

b.   men and women respond very differently to stress.

c.   women talk more than men.

Jeff first called me to get help quitting cigarettes. Three months after kicking the habit, he called again. "Meghan's gone nuts," he announced. We'd never met in person—Jeff lives in Missouri, and we worked together by phone—but his baritone voice made it easy to imagine him as a radio announcer. In fact, Jeff is an airplane mechanic. Among other things, that means he spends most of his time around men. He also grew up with three brothers and no sisters. In short, Jeff was far more familiar with the customs of males than those of females, and as it turned out, this was now causing him some confusion.

"I stopped smoking, just like Meghan wanted me to, but ten days ago she left anyway. You know what Meghan does now? Every day she calls saying we need to talk. Every day she asks me if I think it was the right thing for her to move out."

"Ah. And, well, so—what do you think?"

"I don't know what she wants!" Jeff bellowed into the phone. "She should say what *she* wants!" He sounded angry, which made me think he was sad. He wasn't generally an angry guy, and studies show that, unlike women, men tend to express anger when they are actually feeling depressed.

"How can I help?" I asked. "Is this about smoking? Are you having any cravings for cigarettes?"

"I'm *fine*. She's the problem. My brother says it's a woman thing. Every day she calls, asks me how I'm doing, I tell her fine. She asks me whether I think she should have left. I say I don't know. But she keeps asking! Why does she torture me like that?"

"Mmm. It sounds as though she may want you to invite her to come back."

"That's crazy! If I say she should come back, what's to stop her from laughing at me or at least starting another argument? And then, she always tells me she's going out later with her friends—like our breakup doesn't even faze her. Suddenly she's a party girl!"

"Well, I think you're right that this is a woman thing."

A Science-Driven Gender Adventure

It used to scare me to discuss male-female differences with clients, because hurt feelings abound on both sides of the gender gap. Unconscious sexism runs deep—among males *and females* (see the sidebar "Gender at Work")—and no one wants to be pigeonholed inside an unfair stereotype. While some people cling to outdated gender clichés, others imagine that we're all the same underneath. My own attitude is: Research to the rescue!

Granted, it's likely we will never know the whole story on gender. Scientists continue to investigate just what produces our masculine and feminine behaviors: biology or our environment? Research shows the answer is *both*, because nature and nurture are inextricably intertwined—so much so that the controversy cannot be fully settled. Which is probably good, because it fuels more research into a profound issue. Gender lies at the very core of our personal identities, and most of us want very much to get along with people of other genders, both at work and in our personal lives.

Rigorous studies show tremendous overlap in nearly all male/female differences—meaning we cannot predict any individual's destiny based on gender, and there's no "right way" to be a woman or a man. Science overturns old stereotypes. For example, we now know that except for a slight advantage in spatial reasoning, males are not innately better at math. And women do not talk more than men. At the same time, gender gaps do exist.

In particular, research over the last several decades confirms that, in general, men and women harbor very different attitudes about connection versus independence. As individuals, we are often caught off guard by the consequences. All too frequently, men and women antagonize each other without meaning to, and the standard prescribed cure

GENDER AT WORK

None of us thinks we are sexist, but nearly all of us unconsciously are—particularly when it comes to work. That is what the experiments show.

For example, multiple studies of the same basic design turn up the same results: When people are asked to judge executive resumes, their opinions vary significantly depending on whether they believe the applicant to be male or female. Given an impressive resume, subjects will consistently find a supposedly male candidate to be both competent and likeable. But subjects who are shown the identical resume under a female name will judge the applicant as either likeable but incompetent, or competent but unlikeable (for example, "hostile").

Apparently, we all—both men and women—find it hard to imagine that a high-powered female professional could be both good at what she does and a nice person.

Then how do women ever get hired and promoted? Fortunately, an individual impression can override an unconscious bias. But this makes it absolutely crucial that women present themselves well to create the right impression. And most of the time, that does not come naturally.

Why not? Because, as this chapter reveals, American males and females grow up speaking essentially different languages. Females learn to emphasize personal similarity and to shun overt conflict or competition. Males, in contrast, compete with one another for dominance through one-upmanship. Their conversational style embraces conflict and competition.

Neither style is intrinsically better, but the business world was built by men, and therefore reflects their style. To "fit in," women must learn new behaviors. But it's tricky! Because if a woman simply acts like a man, studies show that she will be shunned, or at least resented, by both sexes.

One of my clients, Celia, had tried hard to impress her male coworkers at an energy company. Initially, they had treated her more like a secretary than a colleague. So, thinking the answer was to emulate them, she pulled back from her naturally warm and nurturing personality. She also adopted a gruffer speaking style. She even copied some of her colleague's one-upmanship behaviors such as rolling her eyes or whistling softly when she disagreed with someone.

The results were disastrous. Far from taking her more seriously, they began to ostracize her. Celia originally contacted me because of psoriasis, so I asked her about possible causes of stress. When she told me about her job, I suggested we repair the work situation to reduce her stress, which might in turn help curb the psoriasis.

Over the next three months, she reclaimed her feminine warmth at the office, but she also learned which "male" behaviors to cultivate and when to use them. She regained credibility, her job became fun again, and her skin cleared up.

Which new behaviors ended up serving her best? Below are the three Celia ultimately found most useful. They may help you too, if you are a female professional. (I also highly recommend Sheryl Sandberg's book *Lean In*.)

1. Assert yourself. Shed your feminine modesty when it's time to state an important opinion, claim credit for your contribution, or negotiate for what you want. Yes, people may like you a little less if you do that, but they will respect you—and be willing to pay you—a lot more.

2. Ask questions carefully. Ask in such a way that emphasizes your intelligence and competence. Studies find that men are much more cautious than women are about this; professional women often pay a price for *appearing* ignorant.

3. Apologize prudently. Refrain from saying sorry too easily or often. Other women may understand that you're being "nice," but men can see it as a sign of weakness or incompetence.

Perhaps above all, Celia learned to be flexible, sometimes emphasizing her feminine caring side, but at other times being more competitive and assertive than at first came naturally to her. Research shows that the men and women who make it to the top of the ladder are, in general, those who've learned to adopt traits of both genders.

Think of the male corporate mogul who wins employee trust by showing compassion. Or of the female executive who gains respect by holding her own in a tough negotiation. Leaders who are gender-flexible not only garner professional success; by example, they invite us all to stretch beyond old limitations, to become greater than we were.

of "talking it over" can make things worse. Misunderstandings arise because usually females are programmed more strongly for social connection, while males attach higher value to independence.

Fight, Flee—or Make a Friend?

Let's first explore the connection-versus-independence gap between male and female social perspectives, then see how that difference can cause trouble, including for Meghan and Jeff.

The difference shows up dramatically in studies of stress. How often have you heard that our natural response to stress is fight-or-flight? And so it is—for *males*. We now know that much of the time, females respond in virtually the opposite manner: Rather than turning aggressive or withdrawing under stress, women typically seek greater connection with others.

How did scientists miss this fact for so long?

Until the end of the last century, animal and human research had focused almost exclusively on males. This wasn't due to some chauvinist conspiracy, but rather to the fact that menstrual cycles can complicate study results. So when experiments with men found that the "normal" stress reaction was fight-or-flight—that is, aggression or withdrawal—scientists assumed it to be true for everyone. It wasn't until 1995 that the U.S. government mandated that research studies must include both genders. After that, the picture changed drastically.

Scientists discovered that "women's responses to stress are profoundly more social," says leading researcher Shelley E. Taylor in her breakthrough book, *The Tending Instinct*. Instead of withdrawing from social contact, women facing stress—whether from illness, unemployment, a death in the family, or simple sadness—often instinctively reach out to friends and relatives.

In some cases, women under stress even become more nurturing, in sharp contrast to men. Research shows that, in homes where both parents work, when Dad comes home from a difficult day, he will likely snap at his family ("fight") and want to be alone ("flight"). But when Mom returns from a hard day at the office, she does the opposite: She hugs her kids more, spends extra time with them, and tells them she loves them. Scientists find that this behavioral shift is so deep-rooted, Mom herself typically remains unaware of it; it's her children who notice and report the extra warmth. (Studies also show, however, that *extreme* stress can inhibit maternal behavior; too much stress is never a good thing for anyone.)

In contrast to fight-or-flight, women under stress will nurture and connect, or, as Taylor puts it, they "tend-and-befriend." Brain-imaging studies show that stress activates women's neuro-anatomy for social bonding, but produces no such effect in men. Moreover, in both sexes, stress releases oxytocin—a hormone that promotes social bonding—but this strongly affects the women only, without much affecting men under stress. That is because oxytocin's influence is reinforced by the female hormone estrogen and weakened by the male hormone testosterone. When men are stressed, testosterone rises, reducing oxytocin's pull.

A meta-review of nearly thirty studies revealed this behavioral difference to be one of the most consistent gaps between the sexes: Under stress, men go it alone, while women reach out.

Why might evolution create this difference? Taylor theorizes that when early men faced danger, they learned to flee or fight to survive. Women, as child-bearers, needed an opposite strategy—unable to take flight with offspring in tow, they sought social support. Thus men's and women's brains evolved along two different tracks. But now that we no longer live on the Serengeti, our opposite stress responses can cause confusion—which brings us back to Meghan and Jeff.

For example, what looked to him like heartless party-girl behavior was actually her feminine reaction to the stress of their breakup. Far from meaning she didn't care, it showed that she cared deeply. Under the stress of her emotional pain, she had reached out to friends. Initially, this confused Jeff, who as a male naturally withdraws under stress. But after discussing the situation with me, Jeff shifted from feeling offended to feeling reassured. Eventually, he and Meghan were able to laugh at the misunderstanding.

However, her socializing wasn't all that annoyed him. He also complained that she kept pestering him with the question of whether she should have moved out. If she wanted to come back, Jeff wondered, why didn't she simply say so?

This too, I reassured him, was "a woman thing."

Perfectly Understandable Misunderstandings

Let me pause here to emphasize that most gender differences arise as much from culture as they do from nature. That is why gender actually varies across cultures. For example, this next misunderstanding between Meghan and Jeff demonstrates one of the best-documented sex differences among white middle-class Americans—but it's one that does not show up as much among African Americans or in the East. It is a gap in communication styles. Essentially, Meghan and Jeff were speaking two different languages—and, more importantly, neither had a clue.

On one hand, this difference should be old news. Linguist Deborah Tannen broadcast it a quarter century ago in her bestseller, *You Just Don't Understand: Women and Men in Conversation.* But on the other hand, as Tannen's ongoing research shows, language habits are so ingrained as to be unconscious. That is why most of us, for all our good intentions, continue interpreting—or rather, misinterpreting—the opposite sex as if they were speaking our gender dialect, which they are not.

So just what is this language gap? Well, it's the same difference that shows up in our stress response: women pursue connection while men aim for independence. Before we return to Meghan and Jeff, here's the gist:

From age three onward, girls and boys learn nearly opposite ways of speaking with their friends. Studies of children interacting show that little girls seek connection through similarity. If Little Girl A declares her favorite color is pink, then girls B and C may suddenly choose pink as their favorite too, even if five minutes earlier they preferred purple or green. In seeking similarity, girls learn to shun overt conflict or personal competition.

Little boys, meanwhile, learn the opposite. Rather than striving for similarity, they compete for dominance. Boys play in larger groups where hierarchy rules. Because each boy is constantly vying to be top dog, their conversations revolve around one-upmanship and asserting independence. If Little Boy A says he can throw a ball to the ceiling, Boy B may claim he can throw it to the roof, while Boy C insists he can throw it to the moon. For boys, ritual conflict and personal competition are the norm.

This explains why many men experience dialogue as a contest they must try to win. In Tannen's famous example, the typical male hates to stop and ask for directions. As she points out, from a man's perspective, doing so puts him in a one-down position. So he'd rather take more time to find his own way and maintain his independence. It's hard for some women to understand this attitude, because for most females, dialogue means connection rather than competition, so for them, seeking help may be not only practical but even pleasurable.

Love Lost (Then Found) In Translation

Keeping the different communication styles of men and women in mind, it's easy to see why Meghan kept asking Jeff if she should have moved out, and also why her question angered him.

Meghan had believed that, by soliciting Jeff's opinion, she was clearly indicating both that she desired to return, and that she wanted his agreement before she did anything. Following the female rules of dialogue, she was seeking similarity and consensus. When she told her girlfriends about it, they immediately understood, which made Jeff's reaction even more baffling to her.

But remember, male dialogue revolves around competing and winning—so in male language, her question sounded to Jeff like a ploy to force his hand without any risk on her part. Indeed, he had imagined that if he said he wanted her back, she might outright laugh at him! As long as they were each operating by their own language rules, every conversation merely reinforced the misunderstanding and made things worse.

Through working with me, Jeff came to recognize what was going on. Finally, when Meghan, as usual, asked whether she should have left, he said, "No, you should be here because we belong together." Within a week, she moved back in.

Yet this young couple still had work to do, for they needed to address why Meghan had left in the first place. As it turned out, their issue involved a sex difference about . . . *sex*.

For the first year, Meghan so greatly enjoyed being in love that she told herself she was sexually "satisfied." But in fact, she experienced orgasm only about half the time. She made a common mistake of withholding this truth until she felt more secure in their relationship. When Jeff proved his love for her by quitting cigarettes, she finally felt safe. So *then* she told him. To Jeff, this was a knife in the back! All along, he'd assumed she was delighted with his lovemaking. To suddenly learn otherwise made him feel like a fool. He told me their breakup went something like this:

She: You know, our sex life could be better.

He: What do you mean?

She: I just mean you haven't completely learned how to make love to me.

He: What?! What is it you think I've been doing?

She: I mean there are ways of touching me that would help.

He: Would help *what*?

She: Help me to have an orgasm.

He: But you always do.

She: (Silence.)

He: You mean you *don't*?

She: Lots of times, I'm not even close . . . You never actually *ask*. I've tried to bring up the subject, but it's uncomfortable for me. You seem to just assume that if you're satisfied, I must be satisfied. If you'd be willing to take more suggestions, instead of thinking you know everything, it would be a lot better.

He: I thought I knew you! I thought we were happy together! You sound so unhappy, maybe you should just leave.

She: All right, if that's what you want!

Some 85 percent of men said their partners climaxed during the most recent sex act . . . but only 64 percent of women reported they actually did.

It took Jeff a while to share this information with me, and he did so with an air of hopelessness. His world seemed to have turned upside down, to have changed in an instant from rosy to bleak. Even after Meghan returned, he was terrified to initiate sex, for fear that he would disappoint.

Gradually, however, he came to recognize this moment in their relationship as a great opportunity. He could finally discover his sexual partner's *actual* desires and needs, as well as share more of his own. Now they could create a truly satisfying sex life.

A 2010 study of 6,000 Americans found that, even in today's sex-savvy culture, men often don't know the real story. Some 85 percent of men said their partners climaxed during the most recent sex act . . . but only 64 percent of women reported they actually did. This indicates that across America, many millions of women are secretly frustrated. The Indiana University researchers hypothesized that while some women may be faking it, others have partners who simply don't notice or ask.

Whyever would millions of women keep such a secret? Having helped numerous female clients address sexual issues, I believe many suffer from shame. They see Hollywood sex in popular movies, where actresses appear to climax on time, every time, and they think, "There's something wrong with me."

And here we have another real difference between the sexes: Research shows that unlike men, most women need other forms of stimulation beyond intercourse in order to climax. That stimulation might be digital or oral, or involve sex toys. To make things more complicated, each woman is sexually unique. Just because a man knew how to please the last girlfriend doesn't mean he knows how to please the next.

Men, take courage.

If you're willing to let go of any know-it-all attitude, your lover will be happy to tell you what she needs—or at the very least, to explore and discover her needs with your help. So why is this so difficult? Well, remember . . . men hate to stop and ask for directions!

Indeed, as Jeff discussed the issue with me, he recalled that Meghan had shyly attempted to give him lovemaking guidance a few times, early on in their relationship. Instead of thanking her, he had felt offended. Because from a classic male perspective, needing to take directions puts a man in a one-down position and makes him feel, literally, like a loser. So he had experienced her directives as an insult.

Happily, Jeff now chose to think differently. He came to see that Meghan never meant to put him down; rather, she had been aiming for more intimacy . . . and better sex. Jeff now understood that Meghan had felt timid, perhaps even ashamed, about expressing her desires. Faced with his initial response, she had simply backed off until that fatal day when she brought up the subject again, only more bluntly.

Now he decided to take the lead. "It's time to be a man again," he told me. "I'm not just going to ask. I'm going to insist that she give me directions, suggestions, outright demands—" He paused, then in his beautiful baritone voice, he drawled, "In a nice way, of course."

Jeff became the lover every woman dreams of—secure enough in himself to explore the differences between him and her, knowing that doing so will bring them closer. He later told me that he and Meghan have made a new agreement. Henceforth, they will strive to learn each other's gender language, letting go of the need to be "right" and choosing instead to be curious. Together, they have begun a grand new adventure.

Use Your Self-Intelligence

No matter what your sexual orientation or relationship status may be, understanding gender differences will lead you to greater success. Scientists continue to make surprising discoveries in this field, so decide now to always keep an open mind.

Read the sidebar "Gender at Work" on page 207, then consider how you're seeing—and being seen by—the opposite sex. For example, if you're female, you may need to claim more credit for your accomplishments. If you're male, you might be underestimating the women around you because they're not blowing their own horns. And guys, next time you need to partner up on a project, remember that women tend to be great collaborators.

Statistics show more women report being depressed, yet far more men commit suicide. Because of the way we're raised, women sometimes dwell in their emotions while men often deny their feelings until it's too late. If you're female, practice taking action to cheer yourself up, such as getting together with friends. If you're male, practice acknowledging your feelings, even privately to yourself or with a trusted intimate. Remember that anger is often a smokescreen for sadness. Often, simply allowing oneself to *experience* sadness will lead ultimately to greater joy.

Whether dating or in a relationship, keep in mind that men and women unconsciously speak different languages. So ladies, if men seem competitive in conversation, don't take it personally. And gentlemen, allow yourselves to show more vulnerability (and less one-upmanship) when talking with the opposite sex. It may feel unnatural at first, but believe me, to us gals it makes you super sexy.

If you're not as wealthy as you want to be, it's possible you're holding on to some gender-related limiting beliefs. Women often subconsciously fear that earning tons of money will make them appear less feminine or cause envy among friends. For men, it's sometimes a dread of too much alpha-male responsibility. In either case, look for same-gender role models who enjoy financial success. Practice appreciating their achievement without envying or judging. It'll help!

Quiz answer: It has been confirmed by science that . . .

    b.   men and women respond very differently to stress.

In a Nutshell

Misunderstandings plague men and women because of their distinct attitudes toward independence-versus-connection. Typically, men value independence more highly, while women treasure connection. Evolution may have wired in this difference so that primitive men and women would survive danger—men by fighting or fleeing, and women (often with children in tow) by seeking help. Today this shows up in males' fight-or-flight response to modern stress, versus women's inclination to tend-and-befriend. Meanwhile, at least in the United States, most males and females grow up learning virtually opposite communication goals—again, differing around the issue of independence-versus-connection—so that women in conversation tend toward consensus and similarity, while men often compete for dominance. Use this knowledge to foster flexibility within yourself and to connect more effectively with everyone in your life.

PART FIVE

VITALIZING YOUR STRIVING SELF

Congratulations, your Self-Intelligence model is nearly complete. In building it, you've progressed from inner to outer, so here you arrive at the sub-self that most dramatically interacts with the rest of the world. It is your *striving self* who sets and achieves measurable goals. It's thus your *striving self* who makes the biggest public impression, who earns the most money, and who receives the loudest applause.

But by now you've discovered enough about interconnection to know that your *striving self* can succeed only because it's got all your other sub-selves backing it up. At first glance, the striving self might even seem to be superfluous. Once you have your *subconscious, conscious, embodied,* and *social selves* all working together, what more could you want?

Well, from studying science, helping clients, and learning from my mentor Jack Canfield, I've come to believe that to be happy and whole, we humans need to strive. I believe that every one of us yearns for a sense of purpose, meaningfulness, and personal agency. I believe that the history of humankind is a history of striving.

My clients are all strivers. Each comes to me hoping to create a change, to make a difference, to achieve a goal. Most of them are already high-functioning individuals, as I imagine you are, too. They seek help either when they've gotten stuck in their effort to achieve some particular goal or when they've grown unhappy and devitalized out of failure to set a particular goal.

That's why this part delivers help for your *striving self* to set and achieve goals. You'll learn specific questions to ask in order to generate the internal motivation needed to reach your dreams. You also will discover what to say—to yourself and others—about your goals, along with what *not* to say, so that you can prevent subconscious sabotage.

We'll continue to work with your thoughts, because thoughts always matter—but here we'll aim your thinking specifically to support a self who takes action. As uber-successful Jack Canfield says, "The difference between winners and losers in life is that winners take action."

Some men have thousands of reasons why they cannot do what they want to, when all they need is one reason why they can.

—AMERICAN CHEMIST WILLIS R. WHITNEY

CHAPTER 17

WHY?

The Question You Must Ask to Access Your Superpower

Prime-your-mind Quiz

Research says you'll remember this chapter better if you test yourself now. How will the answer affect *you*?

As we humans have evolved our capacity for reason and logic, we've come to the point that . . .

a. we quickly recognize and dismiss false reasons about why or why-not.

b. what's most motivating to most of us about why we do things is how logical those reasons actually are.

c. put on the spot, our brains will generate bogus explanations to answer the questions "Why?" or "Why not?"

H ave you ever felt mysteriously frustrated by a personal challenge? Let's take an increasingly common example: weight loss. Each year, millions of Americans cumulatively spend billions of dollars trying and failing to lose weight. On the one hand, perhaps it makes sense. After all, our brains evolved to crave carbs and fat so that we would do whatever it took to get those nutrients, whether it was climbing a 100-foot-tall coconut tree or hunting down a rhinoceros. Today, cheap processed fats and sugary, refined carbs are only a car ride, phone call, or mouse-click away. In this situation, you could say we're geared for gluttony. More and more Americans report that they find it impossible to lose weight and stay fit.

On the other hand, some do succeed. As I'll share in chapter 19, after years of being chubby, I shaped up once I stopped talking about the issue. In chapter 12 we saw how getting more sleep can help a person shed excess fat. But for most of my weight-loss clients, the single biggest step leading to long-term success is first finding their own best reasons *why* they want to get fit and to stay fit for the rest of their lives.

In this chapter, we'll explore the extraordinary force of *why*. This will help you not only to lose weight (if that's one of your aims) but to realize any number of previously unattainable goals.

Why to Ask Why and Why Not to Ask Why Not

Detroit businesswoman Lynn didn't bring up weight loss until her final session. Consulting by phone for six months, we'd focused on marital and business-personnel issues while she and her husband merged his renovation company with her home-organization service. Lynn kidded around a lot on our calls, but I'd come to realize she was a brilliant entrepreneur. I'd also witnessed her pursue goals with courage, flexibility, and focus, so that now, both her marriage and their joint venture were thriving.

When I asked what she'd like to address during our last call, she joked, "Help me track down the lady who stole my sexy body and left me with her fat figure!" Then she got serious. "Until a few years ago, I looked fabulous even while bringing up three daughters and running a business. Now they're all married and I've got two grandkids. When those babies were born, everybody said, '*You* don't look like a grandma!' People always told me I looked like Angela Bassett. Then I don't know but sometime during menopause, that fat lady snuck in when I wasn't looking. "

I laughed. "Do I understand you to mean that you want to lose weight?"

"But my metabolism has changed, and I can't eat the way I used to without getting fat. At our July 4th picnic last week I had seconds of everything. My oldest daughter caught me eating her homemade ketchup with a spoon. My lack of willpower is killing me."

I knew from working with Lynn that she had plenty of willpower. But by telling herself otherwise, she was now creating a false rationale why *not* to succeed. Among other things, we would have to dispel that.

I asked, "Why do you want to lose weight?"

"I'm fifty-three and I don't feel like buying a whole new wardrobe for a fat lady."

"Are you saying that you can't fit into your old clothes and you're feeling unattractive?"

"That's what I'm saying."

"Well, those are okay motives to lose weight, but maybe they're not enough." I suggested to Lynn that we use my "3-D Why-Finder," a trio of questions designed to remove debilitating *why-not's* around a particular goal, while generating an individual's best reasons *why* to succeed.

"'Three-D Why-Finder' as in three-dimensional? That sounds like a cereal-box toy," objected Lynn. I thought she had a point, but asked her to try it anyway.

Psychologists will tell you that we humans love to have *why's* and *why not's* to justify whatever we do or don't do. The science on this can get a little complex, but if you want to geek out on some of those experiments, see the sidebar "When *Why* Gets Weird." The upshot is that, as we evolved our capacity for logical thought, our brains became hardwired to both produce and respond to reasons *why*. In fact, *why* packs such a big psychological punch that it can seriously harm you or immensely help you. To lead your best life, you must take control of your *why's*.

It helps to understand that our left brain hemisphere is so talkative—commanding the bulk of our verbal facilities—that, well, it sometimes fabricates *why's* or *why-not's* out of thin air. (Check out the sidebar for more scientific detail.) And sometimes, those left-brain fibs can be downright destructive. In Lynn's case, she inadvertently invited failure by telling herself she lacked willpower. Even though I knew it wasn't true, I didn't want to debate her belief, because that can backfire. When challenged, the loquacious left brain often just fabricates more reasons to prove it's correct.

Has this ever happened to you? Perhaps you had a limiting belief about *why* you could *not* do something, and you wanted to let go of that belief but found it oddly hard to relinquish? In such cases, here is my advice, and one of the principles behind the "Why-Finder": Don't waste too much time consciously arguing with your left brain over imaginary *why-not's*. Instead, if you find and focus on your most meaningful *why-to's*, they—and you—will prevail.

Exploring the Ways to Your Why's

One easy method to arrive at your strongest *why's* is to use my "Why-Finder." By asking and answering each question numerous times, you'll produce a long list of responses for each. Then you distill those results into a few strong statements. I suggest that, as soon as you finish this chapter, you choose a personal goal that has been frustrating you and try it out:

Self-Intelligence 3-D Why-Finder Questions

1. **The inward Why:** Why will this goal matter to you personally (what difference will it make to you in your everyday life)?

WHEN *WHY* GETS WEIRD

As our brains evolved for higher intelligence, we developed the ability to think rationally, reasoning out logical *why's* or *why-not's* to make decisions. Hence we rule planet Earth. But one side effect is that we're now wired to crave cogent reasons for doing things—and this leaves us with a peculiar pair of vulnerabilities. The first is that we like so much to have reasons for what we do that we will buy into even the *illusion* of reason.

Consider this famous experiment by Harvard psychologist Ellen Langer on people waiting to use a library copy machine. She had an actor attempt to cut in line using three different approaches. When the actor said, "Excuse me, I have five pages. May I use the Xerox machine?" only 60 percent of the subjects allowed the actor to cut in. When the actor added a reason *why*, saying, "Excuse me, I have five pages. May I use the Xerox machine, *because* I'm in a rush?" the compliance rate shot up to 94 percent, demonstrating that yes, we humans like having a reason *why to* do something.

But then the next experiment took an odd twist. This time, the actor offered only the *semblance* of a reason, saying, "Excuse me, I have five pages. May I use the Xerox machine, because I have to make some copies?" That's not a real reason to cut in line since everyone in line was there to make copies. Yet just as when confronted with a valid reason, this time nearly everyone again said yes—a full 93 percent. We humans are so programmed to respond to *why's* that simply hearing the word *because* can trigger automatic compliance.

Quite often, Langer says in her pioneering book, *Mindfulness*, it makes little difference to our reason-hungry brains whether a reason is "legitimate or silly."

As if that weren't scary enough, here's the second, related vulnerability: Our left brain hemisphere readily *invents* false reasons. And, because of the first vulnerability, we can then get misdirected by our own fake *why's*. Double trouble!

University of Virginia psychologist Timothy D. Wilson found that when people are asked to just choose an item—say, to pick the tastiest strawberry jam or the most attractive free posters to hang on their walls—they make good choices, that is, choices which happen to concur with expert opinions and which the people themselves remain pleased with over the long term. (Maybe you've

> **This double brain whammy—both inventing and believing our own false why's—also shows up in experiments involving so-called split-brain subjects.**

noticed that when you enter an art gallery, you immediately know what you like, without having to first figure out why.)

But when individuals were asked up front to state *why* they would choose an item, they confused themselves in their rush to produce "logical" justifications—seizing on irrelevant factors, such as saying that this jam tastes better because it's less lumpy, or that's a better poster because it shows a funny animal. Consequently, these people made poor decisions, for example choosing the worst jams and ending up unhappy with the posters they hung on their walls.

This double brain whammy—both inventing *and* believing our own false *why's*—also shows up in experiments involving so-called split-brain subjects. These are epilepsy patients who, in an attempt to control their seizures, have had the communication bridge between the left and the right sides of their brains (called the *corpus callosum*) surgically severed. Testing these unusual subjects has allowed scientists to more clearly differentiate between left- and right-brain behaviors. They've discovered that the left brain is often a liar, a kind of know-it-all who, if asked *why*, will invent an explanation rather than admit it doesn't know.

My apologies that the science here gets a little tricky, so let's start with a couple of basic brain facts that are true for most people. First, while our right brains can understand simple words and phrases, our primary verbal abilities—including the ability to talk—reside in the left brain. Second, our brain connects to our bodies inverse-diagonally, meaning our right brains control the left sides of our bodies, and our left brains control our bodies' right sides. Likewise, what we see in the left visual field goes to our right brain, while what we see in the right visual field goes to our left brain. Now, in a normal person, this information gets transferred back and forth via the corpus callosum. But in a split-brain subject, neither brain hemisphere has any idea what the other half has seen.

Okay, you got all that? Excellent! So what have researchers done with split-brain subjects? Well, among other things, they've simultaneously shown one image to the left side of the brain and a completely different image to the right side of the brain, and then asked some questions. For example, neuroscientist Michael Gazzaniga presented a snow scene to a man's right brain and a chicken claw to his left brain. Next, the man was asked to choose related images from an assortment of cards. With his right hand (which, you remember, is connected to the left brain) he chose an image of a chicken, apparently to go with the chicken claw. With his left hand (which is connected to the right brain), he chose a snow shovel, to go with the snow scene. So far so good.

But the right side of brain can't talk, remember? So when the man was asked, "Why did you choose the shovel?" only the left brain could produce a reply. Because of his split-brain condition, the man's left hemisphere actually had no clue why his right brain chose the shovel image. So his left brain quickly made up a reason, and the man said: "Because you need a shovel to clean out the chicken coop." In a sense, he was lying about why he'd chosen the shovel, although he was completely unconscious of his dishonesty. Many other studies have shown the exact same tendency of the left brain to tell fibs rather than admit it doesn't know the answer.

The research indicates that we are all liars now and then (even if our brains are fully intact). We are all vulnerable to the unconscious compulsion to invent false justifications for doing or having done things, and then to naturally believe our own falsehoods. It may be helpful to remember this glitch whenever stuck in a personal conflict about who did what and why. Since science shows that none of us can completely know ourselves, recalling this fact may help us to avoid petty arguments and to strive for those greater *why's* that bring out the best in everyone.

2. **The upward Why:** Why will it serve your highest purpose for you to succeed?

3. **The onward Why:** Why can you achieve this goal?

The first two questions help to strengthen your resolve and dispel learned helplessness (a phenomenon explained in chapter 8) by connecting you with your core values, your most fundamental guiding beliefs about what's important in this world. These questions help make your goal *meaningful*, a key factor to success which we'll return to shortly. The third question—"Why *can* you succeed at this goal?"—dismantles left-brain *why-not's* without resorting to direct argument.

Using this process, I asked Lynn each question multiple times, until she had no more to say. (You can pose each question over and over again to yourself in the same manner, or have a friend repeatedly ask you. In my seminars, people pair up to do this exercise.) Next, I helped her to identify the most essential elements of her answers, to form a few shorter declarations. We didn't stop working until she felt a profound inner shift, a new sense of determination and confidence. That is how you, as well, will know the process is complete. Your own "Why-Finder" results will of course be unique, but to give you a clearer idea of the kind of summary statements you want to end up with, here are Lynn's:

1. **Lynn's inward Why:** "I want to achieve my goal of physical fitness because I want to feel happy in my skin, an attractive, admirable, self-assured woman, sexy to my husband, proud of myself, and a positive role model for my children and grandchildren."

2. **Lynn's upward Why:** "It will serve my highest purpose to reach this goal because when I help people organize their homes, I teach them how to lead better lives— and I can help more people, and far more effectively, when I'm in great shape, embodying the values that I teach."

3. **Lynn's onward Why:** "I can succeed because I've conquered bigger challenges than this, and by now my abilities to plan, organize, and follow through are stronger than ever. Also, I'll ask for help from the right people, eat delicious foods so I don't feel deprived, be patient with myself when I make mistakes, keep my *why's* top of mind, track my progress, and establish healthy habits to stay fit for the rest of my life."

Lynn agreed to read through her *why's* every week, or any time she could use a boost. "I can feel it now," she said. "I wasn't committed before. I didn't know how important this was to me."

How Long We've Longed for Meaning

Lynn had made her goal *meaningful*. We human beings yearn for *meaning*. Although this drive has been recognized by sages throughout history, some people dismiss it as merely spiritual and therefore nonscientific. Personally, I believe the need for meaning to be so central to your Self-Intelligence that I would be remiss to leave it out of this book. It was perhaps most famously championed following World War II by a physician whose own quest for meaning saved his life against all odds.

Austrian psychiatrist and neurologist Viktor Frankl had been formulating a new branch of psychology, called logotherapy (from *logos*, or "meaning" in Greek), when the Nazis seized him. In essence, logotherapy posits that we experience genuine fulfillment only when we find meaning—the real *why's* in our lives. When he arrived in Auschwitz, he carried hidden in his overcoat lining his life's work: the manuscript codifying logotherapy. Nazi guards immediately found and destroyed it. Far worse, Frankl's father, mother, brother, and wife all died at Nazi hands. From an outsider's perspective, under Hitler's tyranny Frankl lost everything.

Yet, as he later recounted in his by-now classic book, *Man's Search for Meaning*, Frankl managed to survive for three years in the concentration camps with his mind and spirit intact. He endured freezing temperatures, forced labor, brutal hunger, and torture. He cheated death by focusing on his own best reasons to live: his belief in love, including memories of his beloved wife; his development of logotherapy to help humankind; and his will to someday share his story so that people everywhere could learn and benefit from his suffering.

Ultimately, he actualized all three of those *why's*. After the war, he published nearly 40 books and lectured at more than 200 universities worldwide, both about logotherapy and about his years in the camps. Frankl was able even to love and to marry again, and to bring up a daughter.

One of his favorite quotes was by the nineteenth-century philosopher Friedrich Nietzsche: "He who has a *why* to live can bear with almost any *how*." Certainly, Frankl himself had proven that adage to be true. But he also believed that suffering is *not necessary* for us to evolve. In fact, he found that most suffering can be dispelled precisely by finding one's own sense of meaning.

He frequently recounted stories of patients whom he helped to replace destructive *why-not's* with meaningful *why-to's*. For example, an American diplomat who was unhappy

**We human beings
yearn for meaning.**

with his job came to Frankl. The man had undergone Freudian psychoanalysis for five years. His analyst insisted that the real reason why the man did not like his work was that his boss, the U.S. government, "represented" his authoritative father. But Frankl realized that the patient simply longed for deeper purpose, a genuine *why-to*. So Frankl suggested that he pursue some more meaningful career. The man did so, and never looked back.

Frankl taught that when we feel stymied or unfulfilled, we can do one of two things. We can either choose a new goal to support more meaningful *why's*, as did the diplomat, or we can choose new, more meaningful *why's* to support an existing goal, as did Lynn.

Embrace the Ease of Automatic Habits

I shared one more instruction with Lynn during her last session. This may help you, too. Recent research shows that it can be counterproductive to ask ourselves "Why?" so constantly that it interrupts healthy habits. For example, once someone decides never to buy Twinkies again, they will experience more success from then on by automatically following good routines. In contrast, if they were to pause in front of the Twinkies display at every store, trying to remind themselves why not to buy junk food, it would become harder to stay on track. So embrace your *why's* when making big decisions, or to give yourself a general motivational boost, but once you've set up smart routines, allow the ease of automaticity to help you succeed.

Five months after our call, Lynn's holiday card arrived in a sparkly gold envelope. Inside was a family photo, which I took to be of Lynn, her husband, their three daughters, three sons-in-law, and the two small grandchildren. It was a handsome family, and Lynn looked elegant in her red dress—not skinny like an anorexic model, but dynamic and curvy. And yes, with her wide-set eyes, and high cheekbones, she did indeed resemble Angela Bassett.

"What do you think, Jane?" she wrote. "No 'before' pic, because I believe in destroying criminal evidence, ha-ha. I've lost forty pounds and expect to keep getting foxier until my body stabilizes. Then I'm going shopping. I wanted to send you a box of cereal with a toy in it, but it seems they no longer exist. I'd send you a Happy Meal with a free super-hero, because that's what I am now (invincible!), but that food is good only when it's hot. Trust me, you don't want to eat it cold. My grandkids and I go only once a month to McDonald's now. I eat something beforehand so all I have there is the fries. I'm glad you told me not to completely deprive myself, and am thinking of adding 'McDonald's fries' to my '3-D Why-Finder' list as a reason to live. But seriously, I'm doing great, and hope that you are too. Happy Holidays!"

By defining her deepest, highest, and most self-empowering *why's*, Lynn had come up with the inner strength to achieve her objective. Now it's your turn. Choose a goal that has previously thwarted you, then go ahead and access the Self-Intelligence of *why*. Once you align your aspirations with what you truly care about, then you, too, will become invincible.

Use Your Self-Intelligence

Now that you understand how asking "Why?" affects the brain, use the question wisely.

Surveys by The Energy Project, reaching 20,000 employees, compared people who derive meaning from their jobs with those who don't. People with strong *why's* at work are more than three times as likely to stay with their organizations and 1.7 times more satisfied with what they do. Whether you're a boss, employee or solopreneur, defining a meaningful *why* for your work—and sharing that *why* with people around you—will foster engagement and success.

Whether you want to lose weight or just get more fit, follow Lynn's example and use the "Why-Finder" to discover your *why-to's* and *why-can-you's*. Then immediately begin taking action to establish healthy lifelong habits, reviewing your *why's* regularly to stay on track.

Want to energize your relationship? Write out a list of twenty-five reasons *why* you love your partner, and give it to them. Bonus points for them if they step up to do the same. Or, are you single? You can do this for family or friends, or write out a list of twenty-five reasons why you love yourself. Review it, and *add to it*, regularly. Your self-worth will rise accordingly.

Money is meaningless. It's what you can do with it that matters. If you want more money in the bank, first set an ambitious but attainable goal as to how

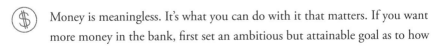

much you want to have and by when (say, $1 million within five years, or whatever's right for you), then apply the "3-D Why-Finder" to make your goal more inspiring, as well as less intimidating due to the *why-can-you's*.

Quiz answer: As we humans have evolved our capacity for reason and logic, we've come to the point that . . .

    c.   put on the spot, our brains will generate bogus explanations to answer the questions, "Why?" or "Why not?"

In a Nutshell

"Why" is one of the most powerful motivators we can use to achieve our goals. We're hardwired to want reasons for what we do or don't do. As long as we understand how the brain works, we can harness the power of "why" to our benefit. But because our talkative left brains will actually invent reasons "why" or "why not" out of thin air, sometimes the wrong *why's* can steer us off track. We humans long to lead meaningful lives, so one effective way to achieve your goals is to access your deepest *why-to's*. It also helps to focus on why you *can* succeed. The science can seem complex, so use my easy "3-D Why-Finder" to find your way around *Why*.

Every artist was first an amateur.

–RALPH WALDO EMERSON

CHAPTER 18

TALENT

Schmalent!
Don't Let the Fallacy Hold You Back

Prime-your-mind Quiz

Research says you'll remember this chapter better if you test yourself now. How will the answer affect *you?*

It is true that . . .

a. most scientists who study "talent" conclude that there's no such thing.

b. Wolfgang Amadeus Mozart was talented from birth.

c. telling someone they're talented tends to increase their confidence.

Before we even finished shaking hands, Jasper—a tall, bald seventy-year-old with a dignified air—began to confess. "I do apologize, but on the phone I described my problem as anxiety. However, it's much more embarrassing than that." He sat down, pressed one fist against his mouth, as if figuring out how to deliver some horrific news, then burst out: "I have writer's block!"

Knowing that this condition can seem, to a creative person, almost as sinister as the bubonic plague, I did not laugh.

Jasper explained that he was retired, having left his banking job five years earlier with plans to become a novelist. He had written for fun throughout high school; in college, he published several short pieces in literary magazines. Publication led his well-meaning parents and friends to enthusiastically praise his "talent," and it was around that time that he began to think of himself as "talented." Soon life got awfully busy, and he found himself writing less. The day after college graduation, he married Betsy. One year later, Jasper was a full-time bank employee and the proud father of twin sons. He began to think of himself as a talented writer on a long hiatus.

"Betsy knew about my talent, so we both looked forward to how well I would do after retirement—you know, the great American novel and all that. But it's been five years since I left work and I've accomplished nothing." He told me that he felt, among other things, confused and defeated. Some mornings he stared at his computer screen, waiting for inspiration. Or he'd start in on a story only to lose interest and discard it. Other times, he'd take a pen and notebook to a nearby state park, hoping Mother Nature might be his muse.

"I thought writer's block only afflicted those poor souls who weren't really talented. But it's paralyzing me. Can you get rid of it with hypnosis?"

I told him that, while hypnosis might help, if he wanted to permanently escape from his writer's block, he should stop thinking of himself as *talented*.

He looked startled. "You don't believe I'm talented?"

"I don't believe *anybody* is particularly talented," I said. "But even if you were somehow genetically superior to most other people, I believe you'd be better off forgetting about it."

Minding Your Mindset

Revolutionary research led by Stanford University psychologist Carol Dweck reveals that seeing yourself as "talented" can dramatically reduce your ability to succeed. Jasper eventually came to realize that ever since college, he'd been suffering from what Dweck calls a *fixed mindset*. Having helped free many clients from creative blocks, I can attest that a fixed mindset is almost always to blame. It afflicts people who believe they are *not* talented, as well as people who believe that they are.

But hold on a minute. This book aims to serve *you*, so before we go any further, let's check *your* mindset. For each one of the following statements, make a note of whether you mostly agree, or mostly disagree:

A. Whether or not you have "talent" in any area is something very basic about you that you can't change much.

B. You can work throughout life to become somewhat better at an art or a sport, but your ultimate progress will be defined by how much "talent" you were born with.

C. No matter how "talented" or not you may be, you can always change your ability a lot.

D. With effort, you can substantially change your level of ability in almost any area.

Did you mostly agree with A and B, or with C and D? If you mostly agreed with A and B, then at this moment you have a *fixed mindset* about talent. If on the other hand, you agreed with C and D, then yours is what Dweck terms a *growth mindset*. (Typically, your mindset about talent will match your mindset about intelligence. To find out for sure, take Dweck's test in the sidebar "Your IQ IQ.")

Fixed-mindset folks believe that talent is an inherited trait; you're either talented or not. Growth-mindset proponents trust that our ability in any area is primarily determined by the encouragement and teaching we receive, plus the effort we put in. If you tested as having a fixed mindset, I invite you to change your mind. Two recent lines of research converge that support the growth mindset:

1. High-tech imaging studies reveal that, due to brain plasticity, our brains are physically re-forming every day throughout our lives, letting go of old neural connections *and creating* new ones. Whether you become worse or better at any particular skill all depends on how (and how much) you apply yourself. The centuries-old notion that human abilities and intelligence were fixed from infancy (or even by the end of childhood) has been utterly overturned.

2. Scores of scientists investigating expertise and top performance have arrived at a myth-busting conclusion: *Talent is either irrelevant or does not exist.*

   Over the last decades, across a wide variety of fields, scientists have investigated the outstanding expertise and extraordinary performance that was long associated with *talent*. Researchers across the world have scrutinized superstars in music, sports, chess, writing, surgery, acting, aviation, ballet, firefighting, computer programming, and other endeavors where top achievers were typically assumed to be talented.

In almost every case of outstanding ability, the scientists found, inborn "talent" had little or nothing to do with it. Yes, it may be that some people are innately better at detecting differences in musical pitch, or that tall people have an advantage playing basketball. But if by "talent," we mean a purely DNA-driven capacity to truly excel at something . . . most researchers conclude there's no such thing.

"Consistently and overwhelmingly, the evidence showed that experts are always made, not born," reports K. Anders Ericsson, perhaps the world's most respected scientist on the topic, as well as editor of the *Cambridge Handbook of Expertise and Expert Performance*. This 900-plus-page tome offers research by more than 100 leading scientists who study ultra-achievers. "These conclusions are based on rigorous research that looked at exceptional performance using scientific methods that are verifiable and reproducible," writes Ericsson. In other words: *talent, schmalent.*

YOUR IQ IQ

Let's use scientist Carol Dweck's test to determine your mindset regarding intelligence. For each one of the following statements, decide whether you mostly agree or mostly disagree:

1. Your intelligence is something very basic about you that you can't change much.

2. You can learn new things, but you can't really change how intelligent you are.

3. No matter how much intelligence you have, you can always change it quite a bit.

4. You can always substantially change how intelligent you are.

Choices 1 and 2 indicate a fixed mindset, while 3 and 4 show a growth mindset. Just as with talent, due to brain plasticity, the growth mindset proves correct: our IQ changes over time, according to how we don't or do use our minds. Although this may still shock some people, it would not have surprised the inventor of the IQ test, Alfred Binet. The Frenchman worked with hundreds of children who suffered learning difficulties largely caused, in his opinion, by a bad education. With improved teaching, he found, the children became smarter. Indeed, he designed the IQ test in order to spot those kids who needed better teachers.

The point isn't that we're all identically intelligent. The point is that with well-guided effort, any one of us can *change* our intelligence. Summing up his findings, Binet wrote that "a few modern philosophers . . . assert that an individual's intelligence is a fixed quantity . . . which cannot be increased. We must protest and react against this brutal pessimism . . . . With practice, training, and above all, method, we managed to increase our attention, our memory, our judgment, and literally to become more intelligent than we were before."

Put simply, IQ is not a fixed trait. Nor does IQ fully describe anyone's mental abilities. For example, research shows that most chess grandmasters have average IQs, and some test below average. Yet these champions are *very smart* at chess. The time they've put in—thousands of hours spent practicing and studying chess—has wired their brains for so-called *pattern recognition*, a particular form of intelligence (one which some scientists say may be our most valuable) that can be acquired only through sustained learning over time.

Scientists can detect clear brain differences between fixed- and growth-mindset subjects, particularly in their responses to making mistakes. Michigan State University researchers gave subjects the same repetitive computer task, then watched what happened in the brain when subjects slipped up. Everyone showed error-awareness whenever they made a mistake. But only some subjects' brains strongly registered so-called *error positivity*, indicating a desire to learn from their mistakes. Those subjects improved their performance over the course of the experiment. Afterward, scientists asked everyone whether they believed intelligence was fixed or could be learned. Sure enough, it was the fixed-mindset folks whose brains had failed to show much error positivity, and whose performance therefore stalled. The growth-mindset subjects were wired to learn, grow, and ultimately succeed.

Dweck got similar results when she brought subjects into the brain-wave lab at Columbia University. Researchers asked the subjects hard questions, then gave them feedback on their answers. All subjects' brains indicated interest in finding out whether they'd gotten answers right or wrong. But a big difference surfaced when scientists then presented information that would help subjects learn the correct answers. Growth-mindset brain waves revealed an eagerness to learn. The fixed-mindset subjects showed no interest at all in learning. The fixed mindset had effectively shut them down.

But then how to explain the likes of Wolfgang Amadeus Mozart or Ben Franklin, Tiger Woods or even Warren Buffet? Research reveals that typically, three factors—none involving special DNA—combine to produce extraordinary achievement: a supportive childhood environment, excellent teachers and, most important of all, *sustained effort.*

"I'm still trying to wrap my head around this," Jasper said after I'd done my best to summarize the research, plus recommended Dweck's book *Mindset.* "If I'm not talented, how come I got published in college?"

"Maybe because you had already been writing for years. You say you wrote all through high school. That's a lot of practice."

"Oh, before that, too. I've always loved to write. Or at least, I *did*, before it became torture." He pressed his fingertips together to form a sort of spherical cage, which he stared down into, as if into a crystal ball. "None of my favorite writers are talented, either, according to this theory. That's rather encouraging."

Eventually, Jasper headed out of my office looking more chipper than when he'd come in. But at the door, he turned back, like Peter Falk in the old *Columbo* series: "Just one more thing. Are you implying that my belief in talent was actually *causing* my writer's block?" I nodded affirmatively.

This is where, in my opinion, the new science gets even juicier. The findings seem, at first, counterintuitive. Studies show that believing yourself to be "smart" or "talented" undermines genuine confidence. It instills a subconscious fear of failure so insidious that it can prevent you from actually making the effort, taking the risks, or embracing the challenges *necessary* to succeed.

For authors, this subconscious fear turns into writer's block. As Ernest Hemingway famously said, "The first draft of anything is shit." To produce something good, even the best writers typically begin by drafting something bad. But writers who believe in talent tend to believe they should be able to create masterpieces fast. So rather than risk penning crap, they find it safer not to try at all.

The Praise That Is Dangerous

When I first read Dweck's work, it explained a mystery that had haunted me for years. While teaching at Rutgers and New York universities, I had naively attempted to encourage my creative-writing students by saying, "You're very smart," or "You're so talented." One day one of my *smart, talented* students submitted a plagiarized poem. It couldn't have been for the grade, because poems weren't graded. What had led this young man to cheat?

Well, brand new poems—which have not yet been honed—can be quite awful at their inception, like ugly babies who need time to grow. Now I understand that my student was afraid to look untalented; even worse, my misguided praise had helped instill that fear in him.

Dweck's research shows that praising people's supposedly inherited traits—intelligence or talent of any kind—subconsciously programs them with a fixed mindset. They internally adopt the labels "smart" or "talented" as their birthright identity. They then automatically resist putting in actual effort, lest such exertion call their supposedly natural abilities into question.

Ironically, the less motivated they become to *work* toward success, the more desperate they may become to *appear* successful. Instead of *trying*, they often end up *lying*. Dweck and her colleagues discovered this sad fact by conducting studies with hundreds of adolescent students. They began by giving all the students the same nonverbal IQ test. Then they divided them into two groups, told all the students they had done well, but instilled only one group with a fixed mindset by praising their intelligence, saying, "That's a really good score. You must be really smart at this."

Immediately the praised group began to exhibit a fixed mindset, for example by giving up quickly when faced with difficult problems. Researchers also gave the students a page to write down their thoughts about the test—supposedly to help out kids at another school—and left a space for the subjects to state their own scores. A full 40 percent of the fixed-mindset subjects lied, reporting higher scores than they'd actually achieved. As Dweck explains: "In the fixed mindset, imperfections are shameful—especially if you're talented—so they lied them away."

Looking back, I'm grateful I didn't punish my student for plagiarizing, but simply requested he write a poem of his own, which he did. (My first inclination was to fail him, but my older and wiser creative-writing program director advised me to be kind, instead.) I can only hope that since then, life has ushered my former student away from a belief in talent and into a growth mindset. Because, yes, *that* is the simple cure: switching to a growth mindset.

Growing Your Growth Mindset

Dweck and other researchers studying athletes, performance artists, businesspeople, and students have found that a fixed mindset can sabotage success in any field and at any age (even as early as four years old). But scientists also have discovered how to do subconscious surgery, as it were, replacing the fixed mindset with a growth mindset.

First comes education, dislodging false beliefs about innate ability while also explaining brain plasticity. Even a child can easily grasp that using our brains will make us smarter. But how to spark that new knowledge into action? You recall that *praise* can implant a fixed mindset, causing creative paralysis. Well, praise of a different sort will accomplish the opposite. Praising *effort* instills a growth mindset and ignites *more* effort.

Remember the students in Dweck's experiment who all took the same nonverbal IQ test? Only half were then programmed with a fixed mindset by praising their intelligence. The other half received almost identical praise, with a key difference. They were told: "That's a really good score. *You must have worked really hard.*" These effort-praised kids immediately adopted a growth mindset. They enthusiastically tackled more difficult problems, quickly improved their overall performance, and soon left the fixed-mindset kids in the proverbial dust.

As Dweck reports, "Since this was a kind of IQ test, you might say that praising ability lowered the students' IQs. And praising their effort raised them." Imagine that! Praising intelligence lowers intelligence. Praising effort raises intelligence and spurs more effort, which will in turn further increase intelligence. Parents, teachers, and bosses, please take note: If you want to help others to be their best, praise people not for what they *are*, but for what they *do*.

But what if *you* are the target of harmful praise? What do you do if someone tells you that you're smart or talented? First, resist letting it bloat your ego. If the situation allows, deflect such flattery by saying, "I work hard," or "It's all about practice," or "I put in the hours." In other words, praise yourself for effort. This will strengthen your own growth mindset, building authentic confidence and motivating you to create real success.

It took a few weeks for Jasper to change his mind. But once he stopped calling himself "talented," he was able to get to work. Is he a household name in fiction yet? No, but he's writing. Is it easy? Nope. Does it require discipline? Yep. Is he enjoying more genuine self-esteem than before? *Yes.*

"I feel free now," he reported. "Every day throwing words onto the page, I'm making a delightful mess, like a kid in a mud puddle. Betsy says I'm both more relaxed and more driven than she's ever seen me. Nice paradox, that."

If you began this chapter with a *fixed mindset*—believing in the existence and importance of talent—I hope that you have begun to change your outlook. If you already boasted a *growth mindset*, I hope that now, you feel even more determined to follow your dreams. May you, too, be freed by the knowledge that your DNA does not determine your destiny. May you be empowered by knowing, with scientific certainty, that you are master of your own success.

Use Your Self-Intelligence

Internalize a growth mindset of valuing effort to reap real results that bring real satisfaction.

As a professional, remember to value people not for what you think they are but for what they *do*. Avoid the Enron effect, in which the illusion of talent trumps actual results. Practice praising others and yourself for strategic effort—including learning from mistakes—to ignite genuine confidence and motivation.

Just as we develop our brains through sustained effort, so do our bodies. Quick-fix fads such as crash diets and two-minute workouts doom people to failure and rob them of personal power. What is one small, daily habit that you could commit to for the long term, to become healthier? Start today, and over time build on your progress to get more fit and *stay* that way.

Adopt a growth mindset toward your relationships. All meaningful relationships—romantic or platonic—need to be nourished through conscious effort. People who believe they shouldn't have to "work" at their relationships tend to end up alone. By embracing the "work," you sustain the fun!

People with fixed mindsets can be vulnerable to get-rich-quick schemes. Don't fall for illusions. With a healthy attitude of steadfastly building value over time, you will be a better judge of where and when to invest.

Quiz answer: It is true that . . .

a. most scientists who study "talent" conclude that there's no such thing.

In a Nutshell

Scientific studies of talent indicate that it's a myth. Superstars in any field may appear to succeed effortlessly, but that illusion results from years of training. Moreover, a belief in talent can actually sabotage success. Praising "talent" instills a harmful *fixed mindset*, while praising effort plants a *growth mindset*, which leads to achievement. When praising yourself or others, forget about supposedly innate traits such as talent or intelligence. Instead, celebrate the effort people make and the good strategies they employ. Praise not what people *are* but what they *do*.

You can't be that kid standing at the top of the waterslide, overthinking it. You have to go down the chute.

—TINA FEY

CHAPTER 19

ACTION

Don't Talk, Just *Do*

Prime-your-mind Quiz

Research says you'll remember this chapter better if you test yourself now. How will the answer affect you?

Thinking or talking about an action that you should take . . .

a. always will motivate you to act responsibly.

b. may lead you to avoid taking the action.

c. produces no particular effect beyond wasting time.

Now I'm a vigorous, trim, fitness enthusiast, but there was a time when I was chubby. It began my senior year of high school, when I caught mononucleosis. The doctor said to relax, rest, eat. For a month I convalesced according to the doctor's orders, consequently gaining ten pounds. Soon after, I went off to college at Indiana University, where the abundance of dorm food helped me put on fifteen more pounds—a lot for someone of my narrow build and five-foot-four-inch height.

The larger I grew, the more I found myself discussing appropriate actions. Enjoying chocolate sundaes with my girlfriends, I'd observe, "You know, I really should start watching calories and going to the gym." Talking about what I should do invariably made me feel better. Most of my Indiana girlfriends could be counted on to politely laugh it off, which also made me feel good.

But one friend, Judy, was a native New Yorker whose communication style was remarkably straightforward. She was annoyed enough by my idle complaining that one day she burst out, "You're a liar! Every day you're saying these lies and I'm sick of it. If you really wanted to lose weight, you would do it." Her words shook me up. For several days, I felt humiliated and resentful. *Boy,* I told myself, *was that Judy mean.*

But she'd done me an enormous favor. She'd told me the truth. And you know what? The truth freed me from my comfort zone. Comfort zones are mostly subconscious, and I might have blithely remained in mine for years had she not spoken up. After that, it became no longer possible for me to maintain a comfort zone of *shoulds.* In fact, the very next day I took action. I began jogging. I began to responsibly choose what to eat and how much. Over just a few months I shed twenty-five pounds (11 kg). It was astonishingly easy to exercise, eat right, and lose weight once I stopped talking about it and decided simply to *do it*. (And, by the way, I did not go on a diet. Research shows diets don't work; if people lose weight on diets, afterward they tend to gain back even more pounds. Instead, I embraced a lifestyle shift of eating smaller portions and fewer carbs.)

It seems natural to talk about our problems and the actions we should take. But sometimes words can backfire. Reflect on whether you've ever had the following experience. You and your partner are going out for the evening, and one of you says, "Darling, on the way home, don't let me forget to stop and buy eggs." The other nods consent. Have you noticed how such interactions can create an immediate sense of reassurance so that now both of you are doomed to forget the eggs?

The False Rewards of "Should Do" Thoughts

Research shows that sometimes merely thinking (even briefly) about what you *really should do* may create a false sense of accomplishment. Consider this strange-but-true experiment: Two groups of college students were each given short menus from which to order food. Both menus included two moderately healthy items—chicken nuggets and a baked potato—and one clearly unhealthy item—french fries. Those three items were all that Group A's menu included. Group B's menu offered those same items plus one additional option that was clearly healthier than all the rest—salad. Salad was a *should-do* option, expected to elicit an inner response of, "I really should order that salad."

So what difference do you think offering the *should-do* option made? Well, the group who got to consider the possibility of ordering salad became three times more likely than the other group to order . . . *french fries!*

Whoa. What the heck happened? Scientists concluded that the mere thought of ordering salad triggered enough subconscious self-congratulations in the participants that they felt entitled to indulge in fries.

And wait, it gets weirder. Ask yourself this: Of the group who saw salad on their menu, which students do you think were the most likely to order fries—those with low to average self-control, or those rated (according to a standardized test) as having the highest self-control? Life is stranger than fiction: those with the highest rated self-control went for the fries.

Now don't slam this book shut and give up on science quite yet. The results actually make neurobiological sense. Why? Because people who regularly practice self-control have conditioned their own brains to enjoy doing the right thing. For them, what usually happens is that self-disciplined behavior triggers the release of neurochemical rewards that help them feel good. But there's one little bug in the system: The subconscious mind often fails to differentiate between what's real and what's imagined. Apparently, the quick thought of ordering salad was subconsciously interpreted as *having ordered* salad. Thus, the brain released its neurochemical reward, which in turn made those students feel self-congratulatory enough to justify pigging out on fries—instead of *actually* ordering salad.

How does this apply to the rest of us? It teaches us to beware of that bug in the brain's system that can lull us into avoiding responsible action. We need to watch out for the false rewards generated by talking—or at times merely thinking—about what we *should do*. We can make this awareness a habit, and we can also rewire our brains for the better by creating an *action habit*—not mere self-restraint but rather a habit of taking responsible action.

For example, when a weight-loss client works with me, we focus less on what to avoid doing and more on what *to do*. Such as: get enough sleep, have a healthy breakfast, eat plenty of protein, walk to the office, pass the elevator and use the stairs. Taking action is more positive—and far more effective—for them than trying to "not eat french fries." Once the clients have established an *action habit*, many old temptations fade away and others become irrelevant (since, for example, eating fries now and then does not, in itself, make you fat). And life becomes more exciting as every client becomes his or her own action hero.

There's a proverb, "If you want something done, ask a busy man." The busy man gets things done because he has an *action habit*.

Getting Out of a Rut and Into an Action Habit

If you look up the "busy man" proverb online, you'll see that on some pages, web users have changed the old saying to a gender-neutral "busy person." In my work, I've found that action-taking can pose bigger challenges for women. Historically, females have been conditioned to behave as passive followers. My tactic is to put these women in the driver's seat by teaching them the *action habit*. When a female client learns to assert herself by taking action, her confidence and self-esteem both blossom.

My client Kristen wanted to travel in Europe, but her husband refused. At first, she strongly objected when I suggested she could simply go without him. She was used to following his lead rather than her own, where travel was concerned. This was true despite the fact that at her job, she was quite assertive and independent.

As a human resources director, Kristen took pride in her problem-solving abilities. So eliciting change became a matter of reframing the issue as her own—rather than her husband's. "Kristen, just hypothetically, if your company asked you to figure out a way to enjoy yourself traveling in Europe without Alex, how would you do it?" I asked. Being a good sport, Kristen accepted the hypothetical problem as her homework assignment.

During the hypnosis part of that same session, I helped her let go of resentment against Alex, which was something we'd been working on already, since her main aim in our sessions had been to improve her marriage. Well, here's some inside info on resentment: Just like over-talking, the bad habit of resentment can impede constructive action. Conversely, letting go of resentment helps propel you forward.

Kristen left the session feeling great, and the following week she arrived excited. She had, she announced, figured things out. She'd begun by asking her best girlfriends, "just hypothetically," if they would travel with her, but most of them were married and, like her, accustomed to relying on their mates. "It made me so mad!" she told me. It had surprised Kristen that their hesitant responses annoyed her. Realizing that she disliked this trait *in them* gave her a new perspective on herself. She'd then done research online and found a group bicycle tour in France that sounded fun . . . hypothetically.

The homework assignment officially ended there, but over the next several sessions, as she began to see how doable her plan actually was, Kristen made her own decision to act. She told me, "I'm going, but it's not till July, which gives both my boss and Alex plenty of notice." A week later, she announced with a big smile, "When I told Alex I was going alone, he almost fell over, he was so shocked." She was proud of herself.

And then came a truly nice surprise. Within two months, by late April, when we finished our sessions, Alex had already signed up to go along. Kristen's determination had impressed him, and he didn't want to be left behind. To slightly rephrase Albert Einstein, "A leader leads by example, whether she intends to or not."

Leaders are people who take action. In my Self-Intelligence leadership workshops, I ask participants to choose a top goal. Then we have a fifteen-minute break during which they're required to take action toward that goal—for example, by making a phone call, setting an appointment, or ordering a book. I learned this powerful exercise from Jack Canfield, and it always works. After taking even just a small action (albeit toward a big goal) attendees exhibit greater confidence, motivation, and energy. Clients tell me the effect lasts long after the workshop . . . as long, in fact, as they continue taking action.

Traditional psychotherapy, which relies on talking things out, can require months or years for patients to improve. Many people go to therapists because they want to feel better about themselves, and often they wait until they feel better before taking more concrete actions to change their lives. But one increasingly popular approach, called behavioral-activation (BA) therapy, embraces action over words. BA therapists urge patients to immediately begin *doing things*—whether it's going for walks, updating a resume, or pursuing a hobby—to enhance their well-being. Studies show that this action-first strategy can free patients from habitual lethargy even after other treatments have failed.

It's not that we should never analyze our personal issues, only that it won't help us to discuss them ad nauseum or make them too complicated. In fact, as you'll see in the sidebar "Keep It Simple, Sherlock," the more simply we can state both our problems and our solutions, the easier it becomes for us to succeed.

Franz Kafka wrote a terrific parable, *Before the Law*, about a man who spends his life waiting for a gatekeeper to let him into the land where he wants to go. The gate is open, but the man is afraid to act without the gatekeeper's invitation, so he expends all his energy beseeching the gatekeeper, who encourages him to talk and talk and talk. Decades go by like this. Just before he dies, the gatekeeper cruelly reveals to him that the man has only himself to blame for his wasted life, announcing that, "this gate was made only for you. I am now going to shut it."

Never relinquish your agency to act by waiting for approval, or by talking—or even *thinking*—your way into a comfort zone of passivity. Whenever you hear yourself discussing what you should do, or would do, or wish would happen—stop talking. Take action.

KEEP IT SIMPLE, SHERLOCK

If you've watched a lot of Sherlock Holmes films, you know how satisfying it is when the detective unveils his solution as being "elementary, my dear Watson, elementary." Complications fall away while the answer shines forth as so basic that it seems downright obvious. *Ahhh.*

Scientific research confirms that we subconsciously prefer whatever appears basic over that which seems complicated. You can use this tendency to your advantage. Simplifying both your problems and your solutions will help you to avert overthinking and act effectively.

Here's a personal example; please feel free to laugh with me at my mistake. I made a problem absurdly complex, and thus ended up unnecessarily suffering for years. The problem was, I'd get so cold at night (due to low blood pressure, poor circulation, hormonal conditions, blah blah blah) that in order to go to bed in the winter, I'd first take a hot bath, then don pajamas, sweatpants, sweatshirt, socks and sometimes mittens plus hat, because . . . there was a draft in my apartment, I wanted to keep utility costs down, the heater was too loud, there was no insulation, blah blah. Then my neighbor Ann asked me why I didn't just get a low-voltage electric blanket. Oh. Eh. Um. Because I'd been too busy making my problem complicated, that's why! Now I'm like Linus with my electric blanket. It's so warm and cozy, I won't give it up for anything. *Ahhh.*

Studies show that when people are given written instructions—whether it's for cooking a meal, choosing a product, or doing a physical exercise—they're more likely to complete the project if instructions are printed in this basic typeface rather than, say, this **FANCY-PANTS TYPEFACE**. The simpler font subconsciously convinces people that the activity is easier, which makes them feel less intimidated and more motivated.

Scientists hypothesize that our brains evolved to prefer simplicity over complication because saving time has helped us survive. In his classic book *Influence*, business psychology guru Robert Cialdini brilliantly describes how top marketers woo consumers by appealing to this time-saving urge. (Have you ever noticed how easy it can be to click a *Buy Now* button?) That's how *they* influence *you*. But you can use the very same insight to *influence yourself* to achieve success. That's Self-Intelligence.

Is there some challenge you've allowed to persist in your life because it seemed too complex to tackle? If so, try redescribing the issue in simpler terms, plainly define your goal, and clearly list the first steps you will take toward success. Notice how good it feels to get rid of that overly complicated inner gridlock. *Ahhh.*

Use Your Self-Intelligence

Ready, set, go! Decide what actions to take, then act ASAP. Is it time to . . .

 Ask for a raise? Schedule lunch with a potential networking partner? Start a business?

 Hire a trainer? Begin swimming? Take a healthy-meal cooking class?

 Book a romantic weekend with your longtime partner? Put the word out to friends that you're single and looking? Make amends with a family member?

 Meet with a financial planner? Enroll in an automatic savings plan? Invest in stock, bonds, or real estate?

Quiz answer: Thinking or talking about an action that you should take . . .

   b.   may lead you to avoid taking the action.

In a Nutshell

 Beware of lulling yourself into inaction by overdiscussing what you should do. Unfortunately, that can trick the brain into believing you've already done it. Condition your synapses to be action-oriented by developing an *action habit*. Talk less, *do* more.

It is very important for every human being to forgive herself or himself because if you live, you will make mistakes . . . . If we all hold on to the mistake, we can't see our own glory in the mirror because we have the mistake between our faces and the mirror; we can't see what we're capable of being.

—MAYA ANGELOU

CHAPTER 20

THE ZEN OF SELF-FORGIVENESS

When Every Mistake Is and Is Not a Mistake

Prime-your-mind Quiz

Research says you'll remember this chapter better if you test yourself now. How will the answer affect *you*?

Studies show that one effective strategy to help you achieve your goals is to . . .

a. upbraid yourself for each failure so that you take full responsibility.

b. make it clear to others that you won't put up with mistakes.

c. let go of guilt or shame as soon as possible.

If you're reading this book cover-to-cover, then by now you've gained deep insight into the power of your subconscious mind to either hold you back—or to propel you forth to achieve great things. You've discovered that by consciously directing your thoughts and actions, you can deliberately rewire your brain, thus reprogramming your subconscious mind in order to do and be your best. And you've explored dozens of scientifically proven Self-Intelligence strategies to turn your life around faster and more easily than perhaps you previously thought possible.

Nevertheless, you are going to screw up. There, I said it.

Despite your best intentions and greatest efforts, the truth is that, along the way to achieving your dreams, you will commit errors. So get ready for the most important question that I'll have asked you throughout this entire book: How do you treat yourself when you make mistakes?

If you pile on self-criticism, chastising yourself with guilt and shame—well, of all the myriad wrong turns we've discussed in these twenty chapters, that would be the very worst. Kicking yourself when you're down triggers a natural brain reaction that guts your self-discipline, robs you of motivation, and can throw you into a slippery spiral of further failure.

Sound like hell? As it happens, scientists call it the *what-the-hell effect*, although not because it creates a hellish experience. The name refers to our brain-wired compulsion to

"Kicking yourself when you're down triggers a natural brain reaction that guts your self-discipline, robs you of motivation, and can throw you into a slippery spiral of further failure.

pile one mistake on top of another, particularly when we're trying to establish new habits. Castigating ourselves for failing once immediately creates a subconscious sense that all is lost, so our brain decides to fail again, as if thinking, "Oh well, what the hell." And then it happens again, and again, thwarting our attempts to stay on a good-habit track. This makes the effect a sinister enemy of positive change since, as you recall, long-term positive change depends on maintaining good habits. In her book *The Willpower Instinct*, Stanford psychologist Kelly McGonigal declares the what-the-hell phenomenon to be "one of the biggest threats to willpower worldwide."

Good-bye Guilt, Hello "Warm and Fuzzy"

Ben came to see me in a state of self-condemnation. A Vietnam veteran and the son of a verbally abusive father, he had survived enormous challenges to create an impressive life. He had built a profitable delivery-service company in a highly competitive market. He had married a lovely woman twenty years his junior, and they now had two fine teenage sons. "But look at me," he demanded. "What a pathetic bum."

Ben was out of shape, to put it mildly. He explained that after being a weight lifter in his youth, in middle age he'd begun slacking off. As he leaned back in my office recliner, his beer belly protruded so far it threatened to pop his shirt buttons. "I bought a gym membership four months ago and haven't gone once," he said.

Ben also was experiencing trouble at home and at work. He believed his wife no longer appreciated him; he was considering divorce. He felt fed up with several employees whose "bad attitudes" he blamed for his company's poor last quarter. Tired of trying to discipline them, he thought maybe he should fire them. He was angry with everybody around him, but most of all he was furious at himself. When asked to choose one issue to focus on first, he said, "I'm a fat, lazy slob. I want you to use hypnosis to make me get off my butt."

I shook my head. As you may remember from chapter 4, contrary to common mythology, hypnosis cannot *make* anyone do anything. Moreover, hypnotic suggestions that seem scolding or upbraiding tend to fail. In contrast, what you might call a "warm and fuzzy" hypnotic approach can work astonishingly well. (In my opinion, Mother Teresa would have made a better hypnotist than would, say, Bobby Knight.) I suggested to Ben that we use hypnosis to give him an emotional hug, as it were—boosting self-forgiveness and helping him to let go of any guilt about his physical shape.

Ben responded well to the session. Afterward, he agreed to refrain, as best he could, from harsh self-criticism. I suggested that whenever he "failed" in any way, he mentally step back to view himself with compassion, the way one might view a one-year-old who was learning to walk, who was repeatedly falling down yet making inevitable progress.

Over the next two months, Ben became more and more comfortable with the process. His mood lifted, he began to laugh at himself more, and then we zeroed in on his fitness goal. He started going to the gym—first a couple of times a week, then three times, then four. He also began to positively reassess other aspects of his life, a happy side effect we'll return to shortly.

The Fortuitous Fact about Self-Forgiveness

Let me ask: Are you hard on yourself when you make mistakes, fail to achieve your goals, or otherwise get off track in life? Here's the rock-solid, scientific truth. If you want to procrastinate less and achieve more, get fit, or accomplish virtually any other worthy personal goal you find difficult, you will have an easier time of it if you first become kinder and gentler toward *you*.

Many people find this hard to believe.

When I teach this in Self-Intelligence workshops, there is always at least one person who becomes so alarmed it's a wonder they don't bolt from the room. Their protests typically go something like this: "That *cannot* be right. The problem is, I'm too easy on myself as it is!" I empathize with their consternation. They just happen to be wrong.

Since the term was coined in 1985 by dieting researchers Janet Polivy and C. Peter Herman, scientists have confirmed that the *what-the-hell effect* plagues pretty much everyone who tries to motivate themselves through guilt. Here are just three of many studies on this subconscious tripwire:

- Some 150 adults were directed to record how much they drank each night, then the next morning to write down how they felt about it. Some of the subjects drank too much. Many of those who had overdrunk beat themselves up with guilt and shame the next day. Well, guess what? Scientists discovered that the *worse* the person *felt* about overdrinking, the *more* likely they were to overdrink on the following night, and on the night after that.

- Researchers tracked students' study habits at a Canadian university for one semester. A great many of the students procrastinated over studying for their first exam.

Some forgave themselves for procrastinating; others chastised themselves. Results showed that those who were *hardest* on themselves for procrastinating the first time became the *most likely* to procrastinate on later exams.

- Psychologists suspected that self-forgiveness would de-activate the what-the-hell effect. They decided to test their hypothesis. They brought weight-watching women into a lab, where research assistants encouraged them to eat donuts. (Really!) Then they gave half of the women a pep talk, reminding them that everyone overindulges sometimes. They exhorted that group to go easy on themselves. Next, *all* the women were served three big bowls of candy, ostensibly to do a taste test but really because scientists wanted to see who would eat more than they needed to and who would resist temptation. Sure enough, those who had not received any self-forgiveness message (and thus were still feeling guilty) overate again, consuming nearly three times as much as the women who got the pep talk. Only the pep-talk group—who'd been led to forgive themselves—resisted binging on the candy.

If berating ourselves doesn't work, why do we do it in the first place? It's because of the way we grew up. Children must be disciplined through mild punishment at least sometimes, because their brains' underdeveloped prefrontal cortices don't yet offer complete self-control. It's hard for parents to know how much correction is appropriate. Many overdo it. Most of us remember having been roundly shamed more than once as children. So it's not surprising that as adults we chastise ourselves for making mistakes.

Nevertheless, as the research proves, for us grown-ups with our fully formed brains, it is self-forgiveness, rather than guilt, that fosters improvement. This likely has to do, in part, with a primary need we have, as adults, for autonomy. On a subconscious level, guilt makes us feel bullied, whereas forgiveness protects our autonomy, leaving us free to *choose* to behave better.

Of course, even with kids, one should carefully balance any shame-inducing punishment with an encouraging dose of forgiveness. I have a confession. In my adolescence, I was a thief. My best friend and I loved to go to the department store, hide small items in our bags or under our sweaters, then sneak off without paying. Both of us had recently suffered traumatic home-life upheavals; perhaps that was why we so easily succumbed to shoplifting. Or maybe we were just being kids, with our underdeveloped prefrontal cortices. At any rate, one Saturday afternoon at the mall, we got caught stealing.

A security guard hauled us into a back office where we were subjected to a good-cop-bad-cop routine. First, an indignant man yelled at us until we began to cry. Then, a pleasant woman came in who spoke softly. She said that what we'd done wasn't so terrible—after all, we hadn't hurt anybody—and that she could see we were basically nice girls. In short, she forgave us. It was in that moment of forgiveness that I knew I would never shoplift or steal anything again. I believe my friend felt the same. (Today my former comrade-in-crime is an award-winning law professor known for, among other things, her integrity and public service.)

Whether dealing with children or adults, forgiveness fosters positive change. Next time you screw up, please bypass self-flagellation and, as best you can, go straight to self-forgiveness, in order to gain whatever education the incident offers. If you adopt a guilt-free habit of transforming blunders into learning, then a mistake is, and is not, a mistake—for every "mistake" becomes a path to wisdom. That is the zen of self-forgiveness.

Oh, one more thing. Did I mention that I'm setting you up for failure? Oops. The more challenges you embrace, the more errors you're likely to make and, if you are a well-meaning person who strives for the good (which I'm betting you are), you may not be able to fully refrain from guilt-tripping yourself now and then. Well, guess what? Forgive yourself for that, too. Doing so will benefit not only you personally, but also those around you, because self-forgiveness generates greater compassion toward others.

The Compound Effect of Self-Compassion

Ben, having grown up with a verbally violent father, found it impossible to completely kick the self-criticism habit. It also turned out that for nearly half a century, he'd been harboring a particularly painful type of guilt. While serving in Vietnam, he had killed people. Without telling me any details, he explained that it was all done under orders but continued to cause him deep remorse. Together, we worked on creating within him an all-inclusive, open-ended attitude of self-forgiveness.

Maybe you can guess what eventually happened. Without any specific prompting from me, Ben became more loving toward his wife, who then followed his lead and became more loving toward him. Ben also came to see his employees differently. While still holding them accountable to high standards, he grew far less critical and much more appreciative, which motivated them to do a better job.

You don't need hypnosis to begin forgiving yourself. You can download a free self-forgiveness audio session at self-intelligence.com, but you may also do this on your own.

Whenever you begin falling into self-recrimination, take a time-out to mentally step back. If possible, sit and relax a few minutes. Perhaps close your eyes. Talk to yourself in a loving manner, out loud or silently. Kindly explain that everyone fails now and then, goofs up now and then, goes off course now and then—and that this is a wonderful thing. It means you are alive and learning.

If you like, during this process you may want to gently stroke your left hand with your right hand, or even physically hug yourself. (And, if this self-forgiveness activity seems funny to you, feel free to laugh out loud!) You might not immediately achieve a dramatic breakthrough, but with practice over time, you will experience a seismic shift. As you stop attacking yourself for failures, you will discover that success comes far more easily in every area of your life.

The last time I saw Ben was at a networking event for business owners. Looking trim in a blue jersey, he boasted a weight lifter's chest and arms. I went to shake his hand but he moved in for a bear hug and, with a rebellious grin, swung me into the air then set me down gently as if it were no effort at all. The guy was fit.

Ben confided that, back when we'd first met, he'd had his doubts about self-forgiveness. "It's like this," he said. "A lot of the guys in 'Nam took heroin. It was almost as sad as seeing a buddy lose his leg. These guys did what they had to, to survive and to get high, but not a damn thing more. That first day in your office when you were going on about being nicer to myself, it kind of rubbed me the wrong way, like if I swallowed your Kool-Aid, maybe I'd be like those kids on smack who just wanted to lie around feeling numbed out." Ben winked to reassure me he was at least half-joking. I asked if, in the end, letting go of guilt was producing any druglike effects.

"I feel physically lighter, I mean beyond the thirty pounds I lost. I used to feel weighed down, tired, like I was still wearing all my old Army gear. Trust me, that gear is heavy. Whenever I get that weighed-down feeling now, it means I'm mad at myself for messing up in some way. So I drink the Kool-Aid; I forgive myself. The heaviness lifts. I'm back in motion. It's all about energy."

True enough. Change cannot occur without it; that's classic physics. So please, let go of old guilt. Reclaim your vitality by practicing self-forgiveness. Enjoy moving forward with unbridled energy by laughing at, and learning from, your own human imperfection. As Tallulah Bankhead once quipped, "If I had to live my life again, I'd make the same mistakes, only sooner."

Use Your Self-Intelligence

Let's spread the good news, sharing the gospel of self-forgiveness.

Want to sustain team motivation? Hold people (including yourself) accountable for their actions, but never shame them. The less blamed or shamed they feel, the more likely they'll be to step up. Regularly and sincerely praise others for their good work.

If you sluff off from exercising or eating right, don't label yourself a loser, because you're *not* a loser. Let go of the guilt. Simply resume your good habits so that you can genuinely congratulate yourself for your long-term commitment.

Guilt-tripping your loved ones might elicit short-term results, but eventually it will backfire. If you must confront your partner or family member about their behavior, keep your tone compassionate, and remember to come back around sometime soon with warm appreciation for all the things they do right. After all, happy intimate relationships require at least a five-to-one ratio of positive-over-negative interactions.

Research shows that people who are anxious about their finances often shop more in order to relieve their anxiety. Uh-oh! A good way to forestall the what-the-hell effect is by tracking your habits. Download a budget app on your smartphone to record all your purchases. Tracking will boost your sense of competence and control, to help you stay the course to financial health.

Quiz answer: Research shows that one effective strategy to help you achieve your goals is to . . .

    c.   let go of guilt or shame as soon as possible.

In a Nutshell

It may seem natural to beat yourself up when you make a mistake—but please resist the impulse. Feeling ashamed can trigger the *what-the-hell effect*, which leads to self-sabotage. Instead, forgive yourself. This will energize you to forge ahead to achieve your goals. It will also lead you to be kinder toward others, thus improving your personal and professional relationships.

CONCLUSION

PARTY ON

Congratulations on your commitment. You not only showed up—you stayed for the party!

I hope you've had fun at this festivity, playing with scientific concepts, juggling new discoveries, and raising your Self-IQ. I hope you're glad to have picked up dozens of self-help prizes to transform your life. I hope you're positively raring to go.

Yet I'm aware that with so many options for personal growth, at this point you might be wondering where to begin. My suggestion? Dream big, aim for the stars . . . and start small.

In the last chapter, we explored why, in order to do and be your best, you must let go of self-shame. Can you guess the most common source of shame that I see in people with admirable ambitions? It's that they don't reach their goals *fast* enough. Or so they think. Our culture promotes the myth of effortless, overnight turnarounds. Diet fads and get-rich-quick scams promise instant gratification. If they worked, we'd all be skinny millionaires.

So pick just one thing to change in your life for now. Perhaps focus first on getting better sleep, or putting more pizzazz into your romantic relationship, or boosting your presentation skills through visualization. Whatever it is, don't aim to please others. Set your own priorities and choose the change that's right for *you*.

Although we've constructed our Self-Intelligence model in a linear fashion, moving from inner to outer, you know that the overall interconnection among your five sub-selves means that improving any part of you improves the whole of you. Allow that fact to reassure you that you can start *anywhere*, as long as you start *somewhere*.

The model also can keep you from falling into a rut. If you feel stuck, simply consider whether you're focusing on the right sub-self for you at this time. For example, one client contacted me for help with dating. This might sound like an issue for the *social self*, but for her it wasn't. Longing to meet her mate, for two years she'd been working on getting out and about. That was understandable, but in her case a deadend because she projected negativity. She needed to start by programming her *subconscious self* and conditioning her *conscious self* in order to generate positive energy. So we began by building her awareness of choice, restoring her personal power to choose optimism over pessimism. Next, she revised her self-story to get rid of an old sense of victimhood. Soon she recovered her natural radiance, becoming a veritable man-magnet.

A journey of a thousand miles
begins with a single step.

—LAO-TZU

Another client had attained impressive artistic abilities, but he lacked the financial success he desired as an entrepreneur. We shifted his attention to his *striving self* so that he began getting measurable bottom-line results in his business. If ever you feel blocked in your quest for greater success, revisit the Self-Intelligence model to consider whether it's time to revise your approach. And if one particular strategy doesn't rock your boat, then try another. The model offers flexibility so that you can do what's best for *you* to reach your true potential.

Please don't let this book be mere brain candy. It's time to spring into gear. Having chosen *one thing* to change in your life, immediately *take action* on that one thing. Order a more comfortable pillow for better sleep. Or text your partner a flirty invitation for a weekend adventure. Or begin scripting your new autobiography. Whatever your goal may be, please take some action toward it within the next fifteen minutes.

Then, for at least a month, focus on consistently following through, using the various scientific tools to create that one change. This will grow easier and easier because, due to brain plasticity, your new habits will be remapping your mind. That means they will become automatic. What then? Well, remain committed to that first improvement—and now also choose one more thing to improve in your life. Then begin taking action on that, as well . . . and so on.

Proceed at your own pace, embracing one positive change after another. Before you know it, your personal confidence and overall competence will dramatically expand. As you build your Self-Intelligence, you will begin to naturally set—and actually achieve—higher goals and bigger dreams. No doubt you'll greatly enjoy all that tangible success. But what will truly thrill you is the Self-Intelligent person you become, both inwardly and out in the world. My mentor Jack Canfield has taught me that it's *who we become* in the process that matters most. Therefore, be ready to become ultra-spectacular.

Every day, scientists are discovering more ways that we can improve our selves and reach greater success. That's wonderful, yet it also can create choice overload (remember that concept from chapter 7). To keep from feeling overwhelmed, you can turn to the model for a bird's-eye view. This will give you a stronger sense of control because the big-picture model is reassuringly simple. (You may recall the subconscious power of simplicity from chapter 19's sidebar, "Keep It Simple, Sherlock"). Reviewing the model regularly will galvanize you to continuously move forward.

These days, as an international coach, speaker, and trainer, I confess to being pretty darn amazing. But weirdly enough, I'm not yet perfect. Hmmm. It turns out the self-transformation party never ends! Therefore, don't delay getting started *and* please don't be impatient to reach the far side of the Milky Way by tomorrow morning.

Recall from the last chapter that if you were to guilt-trip yourself for not going faster, then the *what-the-hell effect* would further slow you down. But by honoring your own pace, you will strengthen your subconscious resolve. This will energize you to put in better effort and make speedier progress, yet it will feel more effortless. Now, that's a fact to celebrate.

So let's celebrate! Pick out your party hat and put on your dancing shoes—*or* go bare-foot. Leap into the pool, or onto the trampoline, or over the jump rope. The choices are yours. Own your life. At this party you can have your cake and eat it too. You can be right *and* happy. You can dance with your mind and think with your body. By consistently deploying your Self-Intelligence, you can obtain long-term results so dramatic they might seem mystical, magical or downright miraculous. And remember, you're never alone, so—

Let's turn up the music, open wide the doors, and invite everybody on board! As you ignite your own success, you will inspire others to improve *their* lives too. You, in your perhaps small—or perhaps, in the end, immeasurably *big*—way, are about to change the world.

CHAPTER
SUMMARIES

When you dream, your brain continues to think, and in some ways it thinks better than when you're awake—particularly in terms of visual problem-solving. Your sleeping brain stops censoring your thoughts, which allows your creativity to expand. This is why so many inventors, scientists, and artists have discovered breakthrough solutions while dreaming. Anyone can learn to direct their dreams. Practice programming your mind to work for you while you sleep.

The kind of visualization that's been proven to work is a form of highly focused mental practice that includes multiple senses—for example, sight, hearing, touch, and kinesthesia. This activates synaptic connections throughout the brain and body, forming strong neural maps for success. Visualization can be used to improve all sorts of skills, including athletic and musical performance, as a complement to quality training. To start with, choose one skill to improve by adding daily visualization to your practice. Soon you will be amazed by your results.

The limbic system—your brain's processor of emotions—responds powerfully to whatever you see, even when you don't consciously realize it. Images often go straight to the subconscious, influencing your mood and behavior without your conscious consent. Exploit this fact by taking in images that elevate your well-being.

Science has rescued hypnosis from the fringe, finding it to be a reliable tool for fixing a wide variety of problems and for generating improvement across numerous areas. Much of the research has been in health care, where studies show that hypnosis can help people to kick bad habits, reduce bodily pain, speed up physical healing, enjoy better sex, and more. Scientists still don't fully understand hypnosis but because the science proves its power, the most highly respected medical institutions advocate its use. It's also the secret to success for many top athletes and other performers. Feeling frustrated with some aspect of your life? Try hypnosis.

Every human culture ever known has told tales, and now research confirms that they influence our brains far more deeply than do dry facts. This is why our inner autobiographies greatly affect our confidence and well-being. So consider what yarn you're currently spinning about yourself. Is your self-story sabotaging or serving you? Most likely, you can revise and improve your story, so that your story improves you.

Because of how the brain works, attempting to suppress negative thoughts tends to create more of them, due to what scientists call ironic rebound. So it doesn't help to berate yourself (or anyone else) for negative thinking. On the other hand, we can direct our minds toward more positivity. In fact, by reading this book you're doing just that—congratulations! The so-called law of attraction, which holds that the universe directly responds to our thoughts, is a spiritual belief, without scientific basis in quantum physics . . . but, hey, it could turn out to be true. The mere fact of our existence offers innumerable grand mysteries that science has yet to solve.

All animals have an innate need to make choices. Research shows that being robbed of choice thus typically leads to an earlier death. Among humans, the act of choosing tends to uplift and invigorate us. Look for opportunities to make your own decisions about things that matter to you, big or small. Also, practice recognizing the choices you already are making. And, if ever you feel overwhelmed by too many options (choice overload), first narrow their number—six or fewer is a good bet—before making your selection. In the end, whether you feel out of control or in command of your own life is up to you. So choose!

To help us survive in the wild, our brains evolved a tendency to focus on the negative. But this negativity bias no longer serves us—especially when research shows that optimists outperform pessimists, and that successful romantic relationships require at least five times as many positive to negative interactions. The solution? Consciously commit to positivity. Aim up. This means disputing your own overly negative beliefs, and it also means buoying up other people. Stop criticizing and start encouraging! Aim your goals up as well. Focus on what you do desire, and set the bar high.

Economists used to believe that we human consumers were rational beings who could be counted on to act in our own best interest. But now, neuroscience shows that almost no one makes purely logical judgments. Subconsciously, our thoughts and feelings remain interdependent, each influencing the other. While it may be wise to "simply follow your heart" or "just trust your gut" in some social situations, don't let your euphoria buy real estate or play the stock market. Financial decisions, in particular, call for a calm, risk-conscious mindset.

Recent studies prove that neurologically, your body language doesn't merely reveal thoughts and emotions, it also creates them. Good posture increases self-esteem. Smiling boosts your sense of humor and emotional well-being. Nodding your head leads to liking. Don't let a difficult day impair how you carry yourself. Instead, adjust your body to improve your mood. (P.S. Having trouble understanding how someone else feels? Adopt their body language to instantly "get" it.)

From boosting student test scores to creating healthy new brain cells in old age, physical exercise strengthens neural connectivity. It's a scientific fact: Exercise makes you smarter. Working out also harmonizes the Big Three neurotransmitters targeted by most antidepressants—norepinephrine, dopamine, and serotonin—meaning exercise makes you happier, as well. To be truly Self-Intelligent, get your body moving.

While scientists still don't know exactly why we humans—and apparently all animals—must sleep to stay alive, they have determined that the great majority of us need at least seven or eight hours' nightly sleep to maintain optimal intelligence. When awake, your brain functions much better if you've gotten a good sleep, partly because when well rested, you metabolize more glucose. Perhaps more astounding, your sleeping brain does a whole lot of thinking that supports learning and memory. Recent research shows that getting ample sleep makes you smarter, healthier, younger-looking, and even slimmer. Say no to sleep macho! Make a self-commitment to get the rest you need to do and be your best.

To thrive, you need other people. Chronic loneliness and social isolation can weaken your immune system, impair brain function and shave years off your life. What matters most is how you feel and think about your relationships. At the same time, research shows that by expanding your network—that is, by playing more social roles—you can protect your inner sense of connection. Your inner and outer social experiences each reinforce the other, creating a snowball effect. So practice improving your social mindset, then use that positive attitude to reach out to good people to strengthen your circle. You'll be far better off—happier, healthier, and probably wealthier.

Laughter's primary purpose is social connection. Indeed, most of the time, what prompts laughter has nothing to do with humor, and all to do with bonding. The neurological mechanisms for this lie deep within the brain, indicating that laughter plays a part in our very survival. In this, we're not alone. Other critters laugh too, including our closest relatives, chimpanzees. So please don't make the understandable but misguided mistake of refusing to laugh at the unfunny. Be an easy laugh, and your life will be easier too.

Playing is how we most joyfully bond with others. This begins in infancy, when mother and baby spontaneously interact, syncing their brain waves in emotional attunement. Later, as youngsters, playing freely with peers builds healthy brains, fostering both Self-Intelligence and social intelligence. Kids who are forbidden to play likely will develop interpersonal problems later on, possibly leading to criminal behavior, including murder. For families, friends, or couples to maintain joyful closeness, they must find ways to play together. So practice letting go of old inhibitions in order to rediscover your innate playfulness. Invite others to play along with you. Share the joy!

Misunderstandings plague men and women because of their distinct attitudes toward independence-versus-connection. Typically, men value independence more highly, while women treasure connection. Evolution may have wired in this difference so that primitive men and women would survive danger—men by fighting or fleeing, and women (often with children in tow) by seeking help. Today this shows up in males' fight-or-flight response to modern stress, versus women's inclination to tend-and-befriend. Meanwhile, at least in the United States, most males and females grow up learning virtually opposite communication goals—again, differing around the issue of independence-versus-connection—so that women in conversation tend toward consensus and similarity, while men often compete for dominance. Use this knowledge to foster flexibility within yourself and to connect more effectively with everyone in your life.

"Why" is one of the most powerful motivators we can use to achieve our goals. We're hardwired to want reasons for what we do or don't do. As long as we understand how the brain works, we can harness the power of "why" to our benefit. But because our talkative left brains will actually invent reasons "why" or "why not" out of thin air, sometimes the wrong why's can steer us off track. We humans long to lead meaningful lives, so one effective way to achieve your goals is to access your deepest why-to's. It also helps to focus on why you can succeed. The science can seem complex, so use my easy "3-D Why-Finder" to find your way around Why.

Scientific studies of talent indicate that it's a myth. Superstars in any field may appear to succeed effortlessly, but that illusion results from years of training. Moreover, a belief in talent can actually sabotage success. Praising "talent" instills a harmful fixed mindset, while praising effort plants a growth mindset, which leads to achievement. When praising yourself or others, forget about supposedly innate traits such as talent or intelligence. Instead, celebrate the effort people make and the good strategies they employ. Praise not what people are but what they do.

Beware of lulling yourself into inaction by overdiscussing what you should do. Unfortunately, that can trick the brain into believing you've already done it. Condition your synapses to be action-oriented by developing an action habit. Talk less, do more.

It may seem natural to beat yourself up when you make a mistake—but please resist the impulse. Feeling ashamed can trigger the what-the-hell effect, which leads to self-sabotage. Instead, forgive yourself. This will energize you to forge ahead to achieve your goals. It will also lead you to be kinder toward others, thus improving your personal and professional relationships.

REFERENCES

An extensive chapter-by-chapter bibliography and other resources
are available for you online at self-intelligence.com.

ACKNOWLEDGMENTS

The biggest thank-you goes to my clients, including those who will recognize their stories in this book, those who encouraged me to write the book, and all those who've proven to me, through their own results, that this scientific self-helpery really works.

Tender gratitude to Ann and Lou Cabral—dearer friends don't exist—who helped create my marvelous downtown-San Francisco office space, from painting walls to hanging pictures to inventing ingenious ways to soundproof (sort of) the tenth-floor window overlooking Market Street.

Speaking of irreplaceable friends, David Dobbin, thank you for not falling asleep when over the phone I've gone on and on about the science of brain plasticity and how we ordinary folks can put it to practical use. Okay, let's say both ordinary and odd. Thank you for being my fellow big-hearted brainiac weirdo bent on saving the world.

Hugs, thanks, and hats off to my brother Farley, whom I'm lucky to count as family and friend, and who comes to my rescue with remarkable patience, including helping me relearn to drive after my move to Durham, North Carolina.

Humble indebtedness to scientists whose research helps people lead better lives. I'm in awe of you.

Grateful praise for my agent Giles Anderson, who gently convinced me to restructure the book so that it would sing for its supper, by which I mean we found a publisher. Thank you Erika Heilman for taking *Self-Intelligence* and its author under your wing during your tenure at Quarto.

Hey, has everyone noticed that this book is drop-dead gorgeous? Happy applause for the Quarto team, including senior editorial project manager Renae Haines, art director Anne Re who designed the interior, and Rick Landers, who designed the cover.

Love and appreciation to members of the Canfield community, my companions on this never-ending journey of self-betterment. Special thanks to the unflappable Marilyn Suttle and to the brilliant strategist Patty Aubery, co-founder of The Canfield Training Group.

Infinite gratitude to Jack Canfield, for continuing to expand my understanding of what's possible.

About the Author

Jane Ransom is an international coach, speaker, and trainer, a master hypnotist, and an incurable science nerd who has helped countless clients achieve breakthroughs using her model of Self-Intelligence over the last decade. A former journalist and professor, she now pairs her communication skills with her passion to serve the world. She helps individuals transform their lives and works with organizations to improve leadership and strengthen employee engagement. Jane's enthusiasm for brain science might have turned her into an eccentric autodidact, if not for the mentorship of Jack Canfield, who taught Jane how to tell people to get off their butts—but in a really nice way. A native Midwesterner, Jane has also lived in New York, Boston, Madrid, Paris, San Juan (Puerto Rico), and San Francisco. In San Francisco, she conducted her hypnosis-coaching practice out of the historic Phelan Building. Recently, she relocated to Durham, North Carolina, a thriving hub of cutting-edge research. Find out more about her at janeransom.com.

INDEX

smiling and, 141
visualization and, 39–40
why and, 231
yarn and, 77
Heath, Chip, 74
Heath, Dan, 74
Heller, Robert, 120
Hemingway, Ernest, 240
Herman, C. Peter, 260
"Holly," 155–157, 159,
    160–161
Huffington, Arianna, 154
human growth hormone
    (HGH), 149
hypnosis
    anchor, 123, 124
    celebrities and, 56
    finances and, 61
    health and, 55, 61
    high-hypnotizables, 54, 55
    history of, 58–59
    "Kathy," 55–56
    low-hypnotizables, 54–55
    name origin, 59
    self-hypnosis, 61
    sex and, 60, 61
    sleep and, 156–157, 163
    social interaction and, 61
    summary, 271
    surgery and, 60
    suspicion of, 57
    usefulness of, 55, 56,
        60–61

I

Iacoboni, Marco, 139
images
    blindsight, 45
    blind spot, 48–49
    emotional contagion and,
        45
    employment and, 49
    extrapolation of, 49
    finances and, 50
    health and, 50
    loved ones, 50
    optic nerve and, 45
    picture superiority effect
        (PSE), 48

relationships and, 50
sensory interaction with,
    47–48
sleep and, 50
summary, 271
"Tom," 43–44, 45, 46–47
value of appearance, 50
work area and, 43–44,
    49–50
Influence (Robert Cialdini),
    252
insomnia, 54–55
inward why, 223, 227
IQ, 238–239
Iyengar, Sheena, 95

J

James, William, 135, 191
"Jasper," 235–236, 242–243
Jaws (film), 73
"Jeff," 205–206, 210, 212–215
"Jonah," 155, 161
"Joshua," 121–122, 123–124
judgment
    animal spirits, 122,
        123–124
    brain and, 124
    emotional influence on,
        127–128
    employment and, 129
    finances and, 130
    health and, 129
    "Joshua," 121–122,
        123–124
    positivity and, 124, 126
    relationships and, 129, 130
    summary, 272–273
    visualization and, 123–124

K

Kafka, Franz, 251
"Kathy," 53–54
Kekulé, Friedrich August, 26
Keller, Helen, 102
"Kevin," 171–172, 173–174,
    175–176, 177, 179
kinesthesia
    "Angie," 133–134, 138

brain and, 135
contagiousness of, 138, 141
embodied cognition,
    135–136
employment and, 141
finances and, 141
head-nodding/head-
    shaking, 136–137
health and, 141
mirroring, 139–140
posture and, 136
relationships and, 141
slumping, 134
summary, 273
Kovacs, Jenny Stamos, 163
"Kristen," 250

L

Lang, Elvira, 60
Langer, Ellen, 94, 224
Lao-Tzu, 266
"Larry," 15–16, 16–17, 18–19,
    20, 195–197, 198–199,
    200–201
laughter
    contagion, 189
    employment and, 187, 191
    finances and, 192
    gender and, 189–190
    health and, 191
    play and, 200, 201
    punctuation effect, 186
    relationships and, 192
    social interaction and, 186
    subconscious and, 186
    summary, 274
    triggers for, 185–186
    "Yvette," 183–185, 186,
        188, 191
*Laughter: A Scientific
    Investigation* (Robert
    Provine), 185, 189
Laughter in Interaction (Phillip
    Glenn), 187
law of attraction, 82, 89, 274
Lean In (Sheryl Sandberg), 208
learned helplessness, 108–109
Lepper, Mark, 96
Lewis, C. S., 92, 179